The Currency of Ideas

A volume in the series

Cornell Studies in Political Economy

EDITED BY PETER J. KATZENSTEIN

A complete list of titles in the series appears at the end of this book.

The Currency of Ideas

MONETARY POLITICS IN THE EUROPEAN UNION

KATHLEEN R. MCNAMARA

CORNELL UNIVERSITY PRESS

Ithaca and London

Copyright © 1998 by Cornell University

First published 1998 by Cornell University Press
First printing, Cornell Paperbacks, 1999

Printed in the United States of America

Cornell University Press strives to use environmentally responsible suppliers and materials to the fullest extent possible in the publishing of its books. Such materials include vegetable-based, low-VOC inks and acid-free papers that are also recycled, totally chlorine-free, or partly composed of nonwood fibers.

Library of Congress Cataloging-in-Publication Data

McNamara, Kathleen R., 1962–
    The currency of ideas : monetary politics in the European Union /
Kathleen R. McNamara.
        p.   cm. — (Cornell studies in political economy)
    Includes index.
    ISBN 0–8014–3432–7 (cloth : alk. paper)
    ISBN 0–8014–8602–5 (pbk. : alk. paper)
        1. Money—European Union countries.   2. Monetary unions—European
Union countries.   3. Monetary policy—European Union countries.
    I. Title.   II. Series.
    HG925.M38   1998
    332.4′94—dc21   97–29728

Cloth printing 10   9   8   7   6   5   4   3   2

Paperback printing 10   9   8   7   6   5   4   3   2   1

For Theo

Contents

Preface to the Cornell Paperbacks Edition

What was long a dream to European leaders has, since this book first appeared, become a reality. A single currency, the Euro, now joins together nations that a half-century ago were more likely to go to war than to merge their monetary futures. As the European Union prepares for the next millennium, the Euro may turn out to be the impetus for further integration as demands increase for political legitimacy and greater policy capacity at the European level. *The Currency of Ideas* provides reasons to believe that these demands will be difficult to meet—but also that the imagination and innovation that have guided the European Union throughout its history may assert themselves again.

This book explains why the governments of Europe pursued monetary integration and how they linked their currencies together in preparation for Economic and Monetary Union (EMU). I show that political elites have shared a strong ideational consensus concerning the desirability of EMU, as a way to lock in monetary stability and neoliberal policies. This consensus does not extend to other crucial areas of governance affected by EMU, however. Nor is this elite agreement on ideas matched by any broader political legitimacy for the institutions of the European Union. This uneven political development means that it will take astute political management and vision by Europe's leaders, as well as active engagement on the part of its citizens, to secure Europe's future.

Much about EMU was unknown a year ago but has since been decided. First, the important question of which states, if any, would join EMU has been answered—but in an unexpected way. Even those observers, like me, who believed EMU would indeed happen predicted that it would probably involve a small core of northern European states. Instead, it will start as a very large monetary area. Eleven states—Austria, Belgium, Finland, France, Germany, Ireland, Italy, Luxembourg, the Netherlands, Portugal, and Spain—all agreed, at a summit on May 2–3, 1998 in Brussels, to go ahead as founding members. Although surprising, this result confirms the book's emphasis on political forces as the key determinant of progress toward a single currency. While member states did indeed make a genuine effort over the past few years to cut spending and balance their budgets, most did not meet the Maastricht criteria for entry into EMU despite their political desire to do so. The inability of Germany, the strongest proponent of strict requirements for entry, to meet all the numerical goals sealed the bargain in Brussels, and political leaders interpreted the entry criteria quite liberally, creating a large EMU. Britain, Denmark, and Sweden, while passing many of the economic tests, decided not to join this first wave of states because of concerns over lost sovereignty; Greece was deemed economically unready. It is likely that all will join eventually.

The European Central Bank (ECB) has now been established in Frankfurt, Germany, with Wim Duisenberg as its president. In a hard-fought Franco-German compromise typical of the EU, Duisenberg will "voluntarily" step down partway through his eight-year appointment, and French central bank president Jean Claude Trichet will replace him. In keeping with the arguments I make about the durability of the monetary policy consensus among European policymakers, both officials are considered "hard money" advocates who view price stability, not growth and employment objectives, as the ECB's purview. The neoliberal ideas that pushed EMU forward now provide the underpinning for the ECB.

Much of the year 1998 has also provided a more benign economic environment than anticipated, which will ease the transition to EMU. Interest rates are at a historic low across the EU, stimulating economic growth in member states now fully out of the recession that gripped them through the mid 1990s. Businesspeople and policymakers, at the national and European Union levels, have slowly worked out the technical details of a single currency. As expected, financial integration in the European Union is proceeding apace.

Mergers and acquisitions are transforming the banking landscape in Europe, small stock exchanges are folding and those in Paris and Frankfurt are becoming deeper and more liquid; the Frankfurt and London stock markets have tentatively agreed to merge.

A bevy of challenges lie ahead once EMU begins, however, many of which are foreshadowed in this book's arguments about the political foundations of monetary integration. In contrast to the exchange rate regimes that preceded it, EMU will require more accountability from the institutions of the European Union and more balanced coordination of a wide range of economic policies. Neither of these necessities is in place. For EMU to work, the European Union must face a task of governance that goes way beyond the elite-level consensus of policy ideas described in the chapters that follow. Although eleven states will fully merge their monetary policies under the ECB, political authority for economic policymaking more broadly will continue to reside with the nation states. The operation of EMU will necessarily have repercussions throughout each national economy, thereby creating a complex and ambiguous situation for policymakers.

There has been some recognition of this challenge. A special economic policy forum has been created for states participating in the Euro. The so called Euro-X Council or Euro-11 club, which had its inaugural meeting on June 5, 1998 in Luxembourg, is made up of the finance ministers of the Euro states. Its mandate is to encourage cooperation across a broad array of policies. The French have argued that it will form a necessary policymaking counterweight to the highly independent ECB. They have promoted the Euro-X as a way to coordinate national budgets to boost growth, to plan structural reforms in pensions and labor markets, as well as to coordinate tax harmonization in an effort to guard against competition over such policies. More fundamentally, the French are widely thought to be promoting the Euro-X as an "embryonic economic government for Europe, and a heavy political counter-weight to the ECB," in the words of *The Economist.*

This ambition has been criticized as an inappropriate politicization of central bank independence. German officials continue to maintain that the fiscal rules and sanctions of the austere Stability and Growth Pact, discussed in chapter 7, will provide adequate oversight of national economic policymaking. Such criticism is misguided, as even the highly independent Bundesbank has long been embedded in a web of political institutions, actively engaged in ongoing dialogue with the representatives of social groups and political bodies within Germany. For the ECB to be a legitimate institution, it must be similarly accountable. Indeed, support for the creation of a Euro-X-type intergovernmental council, to serve as an interlocutor with the ECB, has come from former U.S. Federal Reserve chairman Paul Volcker, who reasoned at an IMF conference recently that no central bank "can long be comfortable as an island unto itself, operating entirely outside a political context. . . ." A high degree of central bank independence has clear merits, but in the European Union, where there is no clear balancing political entity from which the ECB is independent, it may be too much of a good thing.

A final governance issue not yet addressed by EMU's members concerns Europe's presence in the international political arena. The ECB is a truly supranational entity, but it exists in a world of international political arrangements and institutions that continue to be organized on the basis of single, sovereign states. The result creates great difficulties in the representation of the European Union in international institutions, particularly the International Monetary Fund, as well as problems for the coordination of policies among the leading industrial states in the Group of 7 summits. Many in Europe have long promoted EMU as a way for Europe to have a stronger voice in the international system. As of this writing, however, the response on the part of European Union policymakers has been to downplay the need to confront these issues—which ironically may lessen Europe's stature internationally.

In sum, the history of European monetary integration has been both fascinating and profoundly important. The Euro's creation only increases its significance. But this history has played out on a stage filled with central bankers, finance ministers, and heads of state debating their policy ideas; voters have been only a passive audience. The political and economic tensions and achievements that come with EMU make it even more desirable that Europe's citizens be given the means to step forward and play a more central role.

KATHLEEN R. McNAMARA

January 1, 1999
Princeton, New Jersey

Preface

International monetary cooperation has long fascinated me, for international agreements on this topic seem to reach into the domestic political sphere in profound and important ways. As I began to learn about European monetary integration, it struck me that international relations theory didn't have a ready explanation for the Economic and Monetary Union (EMU) plan proposed in the 1989 Delors Report and later agreed to at Maastricht. Realist theories of international relations would not have predicted that the European Union (EU) states would voluntarily give up the levers of economic sovereignty, but liberal theories of integration seemed too sanguine in suggesting that economic interdependence leads inevitably to the demand for international regimes. The notion that the European states might surrender their national currencies and create a new European money was deeply intriguing to me. This book represents my answer to the challenge that European monetary integration presents to our conventional understanding of state behavior.

To make sense of EMU, I found it necessary to delve into the postwar history of European monetary politics, starting with the experience at Bretton Woods and extending through the two recent European fixed exchange rate regimes. The realists, I discovered, were right to emphasize national interest, but they did not pay enough attention to the ways in which interests can be redefined over time and lead to the extensive institutionalization of cooperation. The liberals, on the other hand, were right to pay attention to the importance of economic trends but underestimated the role that political and social processes, particularly the development of shared beliefs among policymakers, play in translating the effects of interdependence into political outcomes.

This book will, I hope, help make sense of the progress of European monetary integration to those for whom international economics is familiar terrain, as well as those who are more at home in the study of international or comparative politics. Whatever happens on the road to EMU, an understanding of its fate can be achieved only through the joining of political and economic analysis.

I have been extraordinarily lucky to have received institutional, financial, and intellectual support at each stage in this project. For their generosity, I am very grateful to the Graduate School of Arts and Sciences at Columbia University; the Fulbright-Hays fellowship program; the John D. and Catherine T. MacArthur Foundation; the Center for the Social Sciences at Columbia University; the Eisenhower World Affairs Institute; the Council for European Studies; the European Community Studies Association; the Centre for European Policy Studies, Brussels; and the Center of International Studies and the Woodrow Wilson School, Princeton University. The final revisions were supported by a research fellowship from the German Marshall Fund. Joseph Noto and G. Matt Webster provided excellent research assistance.

I also extend thanks to all the people who took the time to talk to me both in Europe and in the United States about the European Union and monetary integration, and to those who read and commented on endless early drafts of this project. In particular, for their invaluable and detailed comments on the entire manuscript, I am deeply grateful to Peter B. Kenen, Kathryn Stoner-Weiss, George Downs, Michael Doyle, Joanne Gowa, Beth Simmons, Richard Ullman, and two anonymous reviewers. For their advice on various chapters and aspects of this project, I also thank Sheri Berman, Marc Busch, David Cameron, Michele Chang, Jeffry Frieden, Alberto Giovannini, Daniel Gros, Michal Hershkovitz, Robert Jervis, Erik Jones, Jonathan Kirshner, Paulette Kurzer, Martin Malin, Walter Mattli, Andrew Moravcsik, Jonathon Moses, Wayne Sandholtz, Jack Snyder, and Claire F. Ullman. Peter J. Katzenstein and Roger M. Haydon made the preparation of the manuscript and final revisions a pleasure.

Helen V. Milner and David A. Baldwin have had the largest influence on this work, however. They have continually challenged me to think more deeply and clearly about the politics of international economic relations; the scholarly training and careful mentoring they have given me are gifts too fundamental ever to be repaid.

Finally, my deepest appreciation goes to Tomás Montgomery, for his amazingly steadfast faith and unflagging enthusiasm for both me and this project.

KATHLEEN R. McNAMARA

Princeton, New Jersey

The Currency of Ideas

CHAPTER ONE

Introduction

Why do some international monetary regimes fail while others succeed? Which domestic or international conditions bind nations together in economic agreements, and which break them apart? These
are important questions. International monetary cooperation or discord can have significant effects inside states, enabling or constraining
societies in the pursuit of their national goals. International monetary
arrangements can have significant effects on the international system,
promoting political harmony or strife among nation states. In the
1990s, rapidly increasing international capital flows, the integration
of world markets, and a rash of dramatic exchange rate crises have
brought renewed attention to the political importance of international
monetary matters while demonstrating the limits to our understanding
of their dynamics.

This book is about the politics of monetary cooperation among the
states of the European Union (EU).[1] Such cooperation has long been
a concern of European political leaders. Monetary integration, with
fixed exchange rate cooperation as its first step, has been seen by many
as a way to encourage trade and investment by stabilizing currency
fluctuations among the highly open economies of the common European market. Efforts at monetary cooperation also have a purpose
beyond the economic realm, acting as a central anchor for debates

[1] The European Union (EU) came into being on November 1, 1993, replacing and
encompassing the European Community (EC). In this book, I refer to the EU when
discussing the European states in general terms or in a contemporary context and use
EC only in explicitly historical discussions.

1

about political unification in Europe. The final stage of monetary integration—a single currency for all EU member states, scheduled for 1999—has been viewed by many European leaders as a way to ensure a peaceful, stable future for a continent with a history of violent conflict among its states.

Despite this continued desire for monetary stability, the three fixed exchange rate regimes Europeans have participated in have met with widely varying degrees of success. Although the Bretton Woods international monetary system provided stability during the first decades of the postwar era, the European-only currency Snake collapsed after a few short years of operation in the 1970s. Yet, the next European regime, the European Monetary System (EMS), proved relatively durable throughout the 1980s. Indeed, the success of the EMS was a major impetus for the single currency ambitions of the Maastricht Treaty and its Economic and Monetary Union (EMU). A series of currency crises in the 1990s has marred the EMS experience, however, and added to doubts about the feasibility of EMU. This mixed record constitutes an empirical puzzle for those who seek to explain why international monetary regimes succeed or fail.

The evolution of European monetary cooperation also raises a series of broader theoretical puzzles about the changing historical interaction of political authority and economic markets, and how this interaction shapes the conditions under which societies are governed. For example, if a country's currency is an intrinsic component of national sovereignty, as some argue, extensive monetary cooperation of the kind seen in Europe is surprising. Indeed, in the modern era, states have never before voluntarily sought to give up their own monies for a common currency. Why, then, have they proceeded down this path in Europe?

The evolution of monetary cooperation in Europe is equally puzzling for domestic political reasons. Macroeconomic policy has been tied closely to the distinct ideologies and programs of different political parties, from left to right. Why, then, have political actors from socialist to conservative supported an exchange rate regime that in effect gives away economic policy tools and limits their ability to use macroeconomic policy to distinguish themselves in voters' eyes?

Although the workings of exchange rate politics may seem highly technical and at times arcane, they are worth probing in detail, for

2

the study of European monetary integration has the potential to further our understanding of the role of the state, and the nature of political power, in a world where financial flows seem indifferent to national borders and impervious to national control.

The Argument in Brief

The key to solving the puzzle of European monetary cooperation lies in the historic economic policy convergence that occurred across the majority of the European governments beginning in the mid- 1970s and solidifying in the 1980s. A neoliberal policy consensus that elevated the pursuit of low inflation over growth or employment took hold among political elites, eventually resulting in a downward convergence in inflation rates. This policy consensus redefined state interests in cooperation, underpinned stability in the EMS, and induced political leaders to accept the domestic policy adjustments needed to stay within the system. Though this consensus was by no means unwavering and may be showing signs of wear, it represented a clear break with the divergent economic policy paths and diverse priorities of the European states during the Bretton Woods era. For students of politics, this European reorientation is particularly notable because it occurred across most of the EU states, regardless of political party or domestic institutional structure.

This explanation raises a further series of questions, however. Why was the neoliberal policy consensus crucial to the success of the EMS? Where did it come from, and what were its political foundations? What might cause cracks in these foundations? And if this neoliberal policy consensus is so important, how were the European states able to stabilize their currencies within the earlier Bretton Woods system before such consensus developed in the 1970s? Is neoliberal policy consensus a necessary condition for fixed exchange rate cooperation in other regions of the world as well?

To answer these questions, this book explores the interaction between a changing international economy, one in which capital flows have increased exponentially, and the domestic policymaking process, particularly political leaders' beliefs about macroeconomic strategy. Both changes in the structure of the international economy and the

3

ideational factors that shaped policymakers' responses to structural changes are crucial to the story of European monetary integration.

At the international level, capital mobility plays a critical role in determining the conditions under which international monetary agreements can be sustained.[2] When the level of capital mobility is low, states can both fix their exchange rates and follow their own independent monetary policies, but when capital mobility rises, states must choose between fixed exchange rates or monetary policy autonomy. The following chapters frame the historical evolution of European monetary integration within this macroeconomic constraint, spelling out the basic policy trade-offs states have faced over the postwar era in their quest for monetary stability. This analysis sheds light on more general questions about the effects of capital mobility on domestic policymaking, an issue at the forefront of current debates about globalization.[3]

In order to understand the evolution of monetary cooperation in Europe, it is equally important to look at the process of policy choice, specifically, how political elites measure the costs and benefits of monetary cooperation within a changing international economic context. The ideas political leaders hold about macroeconomic policy are crucial to explaining the path that European states have taken and where they may go in the future. Ideas are defined here as shared causal beliefs.[4] Political actors use these ideas to evaluate the costs and benefits

[2] David M. Andrews, "Capital Mobility and State Autonomy: Towards a Structural Theory of International Monetary Relations," *International Studies Quarterly* 38 (1994), 193–218; Michael C. Webb, *The Political Economy of Policy Coordination: International Adjustment since 1945* (Ithaca: Cornell University Press, 1995); Jonathon Moses, "Abdication from National Policy: What's Left to Leave," *Politics and Society* 22 (June 1994), 125–48; Benjamin Cohen, "The Triad and the Unholy Trinity: Lessons for the Pacific Rim," in Richard Higgott, Richard Leaver, and John Ravenhill, eds., *Pacific Economic Relations in the 1990s: Cooperation or Conflict?* (Boulder, Colo.: Lynne Reinner, 1993); and Louis W. Pauly, *Who Elected the Bankers? Surveillance and Control in the World Economy* (Ithaca: Cornell University Press, 1997).

[3] Important recent contributions to this debate include Suzanne Berger and Ronald Dore, eds., *National Diversity and Global Capitalism* (Ithaca: Cornell University Press, 1996); Jeffry Frieden, "Invested Interests: The Politics of National Economic Policies in a World of Global Finance," *International Organization* 45 (Autumn 1991), 425–51; Geoffrey Garrett and Peter Lange, "Internationalization, Institutions, and Political Change," *International Organization* 49 (Autumn 1995), 627–55; Robert O. Keohane and Helen Milner, eds., *Internationalization and Domestic Politics* (New York: Cambridge University Press, 1996).

[4] An argument congruent with mine is Peter Hall, "Policy Paradigms, Social Learning,

4

of monetary cooperation and chart a policy strategy. Policymakers draw on these ideas to formulate answers to questions of values and strategies: What should the goals of monetary policy be? What instruments can be used in pursuit of those goals? The answers will vary significantly over time and place, redefining national interests in international monetary cooperation.

"Ideas," as one author has put it, "do not float freely," however; they arise from actors' experiences with their environment and interactions with other actors, and they survive implementation into policy only if they are politically salient.[5] Thus, to explain why certain neoliberal economic policy ideas triumphed within the political arena, making European monetary cooperation more likely, I develop a template for understanding why certain ideas become dominant at a given historical point, while others are put aside. A process of policy failure, policy paradigm innovation, and policy emulation unfolded among the states of the European Union, producing a new, neoliberal view of monetary policy in the years between the Snake and the European Monetary System.

In brief, European governments' experience with macroeconomic policy failure in the aftermath of the first oil crisis spurred a search for alternatives to traditional Keynesian policies. The sense of crisis that accompanied the policy failures weakened postwar political and societal arrangements, creating the space for a new conception of the role of government in the macroeconomy. Second, monetarist theory provided a template and a legitimizing framework for a new economic

---

and the State: The Case of Economic Policymaking in Britain," *Comparative Politics* 25 (April 1993), 275–96, and Hall, "The Movement from Keynesianism to Monetarism: Institutional Analysis and British Economic Policy in the 1970s," in Sven Steinmo, Kathleen Thelen, and Frank Longstreth, eds., *Structuring Politics: Historical Institutionalism in Comparative Analysis* (New York: Cambridge University Press, 1992), although Hall limits his analysis to developments within one country. See also Peter Hall, ed., *The Political Power of Economic Ideas: Keynesianism across Nations* (Princeton: Princeton University Press, 1989); "Knowledge, Power, and International Policy Coordination," special issue of *International Organization* 46 (Winter 1992), edited by Peter M. Haas; Kathryn Sikkink, *Ideas and Institutions* (Ithaca: Cornell University Press, 1991); Judith Goldstein, *Ideas, Interests, and American Trade Policy* (Ithaca: Cornell University Press, 1993); and the volume *Ideas and Foreign Policy*, edited by Judith Goldstein and Robert O. Keohane (Ithaca: Cornell University Press, 1993).

[5] Thomas Risse-Kappen, "Ideas Do Not Float Freely: Transnational Coalitions, Domestic Structures, and the End of the Cold War," *International Organization* 48 (Spring 1994), 185–214.

strategy that made neoliberal, anti-inflationary policies a priority rather than employment or growth objectives. This policy paradigm, tempered to include fixed exchange rates, provided a solution at a time of great uncertainty about the workings of the global and domestic economies. Third and finally, Germany's success with a pragmatic version of monetarist policy that emphasized a strong and stable currency provided policymakers with a powerful example to emulate. The willingness of other European governments to follow the German example increased the chance that the EMS would hold together, because the German mark serves as its anchor.

By defining the problem, providing an alternative solution, and demonstrating the policy's effectiveness, these three sources of neoliberal change both promoted and legitimated a convergence in policy preferences among European elites. Because this new view of monetary policy deemed domestically oriented, activist policies ineffective, it created the necessary conditions for sustained exchange rate stability under conditions of capital mobility.

The neoliberal consensus was not directly a function of rising capital mobility; instead, it was the product of European political leaders' interpretations of their shared experiences, the influence of the monetarist paradigm, and the German policy example. Other paths were possible, as demonstrated by the many states in the defunct Bretton Woods system, such as the United States and Japan, which moved to floating exchange rates and less stringent monetary policies. Indeed, this template of ideational change also provides some hints of the problematic nature of policy convergence in Europe, whose tensions have contributed to exchange rate crises and may undermine the ultimate durability of European monetary cooperation.

Interdependence and Ideas in Theoretical Perspective

In arguing that the structure of the international economy shapes the terrain within which politics unfold but that the interpretation of that structure, or ideational processes, dictate the crucial choice of policy content and form, I caution against making assumptions about the effects of economic interdependence on political outcomes without tracing out the linkages between rising trade and capital flows and

6

policymakers' decisions. Change of this sort is at present understudied: although we know that increasing financial interdependence is important, we still do not understand fully the process by which it interacts with domestic politics to shape foreign economic policies and, consequently, outcomes in the international system.[6]

The argument of this book thus differs from several familiar lines of argument in the literature on international political economy. For example, private economic actors, such as firms and industries, are often assumed to be the driving force for international cooperation under conditions of progressive globalization of national economies. Or the distribution of power in the international system and the dynamics of bargaining games among nation states are assumed to be the source of cooperative or discordant outcomes of international economic agreements. My findings cast doubt on the ability of such approaches to account a priori for the European policy outcomes because they make inaccurate assumptions about political actors' interests in monetary integration. In particular, these approaches fail to address the high degree of uncertainty about the microeconomic costs and benefits of different monetary regimes and the contextual nature of actors' preferences for monetary cooperation.[7] More generally, they fail to recognize that economic interdependence has multiple effects that need to be carefully traced through the domestic political process if we are to understand the evolution of international economic regimes.

My findings on European monetary integration indicate that uncertainty creates highly fluid conceptions of interest, both national and

---

[6] Recent notable exceptions include Sylvia Maxfield, *Governing Capital: International Finance and Mexican Politics* (Ithaca: Cornell University Press, 1990); Jeffry A. Frieden, *Debt, Development, and Democracy: Modern Political Economy and Latin America, 1965–85* (Princeton: Princeton University Press, 1991); Paulette Kurzer, *Business and Banking: Political Change and Economic Integration in Western Europe* (Ithaca: Cornell University Press, 1993); and C. Randall Henning, *Currencies and Politics in the United States, Germany, and Japan* (Washington, D.C.: Institute for International Economics, 1994).

[7] A related but more narrowly focused literature in economics has linked uncertainty about means-ends relationships in international macroeconomic policy to difficulties in achieving international economic cooperation. See Richard Cooper, "Prolegomena to the Choice of an International Monetary System," *International Organization* 29 (1975), 63–97; Jeffrey Frankel and Katharine E. Rockett, "International Macroeconomic Policy Coordination When Policymakers Do Not Agree on the True Model," *American Economic Review* 78 (June 1988), 318–40; and Atish Ghosh and Paul Masson, *Economic Cooperation in an Uncertain World* (Cambridge: Blackwell, 1994).

societal. This uncertainty obviously has very real consequences for the politics of monetary cooperation. Because uncertainty can obscure the distributional effects of different exchange rate regimes, it has the potential to "depoliticize" the policy process by lessening societal pressures for particular policies and insulating policymakers from public scrutiny, a dynamic heightened by the institutional independence of many central banks. Congruent with both the broader history of international monetary cooperation and that of European integration, political elites have traditionally exerted a strong influence over European exchange rate decisions. But this "depoliticization" is only superficial: the process of defining the national interest is political in both its execution and its outcomes, as is becoming clearer in the movement toward EMU.

In sum, my goal in this book is thus not to separate ideas and interests as competing causal factors but to show the inherent connection between the two.[8] By clarifying how evolving definitions of interest can shape states' preferences regarding exchange rate cooperation, I seek to overcome the shortcomings of approaches that take preferences as given and static and leave unexplored how one strategy comes to be viewed as more appropriate than another. By focusing on the reasons one set of ideas becomes politically dominant and is subsequently institutionalized as policy practice, I also contribute to the literature on ideas by specifying how ideas matter and where they come from. Although I delineate a range of economic constraints created by globalization, I reject a deterministic view of the forces of international capital in favor of the argument that the process of interest redefinition has historically been dependent on policymakers' shared beliefs. By showing the importance of both international economic conditions and actors' interpretations of those conditions, this book takes seriously the roles of both economic structure and human agency in the evolution of international cooperation.

[8] Study of the role of ideas in formulating interests has been advocated in general by Ngaire Woods, "Economic Ideas and International Relations: Beyond Rational Neglect," *International Studies Quarterly* 39 (June 1995), 161–80; in the area of European integration by Thomas Risse-Kappen, "Exploring the Nature of the Beast: International Relations Theory Meets the European Union," *Journal of Common Market Studies* 34 (March 1996), 53–80; and in the area of international monetary politics by David M. Andrews and Thomas D. Willett, "Financial Interdependence and the State: International Monetary Relations at the Century's End," *International Organization* 51 (Summer 1997), 479–511.

EUROPEAN MONETARY COOPERATION IN HISTORICAL
PERSPECTIVE

European monetary integration is deeply bound up in the evolving
historical interaction between political authority and economic markets. The tension between national policy autonomy and the benefits
of economic interdependence, and the key role played by changing
norms regarding the value of autonomy versus economic openness,
have also been pivotal in earlier studies of international monetary
cooperation.[9] Most centrally, my findings engage John Ruggie's work
on postwar international monetary regimes.[10] Ruggie identified the
balance achieved in Bretton Woods between domestic intervention
in the economy and an open international system as the crowning
achievement of the postwar era. He characterized this balance as the
"compromise of embedded liberalism" and argued that this compromise constitutes the normative basis that contemporary multilateral
cooperative regimes must rest upon if they are to succeed.

The remaining chapters in this book cast doubt on the continued
relevance of this view of international monetary cooperation and show
a very different world emerging since the late 1970s from that captured
by Ruggie. Cooperation in Bretton Woods was based on the idea that
a liberal, open, multilateral system did not have to preclude an extensive role for the state in the domestic economy—that market liberalism
would be "embedded" within a larger context of social goals, like full
employment and the welfare state's "safety net." This premise is no
longer viable in the realm of fixed exchange rate regimes, I argue, in
large part because of the effects of rising capital mobility.[11] The exam-

[9] See Kenneth Oye, "The Sterling-Dollar-Franc Triangle: Monetary Diplomacy,
1929–1937," in Oye, ed., *Cooperation under Anarchy* (Princeton: Princeton University
Press, 1986); Joanne Gowa, *Closing the Gold Window* (Ithaca: Cornell University Press,
1983); and John Odell, *U.S. International Monetary Policy* (Princeton: Princeton University
Press, 1982).

[10] John Gerard Ruggie, "International Regimes, Transactions, and Change: Embedded
Liberalism in the Postwar Economic Order," in Stephen Krasner, ed., *International Regimes*
(Ithaca: Cornell University Press, 1983), 196–232. Ruggie's article provides an astute
characterization of the Bretton Woods experience; he does not, however, identify the
causal mechanisms that produced the compromise of embedded liberalism. In contrast, I
explicitly address the sources of the new norm that made cooperation in the EMS possible.

[11] Recent evaluations of the embedded liberalism thesis include John Gerard Ruggie,
"Embedded Liberalism Revisited: Institutions and Progress in International Economic

ples of the Snake and the EMS show that such regimes can function only if participating states cease to use monetary policy actively to shape their domestic economy. The substantive effect of this monetary policy requirement is an orientation toward more neoliberal strategies of domestic governance.

To put it another way, for international exchange rate stability to be achieved, a new "consensus of competitive liberalism" is necessary. States must be willing to rule out the use of monetary policy as a weapon against broader societal problems, such as unemployment or slow growth. Instead, governments must be willing to stake their credibility on walking the plank of rigorous orthodoxy—support for exchange rate stability and inflation control above all other macroeconomic goals.

At its heart, this new norm of competitive liberalism is rooted in the view that improvement in the international economic position of the nation state warrants taking harsh steps to adjust to changing international market conditions. Thus, while liberal in its emphasis on market forces, the new consensus and its emphasis on inflation reduction are driven more by concerns with national economic competitiveness than by a commitment to liberal ideology. In this sense the consensus is a pragmatic but not predetermined response to changing international conditions on the part of governments that no longer view the preservation of national policy autonomy as a viable goal. The conservative orthodoxy shared by socialists and conservatives alike in Europe is a "second best" alternative, one that could be manageably sold to societal groups as the appropriate remedy to relieve the traumas of stagflation and Eurosclerosis.

This consensus of competitive liberalism, crucial to the success of any multilateral exchange rate regime in a world of high financial interdependence, also has high social costs. These costs were seen as bearable by domestic political actors heavily influenced by the lessons of the first oil crisis, a pragmatic version of monetarism, and the success of the German example. The limits of those lessons have become

Relations," in Beverly Crawford and Emanuel Adler, eds., *Progress in International Relations* (Berkeley: University of California Press, 1991); Eric Helleiner, *States and the Reemergence of Global Finance: From Bretton Woods to the 1990s* (Ithaca: Cornell University Press, 1994); Philip G. Cerny, ed., *Finance and World Politics* (Aldershot, Eng.: Edward Elgar, 1993); and Webb, *Political Economy of Policy Coordination*.

apparent, however. As I argue in the concluding chapter, the macro-economic record in Europe shows that the consensus of competitive liberalism can create exchange rate stability despite rising capital mobility, but it cannot assure politically acceptable levels of employment and growth. In addition, ever-higher levels of capital mobility have made adhering to the requirements of the fixed exchange rate regime more costly, as capital markets periodically challenge the credibility of European governments' decision to refrain from autonomous, expansionary monetary policies.

Cooperation, which many analysts tend to assume is an automatic "good," may come to be judged as not always beneficial, at least when it comes to exchange rate stabilization in a world of large and rapidly moving capital flows.[12] And the demands of the next stage of cooperation—Economic and Monetary Union—may well outstrip the consensus that held the exchange rate regime together, particularly if fiscal retrenchment is a criteria for membership in EMU. Whether the neoliberal consensus will unravel depends greatly on what governments and their citizens believe possible in the present economic environment and on the role they see the European Union playing in helping them govern effectively. The ideational factors I have identified as crucial to the development of the consensus will help determine how calculations about national interest are made on the part of governments and the publics they represent.

The European experience with exchange rate cooperation is central to the broader European integration effort and will continue to affect the daily lives of EU citizens, whatever the fate of the Maastricht Treaty on European Union. But this experience also is a crucial story for analysts of international and comparative politics, because it illuminates the more general issue of how domestic politics and international institutions interact in an interdependent world economy. By offering an understanding of the tensions involved in finding a balance between domestic political needs and multilateral regimes, this book may be

---

[12] Economists have tended to be much more skeptical than political scientists about the automatic value of such cooperation; see, for example, Maurice Obstfeld and Kenneth Rogoff, "The Mirage of Fixed Exchange Rates," *Journal of Economic Perspectives* 9 (Fall 1995), 73–96.

useful in the further development of such regimes, both in an ever-widening European Union and in the regions beyond its borders.

Chapter 2 begins this task by examining in more detail the nature of exchange rate cooperation and theoretical explanations for the variation in cooperation in postwar Europe. Chapter 3 then lays out my argument in detail. Chapter 4 applies the approach to the Bretton Woods international monetary system; Chapter 5 investigates the failure of the European currency Snake; and Chapter 6 examines the European Monetary System. The book concludes in Chapter 7 with an examination of the recent history of the EMS and draws on my findings to speculate on the promises and pitfalls of EMU.

CHAPTER TWO

The Puzzle of
Exchange Rate Cooperation

To promote trade, investment, and political unity, the states of the European Union attempted to achieve exchange rate stability among their currencies within three separate monetary regimes over the postwar era. These efforts met with very different results. In the early postwar U.S.-based Bretton Woods international monetary system, exchange rates were stabilized relatively successfully among all the core European states. In the subsequent European-only Snake of the 1970s, however, stability proved elusive and participation in the agreement waned. Yet the next European exchange rate agreement, the European Monetary System, had an impressive track record of longevity and stability and spurred the EU's agreement on economic and monetary union by 1999. This chapter describes in more detail the differences between the European regimes and evaluates some possible explanations for their varying success in stabilizing intra-European exchange rates.

FIXED EXCHANGE RATE REGIMES

To evaluate the two European agreements, one should first consider how fixed exchange rate regimes function to get a better sense of the role cooperation plays in minimizing exchange rate instability. An exchange rate may be thought of as a relative price: the value of one currency in terms of another. There is a range of ways in which countries can manage the price of their currencies. Setting a fixed exchange rate requires the most government intervention, and at the opposite end of the spectrum is a pure float, where governments let the market determine the price of their currencies. Most real-world cases fall somewhere in between, as governments allow their fixed rates to fluctuate within designated bands of value or intervene occasionally to influence the direction of their floating or flexible exchange rates. The specific reasons a government might choose one type of regime over another are manifold (see below and chapter 3). In general, however, the more open the economy in trade terms, the more governments prefer to fix their exchange rates because of concerns about the effect of exchange rate variability on trade and investment activity. Larger, more closed economies such as the United States and Japan have been less willing to fix their exchange rates than the smaller, more open countries of Europe.

In most fixed exchange rate regimes, national governments agree to take steps to maintain the value of their currencies at a certain rate, plus or minus a few percentage points, in relation to each other. This establishes a numerical band within which each currency is allowed to fluctuate in value. It thus is important to note that all the postwar fixed rate regimes the EU member states have belonged to have been fixed but adjustable exchange rate systems. That is, the exchange rates are pegged to each other but allowed to vary within a band, and governments have been able to periodically make discrete changes or realignments in the set value of their currencies. Thus, when I refer to *fixed* rates, the term *but adjustable* is implied.

To maintain a fixed exchange rate, governments must alter their money supply, in either or both foreign and domestic markets. First, their central bank can intervene in international currency markets, buying or selling currency from central bank reserves, to influence the value of their currencies and achieve the desired rate. This intervention can be "sterilized," meaning the central bank takes steps to neutralize the effects of the intervention on the domestic money supply, although it is unclear how consistently effective this measure is. For the majority of national central banks, foreign exchange intervention occurs on a day-to-day basis, but it can also involve extraordinary efforts requiring large amounts of money when a currency is facing market

pressures for a devaluation (where the value of the currency depreci-
ates) or revaluation (an appreciation of the currency's value). Intervention has its limits: the increasing volume and mobility of international
capital flows have made it very difficult for countries to battle strong
speculation in the currency markets through interventions. Intervention works best when a national central bank can coordinate its selling
and buying with other central banks.[1]

In most monetary regimes, including both the Snake and the EMS,
such intervention has been facilitated by mutual lines of credit among
the central banks of the participating governments. Exchange rate
stabilization was aided in the Snake and later in the EMS by the creation
of a fund to allow for short-term financing of imbalances that threaten
to push exchange rates out of line, but the amount of money available
has not always been large enough to thwart a major run on a currency.
The coordination of these activities is facilitated by regular meetings
of high-level policymakers from the EU member states, namely the
Committee of Central Bank Governors and the Council of Economic
and Finance Ministers (ECOFIN). Staff members headquartered at
the Bank for International Settlements (BIS) in Basle originally oversaw
the operation of the system and the intervention process, along with
a small professional staff in the Commission of the European Community, most notably in the Monetary Committee and in Directorate
General II, Economic and Financial Affairs. With the start of Stage II
of the Maastricht Treaty's EMU project in January 1994, the coordination of many of these functions was moved to the new European Monetary Institute in the transition to a single European currency and
central bank.

The second type of action governments can take to maintain a fixed
exchange rate is to introduce internal measures involving monetary
and fiscal policy changes to make their currencies more highly valued
or weaker on international markets. The most effective and immediate
type of policy change is an increase (or decrease) in short-term national

---

[1] Kathryn M. Dominguez and Jeffrey A. Frankel, *Does Foreign Exchange Intervention
Work?* (Washington, D.C.: Institute for International Economics, 1993); Hali J. Edison,
"The Effectiveness of Central Bank Intervention; A Survey of the Literature After 1982,"
Special Papers in International Economics, no. 18 (Princeton: Princeton University, July
1993).

interest rates to attract capital flows to invest in the national currency (or cause them to divest for better returns elsewhere). Other internal measures, if they are effective in altering the economic situation of a country, can modify the way actors in the international currency markets view the value of the currency or the credibility of its fixed rate and thus its market price. For example, if a country such as Italy, which historically has been prone to inflation and a weak currency, enacts legislation that is effective in reducing the budget deficit, currency markets will ease downward pressures on the lira, in the belief that inflation is less likely. Hence the lira will be more likely to maintain its value against other, less inflation-prone countries.

These policy measures do not always succeed in moving exchange rates in the direction governments desire. With the increasing size and volatility of international financial markets, national governments have found that it is not always easy to counteract the pressures of the markets through central bank interventions or domestic policy reforms. Also, the currency markets have at times acted in ways that seem counter to what the economic fundamentals (inflation or interest rates, for example) would indicate. For example, in 1992 the French franc came under pressure for devaluation against the German mark, even though France enjoyed a lower inflation rate and higher real interest rates than Germany. Currency traders may have believed that France's high unemployment rate would lead its political leaders eventually to put pressure on the central bank to cut interest rates to spur the economy and stimulate growth and employment. Indeed, the heavy selling of French francs in foreign exchange markets meant that French interest rates had to be raised further, slowing growth and increasing unemployment, and thus exacerbating the situation. Coordinated intervention among EMS members, however, particularly the support of the German Bundesbank, and a strong policy stance against inflation by the French government caused speculators to abandon the franc for other currencies.[2] The point is that currency traders act on *expectations* about the economy and government policy as much as they do on present-day policies or economic indicators. Thus, the role of "credibility"—the

[2] See Christian de Boissieu, "The EMS Crisis and the French Franc," in Christopher Johnson and Stefan Collingnon, eds., *The Monetary Economics of Europe: Causes of the EMS Crisis* (Rutherford, N.J.: Fairleigh Dickinson University Press, 1994), 11–17.

belief that a government is committed to an exchange rate regime and will stick to its low-inflationary path of policymaking—becomes very important.[3] What may be equally important, however, is a political commitment to multilateral coordination among members of the exchange rate system in support of the currency under pressure.

EXCHANGE RATES AND COOPERATION

Two measures provide a useful shorthand for clearly evaluating the degree to which EU member states' publicly stated goal of creating a "zone of monetary stability" in Europe was achieved and for drawing out the differences between the Snake and the EMS.[4] They are the scope and longevity of EU member state participation, and the level of exchange rate variability. The two measurements provide a rough indication of the degree to which nations are undertaking the necessary policy adjustments described above to keep their currencies within a fixed exchange rate regime. Although they do not directly measure political cooperation per se, they can be considered proxies that indicate the level of exchange rate cooperation.

Cooperation is thus defined in terms of a general trend in regime outcomes, rather than specific episodes of state behavior or interaction. This characterization departs from Robert O. Keohane's seminal definition of international cooperation: "Cooperation occurs when actors adjust their behavior to the actual or anticipated preferences of others, through a process of policy coordination."[5] In this book, the puzzle I examine concerns regime maintenance more broadly over a period of time—not specific, discrete episodes of negotiated policy adjust-

[3] John T. Woolley, "Policy Credibility and European Monetary Institutions," in Alberta Sbragia, ed., *Europolitics* (Washington, D.C.: Brookings Institution, 1991); Keith Blackburn and Michael Christensen, "Monetary Policy and Policy Credibility: Theories and Evidence," *Journal of Economic Literature* 27 (March 1989), 1–45.

[4] See "Resolution of the European Council of December 5, 1978 on the Establishment of the European Monetary System and Related Matters," in Commission of the European Communities, *European Economy*, no. 3 (July 1979), 95–97.

[5] Robert O. Keohane, *After Hegemony: Cooperation and Discord in the World Political Economy* (Princeton: Princeton University Press, 1984), 51; see also Michael C. Webb, *The Political Economy of Policy Coordination: International Adjustment since 1945* (Ithaca: Cornell University Press, 1995).

ment. This focus means that fundamental domestic-level changes in policy preferences can be considered causal forces producing regime stability or instability. Whereas the traditional definition of cooperation directs scholars to study interactions among states with a preference for cooperation but which face problems in acting collectively to achieve it, I examine preference convergence as a central and important explanation for cooperation or discord.

Although I do not directly measure policy coordination, my assumption is that continued membership in a fixed exchange rate regime and European exchange rate stability cannot occur without conscious political actions on the part of states, both in terms of domestic policy changes and multilateral, coordinated intervention in exchange markets. Some of these national policy changes may be driven in part by domestic political considerations, yet in practice it is impossible for a group of countries to spontaneously and unilaterally achieve significant exchange rate stability vis-à-vis one another's national currencies in an open international economy. A similar approach in the trade realm is largely accepted in the international relations literature, one that equates an international system characterized by free trade as a cooperative one, and a protectionist one with a failure of cooperation. The assumption is that free trade is unlikely to occur spontaneously and unilaterally but requires intergovernmental cooperation of some sort, most frequently within an institutional framework or agreement.

Two empirical observations, discussed below in detail, support the notion that exchange rate instability, not stability, is the tendency in the international political economy, absent international cooperation. One is the past experience of the European states, which indicates that there has been a change in outcome, from instability to stability, with the creation and maintenance of the EMS. The second indicator is the degree of exchange rate stability experienced by countries outside of the European arena. The data I present illustrate the extent to which the recent intra-European experience differs from other national experiences. These data suggest that the European experience with stability in the EMS is unique both over time and across other states, and that this stability unlikely to have occurred without conscious efforts on the part of states to adhere to the EU's multilateral regime.

The caveats to inferring cooperation from exchange rate stability are important ones, however. First, in some contexts, departures from exchange rate stability can themselves be the outcome of cooperation. For example, in a fixed exchange rate regime, realignments (when a government sets a new fixed value for its currency) can be an important tool for cooperation if they are used judiciously and with common consent of the regime members to correct over- or undervaluation of a currency and thus reestablish overall regime stability.[6] But a too-frequent use of realignments indicates that participating governments may not be undertaking the domestic policies necessary to adhere to the agreement and are instead pursuing unilateral goals.

Moreover, within the context of a floating rate system, the goal of states may be to act in a coordinated fashion to induce changes in the value of their currencies, not to stabilize them. A notable example is the Plaza Agreement of 1985, wherein a group of five advanced industrialized countries agreed to coordinate their policies to lower the value of the dollar and then, in the Louvre Accord of 1987, to halt its decline.[7] In this instance, currency values changed because of cooperation, whereas stability might have indicated the failure of cooperation. Attention to the context under which exchange rate outcomes are observed is obviously crucial to understanding the role cooperation may play.

A final important caveat to equating stability with cooperation concerns the role of the market. Obviously, exchange rate outcomes are not only determined by government action but also by the actions of private actors in foreign exchange markets, particularly as these markets have grown in size. The European states at times have undertaken coordinated currency interventions and released carefully orchestrated political statements in an effort to stabilize their currencies but found their efforts inadequate in the face of market skepticism about their commitments. Particular episodes of exchange rate instability should be examined carefully to determine whether markets are over-

---

[6] For a chronology of realignments in the Snake, see Table 1.1 in Daniel Gros and Niels Thygesen, *European Monetary Integration* (London: Longman, 1992), 17; realignments in the EMS are depicted in Wayne Sandholtz, "Choosing Union: Monetary Politics and Maastricht," *International Organization* 47 (Winter 1993), 29.

[7] Yoichi Funabashi, *Managing the Dollar: From the Plaza to the Louvre* (Washington, D.C.: Institute for International Economics, 1988); also see Robert Putnam and Nicholas Bayne, *Hanging Together: The Seven Super Power Summits,* rev. ed. (Cambridge: Harvard University Press, 1987) on macroeconomic cooperation more generally.

whelming efforts at cooperation, instead of assuming a lack of cooperation. In the long run, however, governments do have the ability to influence exchange rate trends, through both domestic policy adjustments and coordinated action, should they so desire. Withstanding market pressures may be costly for governments, but few would argue that exchange rate outcomes are beyond the control of those states that make exchange rates their highest priority.

Evaluating Fixed Exchange Rate Regimes

The difference in the two European regimes is particularly striking in terms of the extent and longevity of national participation. When the Snake was established in 1972, its members included Belgium, France, Germany, Ireland, Italy, Luxembourg, the Netherlands, the United Kingdom, and Denmark, all of which also participated in the Bretton Woods system. Within the first two years of the Snake's existence, however, the United Kingdom, Denmark, Italy, and France exited the agreement rather than abide by the Snake's rules, having found untenable the domestic policy adjustments and the level of coordinated interventions necessary for continued membership.[8] A limited version of the Snake, consisting of Germany and the smaller northern countries, persisted as a "D-mark zone" throughout the 1970s, but for all intents and purposes the Snake ceased to exist as a full-fledged European Community (EC) agreement within one year of its founding.

The high level of discord throughout the entire Snake experience and the inability of the EC countries to solve the problems involved in establishing a regional exchange rate agreement prompted a group of EC experts and policymakers in 1975 to characterize efforts toward monetary cooperation as a "failure" and to state that "national eco-

[8] Norway and Sweden also participated for several years as associate (non-EC) members. France and Denmark both returned to the Snake, although France exited permanently in 1976. For a chronology of national participation in the Snake, see Table 1.1 in Gros and Thygesen, *European Monetary Integration,* 17. A detailed history of its breakdown is found in Loukas Tsoukalis, *The Politics and Economics of European Monetary Integration* (London: Allen and Unwin, 1977).

nomic and monetary policies have never in 25 years been more discordant, more divergent, than they are today."[9]

In contrast, the exchange rate mechanism (ERM) of the EMS, which was founded in 1979 by Belgium, Denmark, France, Germany, Ireland, Italy, Luxembourg, and the Netherlands, and eventually added Portugal, Spain, and the United Kingdom, did not experience any loss of membership until thirteen years later, in 1992.[10] The only then-EC member state not participating in the ERM at the founding of the EMS was the United Kingdom, which entered the agreement in 1990. This strong record of participation throughout the 1980s was marred in September 1992, when a currency crisis caused Italy and the United Kingdom to exit the agreement, and culminated in the loosening of the regime's exchange rate bands in August 1993. That the EMS regime has largely maintained its membership through several severe currency crises stands in contrast to the Snake experience, when comparatively low levels of speculative pressures resulted in states' quick exit from the regime.

The level of exchange rate stability in the two regimes also differs markedly. Table 1 compares the Snake and the EMS in terms of the exchange rate variability among the countries participating in each regimes' ERM as well as the exchange rate experiences of other states not in either regimes' ERM.

As Table 1 shows, the average yearly nominal variability for the ERM countries was more than halved in the EMS period (1979–95) as compared to the Snake experience (1973–78); for those countries outside the ERM regime, both within Europe and elsewhere, currency variability remained about the same or increased.[11] Studies have also

---

[9] Robert Marjolin et al., *Report of the Study Group, Economic and Monetary Union 1980* (Marjolin Report) (Brussels: Commission of the European Community, 1975), 1.

[10] The ERM is the central element of the European Monetary System. Some governments, such as Greece and Britain, have belonged to the broader EMS without participating in the ERM. I follow the technically incorrect but common usage, however, and generally refer to the Snake and the EMS, not specifically to the ERM. For a chronology of membership, see Horst Ungerer et al., "The European Monetary System: Developments and Perspectives," *Occasional Paper* 73 (Washington, D.C.: International Monetary Fund, November 1990), Appendix III, 91–95.

[11] Other analyses of exchange rate variability that come to similar conclusions are Francesco Giavazzi and Alberto Giovannini, *Limiting Exchange Rate Flexibility: The European Monetary System* (Cambridge: MIT Press, 1989), chap. 3; and M. J. Artis and M. P. Taylor,

Table 1. Nominal exchange rate variability against the German mark in the Snake (1973–1978) and the EMS (1979–1995) (standard deviation of log changes, yearly average)

	1973–1978	1979–1995
Belgium	0.76	0.47
Denmark	0.92	0.60
France	1.71	0.62
Germany	n/a	n/a
Ireland	2.31	0.99
Italy	2.35	1.19
Netherlands	0.88	0.22
Average "core" ERM	1.49	0.68
Japan	2.37	2.34
United Kingdom	2.31	1.97
United States	2.66	2.71

DATA SOURCE: International Monetary Fund, International Financial Statistics, various years.

NOTE: values have been multiplied by 100 and are shown to two decimal places.

shown that the ERM states experienced an increase in the variability of their bilateral exchange rates in the 1979–95 period vis-à-vis currencies not in the EMS. For example, Table 2 demonstrates that the European currencies have experienced an increase in exchange rate instability against the U.S. dollar since the 1970s. This increase suggests that the currency stability among the EMS states would probably not have occurred on its own, without the institutionalized cooperation of the regime.[12]

This survey of participation and exchange rate stability in Europe demonstrates the degree to which the EMS, in contrast to the Snake, created a "zone of monetary stability." Although this stability did not match the low levels of currency variation in the early postwar Bretton Woods system, it constituted a significant change from the instability of the Snake years. What are the possible explanations for this evolution in European monetary cooperation?

"Exchange Rates and the EMS: Assessing the Track Record," *CEPR Discussion Paper* 250 (1989).

[12] For further comparative figures, see Ungerer et al., "The European Monetary System," Tables 10 and 11. For a more general discussion of the use of counterfactuals, see James Fearon, "Counterfactuals and Hypothesis Testing in Political Science," *World Politics* 43 (January 1991), 169–95.

Table 2. Nominal exchange rate variability against the $US in the Snake (1973–1978) and the EMS (1979–1995) (standard deviation of log changes, yearly average)

	1973–1978	1979–1995
Belgium	2.43	2.69
Denmark	2.36	2.65
France	2.37	2.64
Germany	2.66	2.71
Ireland	1.94	2.62
Italy	1.98	2.53
Netherlands	2.44	2.70
Average "core" ERM	2.31	2.65
Japan	2.20	2.84
United Kingdom	1.94	2.59
United States	n/a	n/a

DATA SOURCE: International Monetary Fund, International Financial Statistics, various years.

NOTE: values have been multiplied by 100 and are shown to two decimal places.

EXISTING APPROACHES TO COOPERATION

Several general approaches in the international relations literature that seek to explain instances of international economic cooperation are relevant to this puzzle. Four approaches are considered here: hegemonic stability theory, business cycles and cooperation, institutional asymmetry, and interest group theories.

Hegemonic Stability Theory

For many observers of international monetary cooperation, the logical source of regime stability is found at the level of the international system. The theory of hegemonic stability places primary focus on how the distribution of power in the international system increases or decreases the likelihood of cooperation. In general, this approach holds that because the international system is anarchic and states are primarily interested in maximizing their power relative to each other, cooperation is likely only when there is a dominant state, or hegemon, in the international system that is both able and willing to ensure economic and political stability. In this view, hegemonic structures of power are the most conducive to the development of strong, lasting cooperative agreements or regimes, and a decline in the hegemonic state's power should be correlated with the disintegration of such agreements.[13]

Hegemonic stability theory has many variants, some of which offer contradictory hypotheses about how and why cooperation comes about in the presence of a strong state.[14] A key difference among them is whether the hegemon is viewed as a benign provider of public goods and a stabilizer of the international economy, as in Charles Kindleberger's work, or as a more politically motivated, potentially coercive presence in the international system, as in the work of Robert Gilpin and others.[15] All of these theorists, however, have agreed that both Britain in the nineteenth century and the United States in the post–World War II years had the capacity and the willingness to create the necessary conditions for the ordering of nation states into liberal international economic regimes.

Indeed, agreement on the importance of hegemony is perhaps strongest among international relations scholars in the case of monetary cooperation in the Bretton Woods system. The provision of the public goods of liquidity, adjustment, and confidence by the United States lent stability to the Bretton Woods system, and the withdrawal of U.S. leadership correlates closely with the system's collapse. The overwhelming dominance of the United States thus sharply distinguishes Bretton Woods from the European-only Snake and the EMS, in

[13] Robert Keohane, "The Theory of Hegemonic Stability and Changes in International Economic Regimes, 1967–1977," in Ole R. Holsti, Randolph M. Siverson, and Alexander George, eds., *Change in the International System* (Boulder, Colo.: Westview Press, 1980), chap. 6.

[14] Helen V. Milner, "The Political Economy of International Policy Coordination," in Michele Fratianni and Jürgen von Hagen, eds., *The Political Economy of Macroeconomic Policy in Open Economies* (Westport, Conn.: Greenwood Press, 1997), chap. 6, and David Lake, "Leadership, Hegemony, and the International Economy," *International Studies Quarterly*, 37 (1993), 459–89.

[15] Charles Kindleberger, *The World in Depression, 1929–1939* (Berkeley: University of California Press, 1973); Robert Gilpin, *U.S. Power and the Multinational Corporation* (New York: Basic Books, 1975). For an overview of the various strands of hegemonic stability theory, see Gilpin, *The Political Economy of International Relations* (Princeton: Princeton University Press, 1987), 72–80.

which the United States has not participated. Because of the important presence of U.S. hegemony, I do not use Bretton Woods as a third case, on an equal footing with the Snake and the EMS, with which to test competing theories about the sources of cooperation. Instead, chapter 4 evaluates Bretton Woods as a baseline case study providing a contrast with the contemporary era, most notably in terms of the role of capital mobility in setting the requirements for cooperation. This insight is largely neglected in the political science literature on hegemony and Bretton Woods but is crucial to understanding the evolution of monetary cooperation historically.

If hegemony is useful in the Bretton Woods case, can it be reformulated to explain the pattern of European exchange rate cooperation? A modification of the theory that focuses on the rise of a regionally powerful nation would argue that German power is responsible for the success of the EMS and the Maastricht Treaty.[16] Although this argument is intuitively plausible, the lack of consistent, logical hypotheses about the dynamics of hegemony makes it difficult to extend hegemonic stability theory to a regional context, particularly in the monetary realm. This difficulty stems largely from the ambiguity over the nature of power—and the exercise of power—in hegemonic stability theory, as well as by the lack of microfoundations for understanding the benefits and costs of monetary cooperation that accrue to a hegemonic power.[17] Nonetheless, two lines of analysis using the hegemony argument can be constructed: a structural power assessment and a leadership or process-oriented one.

[16] Hegemonic stability has not been used extensively at the regional level by political scientists. One exception is Matthias Kaelberer, "Money and Power in Europe: The Political Economy of European Monetary Cooperation" (Ph.D. diss., Princeton University, 1996), which argues that German hegemony is the key to the success of the EMS. Richard Pomfret, "What Is the Secret of the EMS's Longevity?" *Journal of Common Market Studies* 24 (December 1991), 623–33, offers a counterargument. See also the articles in Kathleen R. McNamara, ed., "Money Talks? Germany in the New Europe," special issue of *German Politics and Society* 14 (Fall 1996), 1–107.

[17] An argument for increased attention to the concept of power in political science more generally is David Baldwin, *Paradoxes of Power* (New York: Basil Blackwell, 1989); Milner, "International Policy Coordination," provides a detailed and thorough review of the issues involved in applying hegemonic stability theory to European monetary integration.

Structural Power Hegemony

Perhaps the most straightforward way of assessing the hegemony thesis is to measure Germany's overall power capabilities—over time and in comparison to the other European states. Is Germany the preponderant power in Europe? The answer is ambiguous: though obviously a key actor with the strongest currency in Europe, Germany does not have the quantitative or qualitative economic and military dominance over its neighbors that marked the United States in the postwar era or Britain in the nineteenth century. The economic elements that theorists like Robert O. Keohane point to as defining hegemony—dominant control over markets and sources of capital, control of raw material supplies, and competitive advantage in the production of goods—apply to some extent, but Germany by no means has the overwhelming control Britain or the United States enjoyed at their peaks.[18] For example, as shown in Figure 1, Germany's GDP in 1990

Figure 1. German GDP over time in relation to its neighbors

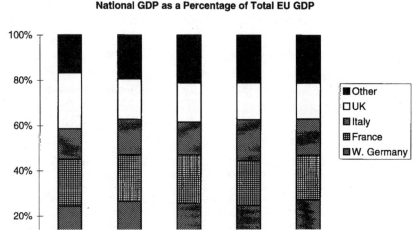

National GDP as a Percentage of Total EU GDP

DATA SOURCE: Commission of the European Communities, *The European Economy*, no. 55 (1993), Table 5, p. 113.

---

[18] These characteristics of hegemons are taken from Keohane's *After Hegemony*, 32–33; on the military aspects of hegemony, see 39–41.

represented 24.8 percent of the total GDP of the EC; France's GDP, however, is a close second at 19.8 percent; Italy is third with 18.2. In addition, the percentage share Germany holds has not changed significantly over time but has remained fairly steady from 1960 to 1994.

Germany also fails on the second crucial index of hegemony that theorists use to determine structural power: military dominance. Here, Germany is far from hegemonic: it certainly does not meet Keohane's criterion of "enough military power to be able to protect the international political economy that it [the hegemon] dominates from incursion by hostile adversaries," having essentially surrendered its military autonomy, in the wake of World War II, to NATO and its European partners.[19]

Hegemony as Leadership

An alternative way to evaluate the role Germany has played in European monetary cooperation is to look to Kindleberger's process-based explanation, which is centered on the concept of benign leadership. Kindleberger argues that an open, stable international economy needs a leader willing to provide three things: a market for distressed goods, that is, open markets even in times of international economic hardship in order to assure the stability of the trading regime; a steady and possibly countercyclical flow of capital to cushion economic downturns; and liquidity for the monetary system as a whole through a rediscount mechanism.[20]

Although since 1979 Germany has been relatively open to free trade, it is not often characterized as a market willing or large enough to counter protectionist tendencies in the system as a whole. But on the second and third points the German example seems to fail the leadership test most severely: the German government, most particularly the Bundesbank, has only rarely and reluctantly responded to calls from both inside and outside its borders to reflate its economy

---

[19] Ibid., 39. Jeffrey Samuel Barkin argues that military power is not a necessary component of hegemony. His focus on the role of finance dominance in producing conflict or cooperation may thus be more appropriate to European monetary cooperation. See Barkin, "Finance Dominance and International Economic Leadership" (Ph.D. diss., Columbia University, 1994).

[20] Kindleberger, *World in Depression.* This is similar to the argument that hegemons

or to ease its discount rate to provide liquidity both internally and to other countries in the EMS.

Instead, Germany has, on balance, followed unilateral policies oriented toward its national goal of price stability. These policies, along with the overall strength of the German economy, made the mark the' anchor currency of both the Snake and the EMS. What this has meant in practice is that these systems have been asymmetrical in terms of the adjustment obligations of the participating states—Germany sets the standard and thus must adjust less than its partners.[21] This conclusion is generally found in econometric studies of Germany's role in the EMS, which tend to debate whether the system is technically asymmetrical or not, rather than address how the leadership implied by asymmetry may translate into system stability or instability, as is done in the political science literature. In this sense, the mark in both European exchange rate regimes has played a role similar to that of the U.S. dollar in the Bretton Woods system or the pound sterling in the gold standard.[22] Yet the reluctance of Germany to act as the lender of last resort in the EMS and its fairly consistent unwillingness to compromise on the rules for European monetary cooperation cast doubt on the view of Germany as a benign leader of the system, providing the "public good" of price stability. Finally, the role of other countries, particularly France, in creating and maintaining institutions such as the EMS bears out the conclusion that cooperation has come about for reasons other than hegemonic action.

Nonetheless, if used as a starting point, hegemonic stability theory can provide important insights into the motivations of states in con-

provide for liquidity, adjustment, and confidence in monetary systems, as is argued by Benjamin Cohen in *Organizing the World's Money* (New York: Basic Books, 1977).

[21] See Gros and Thygesen, *European Monetary Integration,* 136–49; Giavazzi and Giovannini, *Limiting Exchange Rate Flexibility;* and David Cobham, "European Monetary Integration: A Survey of Recent Literature," *Journal of Common Market Studies* 24 (June 1991), 363–38. For an opposing view, however, see Michele Fratianni and Jürgen von Hagen, "Asymmetries and Realignments in the EMS," in Paul De Grauwe and L. Papademos, eds., *The European Monetary System in the 1990s* (London: Longman, 1990), and Fratianni and von Hagen, "The European Monetary System Ten Years After," *Carnegie-Rochester Conference Series on Public Policy* 32 (1990), 173–242.

[22] Ronald McKinnon, "The Rules of the Game: International Money in Historical Perspective," *Journal of Economic Literature* 31 (March 1993), 1–44; Alberto Giovannini, "How Do Fixed-Exchange Rate Regimes Work? Evidence from the Gold Standard, Bretton Woods, and the EMS," in Marcus Miller, Barry Eichengreen, and Richard Portes, eds., *Blueprints for Exchange Rate Management* (London: Academic Press,1989).

structing cooperative regimes. As Keohane has noted, "Theories of hegemony should seek not only to analyze dominant powers' decisions . . . [but should also] explore why secondary states defer to the leadership of hegemonic regimes."[23] Unfortunately, most of the literature on hegemonic stability avoids what turns out to be the critical question in the European case: why did the European states decide to participate in a system centered on the German mark and agree to move forward toward a monetary union mirroring German institutions and policy priorities?

One less common type of hegemony argument may get us closer to understanding the dynamics of German power in exchange rate politics. This strand focuses on how hegemonic states use ideology to create support among other nations for an international order or regime. Although not considered a key element by hegemonic stability theorists, ideological consensus has been cited by Charles Kupchan and John Ikenberry, among others, as a necessary element in explaining how hegemony works. Kupchan and Ikenberry focus on the nonmaterial aspects of hegemonic rule, the "component of power that is not reducible to the coercive capacities of the hegemonic state."[24] Chapter 3 examines the role that norms and ideas play in creating support among other nations for an international order, such as the German-mark-based EMS. It provides an understanding of the role of Germany that is otherwise not possible if one focuses on the traditional measures of power or leadership advocated by traditional hegemonic stability theorists.

Business Cycles and Cooperation

A further set of explanations for cooperation analyze the role of business cycles in producing conditions conducive to international

---

[23] Keohane, *After Hegemony,* p. 39.

[24] See G. John Ikenberry and Charles Kupchan, "Socialization and Hegemonic Power," *International Organization* 44 (Summer 1990), 283–315; quote on p. 289. Robert Cox draws on neomarxist precepts to argue that power always takes a consensual form in hegemonic orders as the hegemonic state attempts to establish the legitimacy of its dominance. Cox follows Gramsci's notion of hegemony, which focuses on the ability of dominant groups to create an ideological consensus with subordinate groups to perpetrate capitalism, despite its flaws. See Cox, "Social Forces, States, and World Orders: Beyond International Relations Theory," *Journal of International Studies: Millennium* 10

Table 3. Average annual economic indicators for the first three years of the Snake and the EMS

		Belgium	Denmark	France	Germany	Ireland	Italy	Nether-lands
% change GDP	1973–76	3.5	2.1	3.1	2.3	3.5	4.1	3.4
	1979–82	1.1	1.3	2.1	1.1	3.0	3.0	0.3
Unemployment	1973–76	4.3	3.5	3.5	2.4	7.1	6.0	3.9
	1979–82	10.1	8.1	6.9	4.1	9.4	7.8	7.8
Inflation	1973–76	10.4	10.8	10.6	6.1	16.8	15.9	9.2
	1979–82	6.9	8.5	12.4	5.3	17.2	17.6	5.8

DATA SOURCE: Economic Commission for Europe, *Economic Survey of Europe in 1992–93* (New York: United Nations, 1993), Appendix A, Tables A.1, A.9, A.12.

agreements. In this view, cooperation is more likely in times of economic prosperity than in economic downturns. Such logic would argue that the very difficult economic conditions of the 1970s made it less likely that states would be able to stay within the Snake. The EMS, in this view, benefitted from the improved economic environment of the 1980s, as states may have found it easier to stabilize their exchange rates within a monetary system during upturns in the business cycle.[25] Yet a survey of economic conditions does not bear out the business cycle argument.

The Snake certainly was hampered by being launched during a period of world economic crisis, but two of the severe shocks that hit the Snake during its first years (the early 1970s)—the oil crisis and inflation—recurred at the time of the founding of the EMS in 1979. Indeed, high inflation continued to create an inhospitable environment for exchange rate cooperation for several years. European states also faced a harsh recession in the early 1980s, with growth slower and

---

(Summer 1981), 126–55. See also Susan Strange, *States and Markets* (New York: St. Martin's Press, 1994).

[25] Michael D. Bordo and Tamin Bayoumi, "Getting Pegged: Comparing the 1879 and 1925 Gold Resumptions," *NBER Working Paper*, no. 5497 (March 1996) find that the external economic environment was crucial to the success or failure of exchange rate pegging in the gold standard. This argument is more conventional wisdom than developed theory in the political science literature, but it is a common part of public discussion on European integration. See Peter Ludlow, *Beyond Maastricht*, CEPS Working Document 79 (1993); Susan Strange, "The Persistent Myth of Lost Hegemony," *International Organization* 41 (Autumn 1987); 553–54, treats the proposition briefly. See also Timothy J.

unemployment higher than in the Snake years, yet there were no defections from the EMS during this period (see Table 3). Although the difficulty of trying to stabilize currency fluctuations in times of economic stress may explain the de facto collapse of the Snake within months of its founding, a similar level of economic stress during the first years of the EMS did not produce the same result.

A variation on the external economic environment argument focuses on effects of a strong dollar in the early years of the EMS: by reducing upward pressures on the German mark, the strong dollar may have stabilized European exchange rates.[26] This argument has been challenged, however, on theoretical grounds, because of disagreement over the effects of dollar weakness and variability in European exchange rates. It also is questionable on empirical grounds, because the weakening of the dollar after the Plaza Agreement did not lead to the collapse of the EMS but corresponded to increasing stability.

Institutional Asymmetry and Cooperation

A third explanation that might explain the differing durability of the two EC agreements focuses on their institutional frameworks, arguing that the EMS was structured in such a way as to make cooperation more likely than in the case of the Snake. Following this logic, Joseph Grieco has argued that cooperation was possible in the EMS because institutional innovations in the EMS spread the burden of economic adjustment more evenly.[27] Grieco maintains that the Snake failed because its rules had an asymmetrical bias, whereas the EMS worked because the rules were changed to reduce asymmetry between Germany and the rest of the EC member states. He cites this failure in support of his thesis that relative gains concerns are of paramount importance to states when they are negotiating multilateral agreements.

Nevertheless, the innovations Grieco cites as critical to changing the asymmetric bias of the regime were in fact more cosmetic changes than meaningful institutional developments. For instance, the divergence indicator, which Grieco cites as a "core new element of the EMS . . .

McKeown, "Hegemonic Stability Theory and Nineteenth-Century Tariff Levels in Europe," *International Organization* 37 (Winter 1983), 73–91.

[26] For a discussion of the relationship between the dollar and stability in the EMS, see Ungerer et al., "The European Monetary System," 12–20.

[27] Joseph Grieco, *Cooperation among Nations* (Ithaca: Cornell University Press, 1990), 222–23.

constituted in such a way as to impose a somewhat greater obligation on Germany" than on the other states, was quickly judged a failure for technical and procedural reasons, and it has played an insignificant role in the EMS.[28] Another innovation he mentions—the doubling of the financial resources available to weaker members in the form of increased lines of credit among the participating central banks—was helpful but not significant enough to transform the EMS in the face of growing capital flows. Also, the EMS agreement initially allowed for use of the funds only when a currency threatened to move outside the designated fluctuation margins. Most interventions were made intramarginally, so these funds were not available until the Basle-Nyborg Agreement of 1987 modified the financing rules.

Contradicting Grieco's assertions that the EMS distributed the burden of adjustment more evenly, most observers have concluded that both the Snake and the EMS are asymmetric institutions because of the central role that the German mark has played.[29] Thus, because the institutional structures of the Snake and the EMS are so similar, institutional structure cannot be considered a viable explanation for the differing outcomes evidenced in the two agreements.

Interest Group Theories

A final explanation for cooperation has its roots in interest group or pluralist theories. This approach argues that national policy choices can largely be understood as a function of government reaction to pressures from domestic groups representing specific interests within industry, labor, finance, and agriculture.

This approach is found in certain versions of neofunctionalist theories of European integration.[30] For some neofunctionalists, interest

[28] Ibid., On the fate of the divergence indicator, see Giavazzi and Giovannini, *Limiting Exchange Rate Flexibility*, 82.

[29] This is not to say that the question of the burden of adjustment and the degree to which Germany is willing to compromise have not been contentious political issues. For an overview of some of the studies on the asymmetrical bias, see the previous citations in note 21.

[30] The neofunctionalist literature is more complex and differentiated than the brief summary given here. Ernst Haas has contributed some of its central works: *The Uniting of Europe* (Stanford: Stanford University Press, 1958), and *Beyond the Nation State* (Stanford: Stanford University Press, 1964). For his own critical review of neofunctionalism, see

groups play a significant role in producing integration by pushing for the building of international institutions that will bring economic gains to society. These institutions entail functional linkages among issue areas and, if managed skillfully by political elites, create positive spillovers that further the integration process. The "stop-and-go" history of success and failure in the area of European monetary cooperation contradicts the general assumption of neofunctionalist theory that the integrative process is automatically self-sustaining through the process of spillover.[31] A more explicit focus on interest group theory and exchange rate policy may, however, be able to do a better job of accounting for the differences between the Snake and the EMS.

A pioneering assessment of the role of sectoral interests in monetary integration has been undertaken by Jeffry Frieden.[32] Frieden developed an innovative framework to identify the distributional consequences of increased international capital mobility, arguing that higher levels of international financial flows produce important new sources of agreement and disagreement over the shape of national monetary policies. The main thrust of his argument is that capital mobility not only exacerbates cleavages between tradable-goods and nontradable goods producers but also creates divisions between internationally oriented, diversified investors and domestically oriented, undiversified investors. These cleavages play out in the policy arena, where the winning coalition convinces the national government to pursue specific

---

also Haas, *The Obsolescence of Regional Integration Theory* (Berkeley: Institute of International Studies, University of California, 1975). See also Leon Lindberg and Stuart Scheingold, *Europe's Would-Be-Polity* (Englewood Cliffs, N.J.: Prentice-Hall, 1970). Reviews that critique this literature in the context of later theories include Henry R. Nau, "From Integration to Interdependence: Gains, Losses, and Continuing Gaps," *International Organization* 33 (Winter 1979), 119–47; and Robert Keohane and Joseph S. Nye, Jr., "International Interdependence and Integration," in Fred I. Greenstein and Nelson Polsby, eds., *International Politics: Handbook of Political Science*, vol. I (Reading, Mass.: Addison-Wesley, 1975), 363–415.

[31] A recent examination (and rejection) of neofunctionalist arguments is Andrew Moravcsik, "Negotiating the Single Act: National Interests and Conventional Statecraft in the European Community," *International Organization* 45 (Winter 1991), 19–56. For further discussion of the strengths and weaknesses of neofunctionalism, see Kathleen R. McNamara, "Common Markets, Uncommon Currencies: System Effects and the European Community," in Jack Snyder and Robert Jervis, eds., *Coping with Complexity in the International System* (Boulder, Colo.: Westview Press, 1993), especially 308–10.

[32] Jeffry A. Frieden, "Invested Interests: The Politics of National Economic Policies in a World of Global Finance," *International Organization* (Autumn 1991), 425–51.

macroeconomic and exchange rate policies that will benefit its interests.

In his analysis, Frieden draws on macroeconomic theory to identify two general, interrelated dimensions of policy choice critical to economic actors: the first concerns the degree of exchange rate flexibility and implies a trade-off between exchange rate stability and macroeconomic policy autonomy; the second, the level of the exchange rate, high (appreciating) or low (depreciating). As Frieden argues, "International traders and investors and the producers of export-oriented tradable goods tend to suffer from exchange market volatility, since it makes their business riskier," but they are less concerned about macroeconomic policy autonomy, since they are not tied to one national economy for their business.[33] Accordingly, internationally oriented firms will prefer a fixed exchange rate, with industry desiring a weak currency and financial interests favoring a strong currency. In contrast, producers of nontradable goods and services, as well as producers of goods for the national market that compete with imports, will both prefer national macroeconomic policy autonomy over stable rates, since their business is domestically oriented.

The exchange rate stability of the EMS and the subsequent plans for monetary union contained in the Maastricht Treaty can be predicted to find support from firms in the financial sector, major exporters, and diversified multinationals; monetary integration will be opposed by domestically oriented industries. The logic of Frieden's framework implies that the longevity of the EMS and the drive to full monetary union would be explained by support for monetary cooperation from the previously identified groups of economic actors because of the benefits they receive from exchange rate stability. Governments are assumed to be highly motivated to participate in agreements designed to capture such benefits in response to domestic pressures from these interest groups.

Unstable Preference Structures

How persuasive are these sectoral preferences in explaining the variation in cooperation, from the failed Snake to the relatively success-

[33] Ibid., 444–45.

ful EMS and the Maastricht Treaty?[34] Although the sectoral interests approach is promising, there is significant uncertainty, both in theory and in practice, about the size and the distribution of the gains from monetary cooperation among specific economic actors. This uncertainty is a consequence of the highly contingent and complex nature of the interactions among government monetary policy actions, the level of the exchange rate, and the variability of the exchange rate. This contingency and complexity produces a highly unstable societal preference structure, one lacking a clear political equilibrium.

For example, Frieden argues that producers of tradable goods should prefer monetary expansions, as reflationary policies generally lead to currency depreciations, making exported goods cheaper on world markets. Not captured in the analysis, however, is the fact that monetary expansions create inherent conflicts with the tradable sector's goal of exchange rate stability. So what is an export-oriented firm to prefer? The problem for the sectoral interests approach is that it is difficult to formulate an answer in the absence of highly specific information about the particular institutional and temporal context under which the decision is being made. The task of generating an aggregated, single framework of European sectoral preferences is thus complicated considerably.

First, an export-oriented firm's preference will most likely depend on the overall macroeconomic situation of the national economy and its trading partners—is the exporter's currency highly overvalued or only moderately strong? Is the exchange rate system relatively stable overall and thus could possibly withstand a one-time devaluation, or is the level of variability already excessive, making exchange rate stability a first priority? The firm's policy preference will also depend heavily on a second factor: the degree to which businesses believe inflation will be worsened by a monetary expansion and depreciation. European public debates on exchange rate and monetary policy have been dominated for the past decade by the view that a strong currency is necessary

[34] Frieden points out that his theoretical framework is only an attempt to predict the "interest at play, not necessarily . . . the outcome of political conflict among them." Ibid., 450. Indeed, this is not uncommon among detailed studies of changing interest group preferences; for example, Ronald Rogowski's study of the effects of changing international conditions on trading interests, *Commerce and Coalitions* (Princeton: Princeton University Press, 1988) also does not consider policy outcomes.

to protect against the "vicious circle" effects of depreciation and infla-tion experienced during the 1970s. Macroeconomic policy autonomy may not be privileged as a worthwhile or realistic goal, because many business and government elites fear that expansionary macroeconomic policies in the highly open economies of Europe will only bring more inflation, not growth or employment. In addition, many European export industries that might be assumed to prefer a depreciating ex-change rate to render their products more competitive in world markets may in fact prefer exchange rate stability because they rely on imported inputs for the production of their goods.[35] These classic "open econ-omy" effects have had a major impact on the way social groups think about exchange rate policy in Europe but run counter to Frieden's sectoral interest approach.

The obstacles to tracing the distributional consequences of different exchange rate regimes have been the focus of recent theoretical work by macroeconomists analyzing events in Europe. Alberto Giovannini has considered three major economic models that evaluate the effects of alternative exchange rate regimes: the Mundell-Fleming model, the rules-versus-discretion model, and the transaction costs model. He examines each model for its ability to identify the societal interest groups that should prefer one type of monetary regime over another but concludes that the models are unable to produce consistent hy-potheses regarding the economic interests in favor of fixed versus flexible exchange rates. Giovannini points out that the economic effects of a monetary regime are often highly contingent on country-specific or time-specific institutional and contextual factors and on a range of other variables, such as the source of economic shocks or the business cycle. Thus, he concludes that "there are no stable constituencies for or against monetary union." This view is echoed by Paul Krugman, who has argued that the underdevelopment of the microfoundations of international monetary theory leaves us without "anything we can properly call a model of the benefits of fixed rates and common curren-cies."[36] This microeconomic uncertainty casts doubt on the view that

[35] This argument is made in Ronald McKinnon, "Optimal Currency Areas," *American Economic Review* 53 (September 1963), 717–25.

[36] Alberto Giovannini, "Economic and Monetary Union: What Happened? Exploring the Political Dimension of Optimum Currency Areas," in Giovannini, ed., *The Debate on Money in Europe* (Cambridge: MIT Press, 1995), 312, 308; Paul Krugman, "What Do We

the economic benefits of monetary cooperation are compelling enough to stimulate strong and highly differentiated interest group pressures of the type proposed by Frieden, because the groups have trouble formulating and thus acting on a fixed and compelling preference.

The Empirical Record

Even if the distributional effects of exchange rate regimes are not well understood theoretically, societal groups may hold strong beliefs about the impact of different policies on their economic interests and engage in political action to see those interests protected. A preliminary assessment of the empirical data, however, does not support Frieden's contention that "Europe's leading financial and multinational firms have been the stronghold of support for breaking down remaining barriers to EC financial and monetary integration." There is little evidence to indicate that they have been proactive in pushing for specific policies, nor has the level of sectoral demands increased substantially as more firms have become internationalized. This conclusion is drawn from my interviews with EC observers and officials, as well as with the very representatives of the business interests Frieden's theory would predict to be strongly in favor of monetary integration and exchange rate stability.[37]

On the question of fixed exchange rates and EMU, for example, financial services representatives have demonstrated decidedly mixed reactions, not the positive endorsement Frieden predicts. In part, they dislike increased exchange rate stability and a single currency because they are reluctant to lose lucrative foreign exchange transactions business and the opportunity for large gains from currency trading, al-

---

Need to Know about the International Monetary System?" *Essays in International Finance,* no. 190 (Princeton: Princeton University, July 1993), 3.

[37] The Frieden quote is from "Invested Interests," 441. Those interviewed and quoted on the following pages include staff members from the Directorate General II of the European Union; financial journalists; expert observers of EU policymaking; banking and business interests in London and Brussels; and officials from the Union of Industrial and Employers' Confederations of Europe (UNICE), the European Trade Union Confederation, the Roundtable of European Industrialists, and the Association for Monetary Union in Europe (AMUE) (London, September 1991; Brussels, October 1991, October 1993, and May 1994; and Paris, June 1994).

though they do favor the increasing investment opportunities that come with monetary integration.

The remarks of the chief economist of a large, multinational bank are indicative: he stated that his bank had undertaken several lengthy studies to determine the effects of monetary integration on its business yet was unable to come up with a decisive position for or against.[38] Although bankers may join organizations like the Association for Monetary Union in Europe (AMUE) so as to remain within the policy debate, some have stated publicly that their AMUE support does not extend to spending time and money to see monetary integration move forward. One AMUE official noted that "the financial sector is involved in the AMUE because any change toward EMU obviously impacts them directly and they need to stay informed, but that it not the same as saying that they are pushing for EMU. They are most concerned with being well informed about the progress of the EMU project, so that they may plan accordingly."[39]

That being said, financial interests have not actively opposed steps toward exchange rate stability or European monetary union. My interviews indicate that banking interests do not want to be seen as against the "European project" because of their own "selfish" interests and because they also do not want to be excluded from the EU's decision-making process in an area of importance to them. Also, in line with the predictions of Frieden's framework, some specialized banks believe that they may gain markets with increased financial liberalization and a single currency, but such banks make up a minority of the European financial actors.

Have other, nonfinancial business interests been more active in pressuring their governments for increased exchange rate coopera-

---

[38] See also a 1990 survey done by Ernst and Young for the AMUE, which concluded that although more than half the European non-financial businesses surveyed believed a European currency would have a positive impact on their overall business strategies, "it is evident that a majority of the banks felt that the lack of a European currency has not been an obstacle to any aspect of their strategy." On balance, the effect of monetary integration was judged in the study to be neutral for the banking sector. Ernst and Young, *A Strategy for the ECU* (London: Kogan Page, 1990), quote on p. 47; see also Figures 9 and 10.

[39] These views were expressed at a private roundtable discussion, "Is EMU Dead?" at the Philip Morris Institute for Public Policy Research, Brussels, Belgium, May 6, 1994. The banker in question noted that an examination of the AMUE' balance sheet would reveal that the financial sector is not a major contributor to the organization.

tion? In general, most export-oriented firms in Europe favor exchange rate stability because of the possibility that wide swings in currency values could dampen trade within the EU, either through escalating transactions costs or, more importantly, because depreciating currencies could generate protectionist responses within the EU.[40] Multinational industrial representatives have tended to be the most prominent members of the AMUE, because they would clearly benefit from a single currency (primarily through the reduction in transaction costs). It is difficult, however, to find evidence suggesting that they have been active on the issue of monetary integration or that their interest in this issue has increased as intra-EU trade has risen.

The comments of a Brussels-based representative of an export-oriented, multinational beer and spirits company help explain why this is so: "Multinational companies [like ours] would find a single currency a marginal improvement, but only marginal. [We] are already quite adept at dealing with currency risk through hedging and so on. . . . Of course, if they ask us, we say we are for it, but it doesn't go beyond that." He further pointed out that "the people who would really be helped would be smaller businesses, who at present do not export because of the high barriers to learning about how to deal with different currencies and exchange rate risks. . . . However, they have not pushed for monetary integration because it is not in their immediate business interests."

Even the AMUE, which Frieden describes as the "private-sector lobbying organization for rapid currency union," was in fact created as the Committee for Monetary Union in Europe in 1987 by former French president Valéry Giscard d'Estaing and former German chancellor Helmut Schmidt as an "elder statesmen's group"; the majority of the initial members were national and EU officials who were longtime supporters of political and monetary integration, not business representatives. In 1988 Giscard and Schmidt decided to try to encourage businesses to support the idea of monetary integration, and they recruited Giovanni Agnelli of FIAT and C. J. Van der Klugt of Philips, among others, to become active in the new, renamed group.

[40] Barry Eichengreen, "A More Perfect Union? The Logic of Economic Integration," *Essays in International Finance*, no. 198 (Princeton: Princeton University, June 1996).

According to a senior AMUE official, the group has not been involved in the two major policy initiatives—the Delors Committee and the Maastricht Treaty negotiations—that have spurred EMU. In his experience, rather than lobby in the traditional sense, the AMUE has proved reactive in nature; the business representatives on the AMUE board hold the view that the most important benefits of monetary union lie in the political realm, as a way to further bind the EU countries together for peace and prosperity.[41]

Although this evidence is suggestive, a more systematic empirical test of the sectoral interest approach is necessary to confirm or deny conclusively the proposition that business interests are the key source of monetary cooperation in Europe. Alternatively, an empirical test of the influence of business may be impossible to construct because of the structural nature of the power wielded by multinationals. A dynamic of anticipated preferences might be occurring whereby policymakers act on what they believe to be the interests of business in monetary integration, without any actual lobbying or articulation of preferences on the part of multinational corporations.[42] Certainly, on a general level, European multinational businesses have supported the efforts of their governments to limit exchange rate variability over the postwar era, and the trend of increased openness in the European economy does correlate very broadly with the movement toward monetary integration.[43] Public opinion polls, such as those carried out by the European Commission's *Eurobarometer* surveys, tend to report high levels of support among business for monetary integration, although the interview data discussed indicate that these surveys may be problematic.

In sum, there has not been the type of highly differentiated sectoral demands for various macroeconomic and exchange rate policies that Frieden's specific-factors theory predicts. The lack of strong preference articulation on the part of financial and industrial concerns may indi-

---

[41] See also the initial statement of the AMUE, at that time called the Committee for Monetary Union in Europe, "Un programme pour l'action" (Paris: AMUE, 1988); the founding membership list is on p. 56.

[42] Charles Lindblom, *Politics and Markets* (New York: Basic Books, 1977).

[43] See the statistical survey in Jeffry A. Frieden, "The Impact of Goods and Capital Market Integration on European Monetary Politics," *Comparative Political Studies* 29 (April 1996), 193–22.

cate the structural power of business, or it may indicate instead that the causal linkages between the firms' interests and government policies in this area may be too ambiguous or, indeed, too contradictory for interest groups to act decisively. Given the amount of uncertainty in the underlying economic theories about exchange rates, this latter interpretation seems more plausible.

Generally speaking, the role of business groups in the EU varies substantially over issue area and type of policy, and the level of problems with collective action inherent in an issue works well in predicting the way business influences policy.[44] For example, interest groups are active both in Brussels and at the national levels on specific, narrowly drawn issues, such as food product regulations, that do not give rise to serious collective action problems. Some larger issues, such as the reinvigoration of the single market program, have been moved along with business input but only through the actions of a select group of key industrialists on a very elite level. The role of Wisse Dekker, chief executive of Philips, in providing a blueprint for the Single Act program is one example.[45]

Domestic political interests matter a great deal in the evolution of monetary cooperation in Europe but not in the manner assumed by traditional analyses of sectoral interest theories. Policymaking on European monetary integration issues is a highly insulated process, occurring at the level of national governmental elites and their counterparts in the European Commission in Brussels. To explain the evolution of European monetary integration, one must turn to government leaders and their beliefs about macroeconomic strategy.

My framework for evaluating different exchange rate regimes shows that the European Monetary System demonstrated a dramatically greater degree of cooperation than did the Snake. In reviewing four

[44] The classic work on collective action problems in interest groups and policy formation is Mancur Olson, *The Logic of Collective Action* (Cambridge: Harvard University Press, 1965), and Olson, *The Rise and Decline of Nations* (New Haven: Yale University Press, 1982); Joanne Gowa extends this argument in "Public Goods and Political Institutions: Trade and Monetary Policy Processes in the United States," *International Organization* 42 (Winter 1988), 15–32. Gowa asserts that different areas of monetary policy are subject to different levels of collective action problems, with exchange rate policy having the highest level.

[45] Dekker's role has been widely acknowledged in accounts such as Wayne Sandholtz and John Zysman, "1992: Recasting the European Bargain," *World Politics* 42 (October

possible explanations theorists use to identify the sources of regime stability, I argued that the theory of hegemonic stability is crucial in explaining other important historical examples of monetary cooperation, namely the Bretton Woods system, but it cannot persuasively account for variation in the European-only cases. The other explanations for the contrasting experience of the Snake and the EMS—business cycle theory, institutional asymmetry, and interest group activity—provide some useful insights but are inadequate.

Figure 2. Explanations for exchange rate cooperation and non-cooperation

	Business cycle (boom or bust)	Institutional structure	Interest group pressure	German hegemony	Neoliberal consensus on monetary policy
Snake (non-cooperation)	BUST	ASYMMETRIC BIAS	LOW	NO	NO
European Monetary System (cooperation)	BUST	ASYMMETRIC BIAS	LOW	NO	YES

Figure 2 follows J. S. Mill's "method of difference" to analyze these competing approaches. It shows that the factors identified as causally important in the approaches I surveyed were all constant over the Snake and the EMS periods. One further explanation remains to be explored, one centered on the development of a neoliberal consensus on monetary policy. This approach provides a link between changes in the independent or explanatory variables and the pattern of cooperative and non-cooperative outcomes in European exchange rate institutions, in contrast to existing explanations.

1989), 95–128. A detailed analysis is found in Maria Green Cowles, "Setting the Agenda for a New Europe: The ERT and EC 1992," *Journal of Common Market Studies* 33 (December 1995), 501–26.

CHAPTER THREE

Capital Mobility and Ideas in European Monetary Cooperation

The exchange rate stability of the European Monetary System is an anomaly in today's global economy. The success of the EMS has been viewed by many European elites as a key impetus for a single European currency and a fully integrated Europe, yet its political underpinnings are not well understood. This chapter argues that the answer to the puzzle of European monetary cooperation lies in a new neoliberal policy consensus about the goals and instruments of monetary policy that developed across the European states beginning in the mid-1970s, a consensus shaped by changing beliefs about macroeconomic policy and framed by increasing international interdependence.

CAPITAL CONSTRAINTS: MUNDELL'S HOLY TRINITY

To understand the evolution of European monetary cooperation, it is necessary to start by understanding how changes in the world economy have reconfigured the set of options governments face when deciding whether to participate in a fixed exchange rate regime.[1] A variant of the Mundell-Fleming model, a central framework in modern

---

[1] A classic treatment of many of the issues surveyed here is W. M. Corden, "Monetary Integration," *Essays in International Finance*, no. 93 (Princeton: Princeton University, April 1972).

43

macroeconomic theory, is useful for this purpose. The theoretical proposition is formally known as Mundell's "assignment problem" but is commonly referred to as the "Holy Trinity."[2] It sketches out the interaction between domestic policy choices and multilateral exchange rate cooperation as capital markets become increasingly integrated and the volume of capital flows rises.[3] The Holy Trinity holds that' policymakers can choose only two out of three policy options at any one time: free capital flows, a fixed exchange rate, and monetary policy autonomy. Thus, if a state wishes to keep its exchange rate fixed in the context of international capital mobility, national monetary policy must be used to maintain exchange rate parity and cannot be directed toward other internal goals.

The logic behind this proposition can be illustrated with a simple example. If Belgium decided to use its monetary policy in the hope of stimulating growth or employment, national monetary policy would be relaxed and interest rates would be lowered. The fall in interest rates would have the effect of encouraging investors to move their funds out of Belgium markets and thus sell their Belgian francs in a search for higher rates elsewhere. As a result of the capital outflow, a balance of payments deficit would be created and the Belgian franc would tend to depreciate. This pressure would force the Belgian central bank to intervene by buying up Belgian francs and selling foreign money in exchange until the franc stabilized at its assigned fixed rate.

[2] Robert Mundell, "The Monetary Dynamics of International Adjustment under Fixed and Flexible Exchange Rates," *Quarterly Journal of Economics* 74 (1960), 227–57. See also Peter B. Kenen, "Macroeconomic Theory and Policy: How the Closed Economy Was Opened," in Ronald W. Jones and Peter B. Kenen, eds., *Handbook of International Economics*, vol. 2, *International Monetary Economics and Finance* (Amsterdam: North Holland, 1985), especially 662–65. This proposition was dubbed "the unholy trinity" by Benjamin Cohen in *Organizing the World's Money* (New York: Basic Books, 1977).

[3] Political analyses focusing on various aspects of the Mundell-Fleming framework are David Andrews, "Capital Mobility and State Autonomy: Towards a Structural Theory of International Monetary Relations," *International Studies Quarterly* 38 (1994), 193–218; Louis W. Pauly, *Who Elected the Bankers? Surveillance and Control in the World Economy* (Ithaca: Cornell University Press, 1997); Michael C. Webb, *The Political Economy of Policy Coordination: International Adjustment since 1945* (Ithaca: Cornell University Press, 1995); and Jonathon Moses, "Abdication from National Policy Autonomy: What's Left to Leave?" *Politics and Society* 22 (June 1994), 125–48; Benjamin Cohen, "The Triad and the Unholy Trinity: Lessons for the Pacific Rim," in Richard Higgott, Richard Leaver, and John Ravenhill, eds., *Pacific Economic Relations in the 1990s: Cooperation or Conflict?* (Boulder, Colo.: Lynne Reinmer, 1993).

This currency intervention would have the same effect, however, as a contraction of the money supply: it would undo the effects of the initial expansion and raise Belgian interest rates to their original levels. This process could be stymied only if capital mobility is low and investors are not prone to moving their money among different national markets. Alternatively, the Belgian government could cease to defend its fixed exchange rate so as to sustain the effects of the original policy initiative.

Fixed versus Floating Exchange Rates

The first of the three policy options a government has in the international macroeconomic realm is its choice of exchange rate regime. A government can choose to keep its exchange rate nominally fixed (against another currency, a commodity such as gold, or a "basket" of currencies), or it can let the currency float, with its value largely determined by market forces. In the modern era, Europeans have for the most part preferred to fix their currencies so as to limit exchange rate fluctuations. Bretton Woods, the Snake, and the EMS are all examples of fixed but adjustable exchange rate systems set up with the intent of keeping exchange rate fluctuations to a minimum among member states. Many of the European states have allowed their currencies to float over certain periods, however—notably the interwar years and in the years following the failure of the Snake in the 1970s.

Exchange rates are of particular concern to states that are highly open; because trade makes up a higher percentage of overall GDP for the European states than for the United States or Japan, as indicated in Table 4, they have a stronger incentive to make exchange rate stability a priority. In contrast, a relatively small proportion of the U.S. economy is dependent on international trade, which may explain the willingness of American officials to maintain a floating exchange rate since the demise of Bretton Woods. Another important fact is that the majority of the European states trade heavily with each other, making it again more likely that they would try to stabilize rates within the EU.

Although the level of intra-European trade is a good initial explanation for why European governments might be sensitive to currency fluctuations within the EU and less so to fluctuations outside their common market, there is surprisingly little empirical evidence or academic agreement on the degree to which exchange rate uncertainty

45

Table 4. Openness in the European Community, United States, and Japan: Exports and imports as a percentage share of GDP

	1965		1975		1985		1995	
	EXP	IMP	EXP	IMP	EXP	IMP	EXP	IMP
Belgium	42.6	42.9	53.7	53.3	76.8	74.3	72.0	66.2
Denmark	29.2	30.7	30.1	31.0	36.7	36.3	36.4	30.6
Germany	17.9	17.6	24.5	21.6	32.5	29.0	34.7	25.7
France	13.8	12.9	19.5	18.8	23.9	23.2	23.0	21.2
Italy	14.0	11.8	19.8	19.9	22.8	23.2	24.3	20.7
Netherlands	42.9	43.6	49.9	46.5	60.8	56.0	52.6	47.0
United Kingdom	19.3	20.1	26.0	27.8	28.8	27.8	27.3	27.7
EC12	18.7	18.9	24.4	27.9	30.8	29.5	31.3	27.4
Japan	10.5	9.1	12.8	12.8	14.5	11.1	9.1	7.3
United States	5.2	4.4	8.6	7.6	7.5	10.4	11.1	12.9

SOURCE: Commission of the European Communities, *European Economy* 59 (1995), Tables 38 and 42. Figures for Germany and EC12 represent West Germany only.

and currency transaction costs hinder trade flows.[4] Whatever the inconclusiveness of these scholarly studies, the level of government support in Europe for fixed rates over flexible rates has been fairly constant, as is demonstrated by the attempts at cooperation during the postwar era. As I argued in chapter 2, the trend toward openness correlates very generally with increasing government commitment to exchange rate stability, but it remains to be explained how openness translates into political decisions regarding European monetary regimes.[5]

[4] The European Commission presents the case for the high costs of exchange rate variability on trade in Michael Emerson et al., *One Market, One Money: An Evaluation of the Potential Benefits and Costs of Forming an Economic and Monetary Union* (Oxford: Oxford University Press, 1992), chap. 3. More skeptical accounts include the International Monetary Fund, "Exchange Rate Variability and World Trade," *Occasional Paper* 28 (1984); Avinash Dixit, "Entry and Exit Decisions under Uncertainty," *Journal of Political Economy* 97 (1989), 620–30; John Williamson, *The Exchange Rate System* (Washington, D.C.: Institute for International Economics, 1985); Paul Krugman, "Deindustrialization, Reindustrialization and the Real Exchange Rate," *NBER Working Paper,* No. 2586 (1988); A. R. Chowdhury, "Does Exchange Rate Volatility Depress Trade Flows? Evidence from Error-Correction Models," *Review of Economics and Statistics* 75 (1993), 700–706; L. Bini-Smaghi, "Exchange Rate Variability and Trade: Why Is It so Difficult to Find Any Empirical Relationship?" *Applied Economics* 23 (May 1991), 927–35; and J. E. Gagnon, "Exchange Rate Variability and the Level of International Trade," *Journal of International Economics* 34 (May 1993), 269–87.

[5] Jeffry Frieden, "The Impact of Goods and Capital Market Integration on European Monetary Politics," *Comparative Political Studies* 29 (April 1996), 193–222.

The European governments have a second trade-related reason for favoring exchange rate stability: the EU's Common Agricultural Policy (CAP), an agricultural stabilization and subsidization program established in the early 1960s that sets common prices for food products among its members (see chapter 5). Fluctuations in national currencies greatly increase the complexity and costs of administering this politically important program, thereby reinforcing governments' preference for exchange rate stability. Even though a series of reforms have streamlined the CAP, exchange rate variability continues to create problems within the program.

Autonomous versus Surrendered Monetary Policy

The second element of Mundell's framework is national monetary policy. The key trade-off is between directing monetary policy internally in an effort to shape the domestic economy or using monetary policy to achieve an external goal—the maintenance of exchange rate stability. As described in the Belgian example above, the basic insight is that if capital mobility is high and the state is participating in a fixed exchange rate regime, governments can use their monetary policy only for external purposes. If, however, financial flows are low, there is more room to use monetary policy for internal, nonexchange-rate-related purposes without jeopardizing the fixed exchange rate target.

For the majority of the postwar era, the internal goals of monetary policy were those of macroeconomic demand management. Demand management is the attempt to fine-tune the economy using the contraction and expansion of monetary policy to speed up or slow down economic growth, decrease unemployment, or control inflation.[6] This "activist" monetary policy was part of the broader Keynesian arsenal of policy instruments taken up by governments in the 1960s. Keynesian policies can be thought of as independent or autonomous in the sense that they are tailored to domestic political concerns about the direction of the national economy and are not merely directed to an external exchange rate target. In contrast, externally oriented national mone-

[6] For an overview of these issues, see Niels Thygesen, "Monetary Policy," in Andrea Boltho, ed., *The European Economy: Growth and Crisis* (Oxford: Oxford University Press, 1982), 329–64.

tary policy is targeted toward ensuring that the national currency holds its value in international markets. Central bank interventions (buying and selling on international currency markets) are undertaken to support the currency, or interest rate changes are implemented to stabilize a depreciating (or appreciating) currency. Monetary policy is not autonomous but is subordinate to exchange rate considerations.

A crucial part of the external face of monetary policy is rooted in market perceptions about inflation. Controlling inflation is one of the most important actions a government can take to stabilize its exchange rate, because the relative pace of inflation helps determine the future value of the exchange rate in the eyes of the market. But investors use *expectations* about inflation rate differentials—not simply the present inflation rate—to gauge the direction of exchange rates. If a government's monetary policy actions are viewed as expressing a truly credible, long-term commitment to fighting inflation, inflationary expectations are likely to be low.[7] Thus, if capital mobility is high and monetary policy is oriented toward the external goal of exchange rate stability, the internal goal most congruent to this situation is price stability, because low inflation supports the value of a currency and keeps it stable. Success at inflation fighting on the part of only a few members of an exchange rate regime might, however, in the short term mean currency appreciation instead of stabilization. A regime-wide reflation or expansion could be achieved without currency instability only if effectively and precisely coordinated.

Capital Controls versus Capital Mobility

The final policy option in Mundell's framework concerns the level of capital mobility. Is capital relatively free to move across national borders, or are there significant barriers to capital movements? Cross-border portfolio transactions, such as the trading of currencies or

[7] Robert Barro and David Gordon, "A Positive Theory of Monetary Policy in a Natural Rate Model," *Journal of Political Economy*, 91, no. 4 (1983), 589–610; on its application to the EMS, see Francesco Giavazzi and Marco Pagnano, "The Advantages of Tying One's Hands: EMS Discipline and Central Bank Credibility," *European Economic Review* 32 (June 1988), 1055–75; and John Woolley, "Policy Credibility and European Monetary Institutions," in Alberta Sbragia, ed., *Euro-politics* (Washington, D.C.: Brookings Institution, 1991), 157–90.

financial claims, international banking, and the provision of commercial banking services, constitute international capital flows. There are also significant flows associated with foreign direct investment, such as the financing of production facilities abroad. Western Europe has moved from high levels of openness at the turn of the last century to closure and capital controls in the period surrounding World War II to the reemergence of capital mobility in the contemporary era. A complete analysis of this phenomenon cannot be undertaken here, but a simple assessment of the calculus of decisions states confront in the area of capital mobility is helpful.[8]

The most fundamental benefit of allowing capital mobility is, at least in theory, that capital will be allocated to uses that produce the highest returns and are the most productive. Capital movements are necessary to have truly integrated global markets for goods and services and thereby achieve the welfare maximization that forms the basis of the theory of comparative advantage. If capital is not free to move, it will distort trade and investment decisions, and result in inefficiency and loss of aggregate welfare.

More specifically, allowing inflows of capital may assist governments in financing public spending through the sale of national financial instruments, such as treasury bonds, to foreign investors. Allowing outflows may assist national investors in accumulating more wealth through their overseas investments than would be possible if they were only allowed to build national portfolios. Thus, governments seeking to create the conditions for growth in their own economies and encourage the creation of wealth, at least among certain of their citizens, find capital mobility an attractive prospect.

Yet freedom of choice also means that when capital can flow to the highest return regardless of national affiliation, it may produce divestment from domestic firms and industries or a drop in the use of national financial instruments, be they stocks or bonds, and thus difficulties in financing private and public debts. Also, some argue that

---

[8] A thorough historical analysis is provided in Eric Helleiner, *States and the Reemergence of Global Finance* (Ithaca: Cornell University Press, 1994). An overview of the recent literature on this topic is Benjamin Cohen, "Phoenix Risen: The Resurrection of Global Finance," *World Politics* 48 (January 1996), 268–97; see also Richard J. Herring and Robert E. Litan, *Financial Regulation in the Global Economy* (Washington, D.C.: Brookings Institution, 1995).

the downside to capital mobility is the potential for financial instability to disrupt the "real" economy (that is, the nonfinancial sectors) when financial speculation leads to irrational collective outcomes. For example, many observers argue that foreign exchange markets do not always function optimally but instead are prone to excessive, destabilizing volatility or to over- or undervaluation of currencies.[9] An overly strong currency may damage national industrial competitiveness; an overly weak one may aggravate domestic inflation.

In practice, the choice of whether to control capital or not has rarely been a dichotomous decision on the part of states. States have generally sought to gain the benefits of free financial movements while attempting to avoid the costs, with varying degrees of emphasis on openness or insulation. The early postwar period was marked by a consensus on the value of capital controls as a way to guard against what was seen as the damaging speculative flows of the nineteenth-century gold standard (see chapter 4). In this unique period in the political economy of the last century, low levels of capital mobility meant that governments could maintain a high level of monetary policy autonomy and still fix their exchange rates.[10]

Capital mobility began to accelerate in the late 1960s due to a remarkable confluence of events. Briefly, the factors leading to increasing levels of capital flows included the demise of the Bretton Woods fixed exchange rate system, which prompted the growth of foreign exchange markets; the balance of payments crises brought on by the OPEC oil shocks; the development and use of new financial instru-

[9] Mahbub ul Haq, Inge Kaul, and Isabelle Grunberg, eds., "Overview," in *The Tobin Tax: Coping with Financial Volatility* (New York: Oxford University Press, 1996, 1–14). See also Tony Porter, "Capital Mobility and Currency Markets: Can They Be Tamed?" *International Journal* 51 (Autumn 1996), 669–90.

[10] Figures comparing capital flows in the pre-1914 gold standard era to the present can be found in Philip Turner, "Capital Flows in the 1980s: A Survey of Major Trends," *BIS Economic Papers* 30 (April 1991), 13–20. For an overview of the data on international capital flows, see International Monetary Fund, *Determinants and Systemic Consequences of Capital Flows* (Washington, D.C.: International Monetary Fund, March 1991), 3–7. Other relevant literature includes Susan Strange, *Casino Capitalism* (Oxford: Basil Blackwell, 1986); Charles Kindleberger, *International Capital Movements* (New York: Cambridge University Press, 1987); Mark Allen et al., *International Capital Markets: Developments and Prospects* (Washington, D.C.: International Monetary Fund, 1989 and 1990); and Maurice Obstfeld, "International Capital Mobility in the 1990s," *CEPR Discussion Paper* 902 (February 1994).

ments; technological advances; and a gradual reduction in capital controls. In some cases, increased capital mobility was the product of conscious government policy; in others, it was independent of government action or in spite of government action, as with certain national capital regulations, which had the unintended consequence of spurring the development of offshore capital markets.[11]

Many observers point to the difficulties states face in establishing effective capital controls as an indication of the universality and power of capital flows. Capital controls were used throughout the postwar era to reinstate some degree of policy autonomy by preventing or slowing down the adjustment that would occur if financial transactions were free from controls. As capital mobility has increased, however, capital controls have become less effective in all but the very short term, because of the increased volume and responsiveness of capital.[12] As the *Economist* noted, "In international finance, regulators are at a great disadvantage because money is so slippery," pointing out that, for example, when governments attempted to place new restrictions on rising financial flows in the wake of the breakdown of Bretton Woods, these regulations only spurred more innovations to circumvent them.[13] One argument for why policies of capital decontrol converged among several industrialized states in the late 1970s and early 1980s is simply that governments realized controls were no longer effective. Multinational corporations and financial institutions can use strategies

[11] An overview of the literature in this area is provided in Gerald A. Epstein and Juliet B. Schor, "Structural Determinants and Economic Effects of Capital Controls in OECD Countries," in Schor and Tariq Banuri, eds., *Financial Openness and National Autonomy: Opportunities and Constraints* (Oxford: Clarendon Press, 1992), 136–62.

[12] See Daniel Gros, "The Effectiveness of Capital Controls: Implications for Monetary Autonomy in the Presence of Incomplete Market Separation," *Staff Papers of the International Monetary Fund*, vol. 34/4 (December 1987), 621–42. Gros's study mainly addresses the types of quantitative controls employed in the EMS, concluding that international capital flows effectively offset the actions of national monetary authorities and controls "provide only temporary autonomy for national monetary policy" (639). The French experiment with capital controls in the early 1980s is an example of how difficult it is to put the genie back in the bottle, once freed. See Michael Loriaux, *France after Hegemony* (Ithaca: Cornell University Press, 1991), chap. 8. Others still advocate the creation of new types of capital controls, most notably Barry Eichengreen and Charles Wyplosz, "The Unstable EMS," *Brookings Papers on Economic Activity* 1 (1993). On the technical issues, see Peter B. Kenen, "The Feasibility of Taxing Foreign-Exchange Transactions," in ul Haq, Kaul, and Grunberg, eds., 109–28.

[13] "Fear of Finance: A Survey of the World Economy," *Economist*, September 19–25, 1992, 12. This survey provides an overview of the growth of international capital mobility.

of evasion and the threat of exit to undermine national regulations.[14] Others, however, note that international financial markets are far from perfectly integrated, because investors continue to view national and international assets differently, not as perfect substitutes for each other. Empirical studies have concluded that the majority of national savers still tend to favor local investments over potentially higher-yielding foreign assets.[15]

It is important to remember, however, that capital mobility does not constitute a force outside political authority.[16] Although technical difficulties do exist, the political costs of capital control are the most significant barrier to regulating capital mobility. Some of these political costs are obvious: the international investment community is a potent political force opposing efforts at capital control. Some of the political pressures may be more subtle: as Goodman and Pauly note, although there is little evidence that firms use strategies of evasion and exit in response to capital controls, the potential for these actions exerts a structural power on national policymakers that need not be exercised to have effect.[17] What is also less obvious is that a government seeking to ensure politically acceptable levels of economic growth may eschew capital controls in the fear that they will dampen economic activity.

Finally, capital controls may be opposed because they run directly counter to the ideology of neoliberalism. Whereas the consensus at the end of World War II favored the regulation of capital movements, by the 1980s an ideology of decontrol and deregulation had gained

[14] John B. Goodman and Louis W. Pauly, "The Obsolescence of Capital Controls? Economic Management in an Age of Global Markets," *World Politics* 46 (October 1993), 50–82.

[15] There remains a high degree of correspondence between national saving and investment rates, despite capital mobility. Martin Feldstein and Charles Horioka, "Domestic Savings and International Capital Flows," *Economic Journal* 90 (1980), 314–29, is the classic investigation of the savings/investment question. See also Barry Bosworth, *Savings and Investment in a Global Economy* (Washington, D.C.: Brookings Institution, 1993); Atish Ghosh, "International Capital Mobility amongst the Major Industrial Economies: Too Little or Too Much," *Economic Journal* 105 (January 1995), 107–28; and International Monetary Fund, *Capital Flows*.

[16] Louis W. Pauly, "Capital Mobility, State Autonomy, and Political Legitimacy," *Journal of International Affairs* 48 (Winter 1995), 369–89; Suzanne Berger and Ronald Dore, eds., *National Diversity and Global Capitalism* (Ithaca: Cornell University Press, 1996).

[17] Goodman and Pauly, "The Obsolescence of Capital Controls?" 59.

influence within Europe and most of the OECD states. In particular, EU authorities had equated freedom of capital movement with a broader series of market reform efforts, most centrally the Single European Act and its "four freedoms" (free movement of goods, services, people, and capital).

Mundell's Holy Trinity and European Monetary Cooperation

Although Mundel's framework is generally accepted in economic thinking, it has not been subjected to systematic empirical analysis. This is surprising, for the proposition that only two out of the three conditions—capital mobility, fixed exchange rates, and policy autonomy—can be met at any one time provides a useful framework for interpreting the broader history of international monetary regimes.[18]

Figure 3. Capital mobility and international monetary systems: The "Holy Trinity" in historical perspective

| | Economic Policy Options | | |
| | --- | --- | --- |
Monetary regime	Capital mobility	Autonomous monetary policy	Fixed exchange rates/cooperation
Bretton Woods	NO (low levels)	YES	YES
European Currency Snake	YES (rising)	YES	NO (attempted, but failed)
European Monetary System	YES (high)	NO	YES

NOTE: Only two of the three policy options can be met at any one time.

Figure 3 depicts the Bretton Woods system as a cooperative fixed exchange rate regime in the context of relatively low capital mobility and autonomous policymaking. In contrast, the European Snake coex-

---

[18] One exception is the econometric study by Andrew Rose, "Exchange Rate Volatility, Monetary Policy and Capital Mobility: Empirical Evidence on the Holy Trinity," *NBER Working Paper*, no. 4630 (January 1994). Rose's results weakly support Mundell's proposition.

isted with continued autonomous policymaking during a time of rising capital mobility, which made fixed exchange rates unsustainable. The achievement of fixed rates in the EMS, on the other hand, was marked by high capital mobility and relatively little policy autonomy.[19]

To make sense of the dynamics involved in the contemporary European cases, one must turn to the Bretton Woods regime. The Bretton Woods system, which included all the states of what is today the European Union, was created in 1945 and lasted until 1971. Bretton Woods was set up so as to allow domestic policy autonomy to coexist with fixed exchange rates in what John Ruggie has called the "compromise of embedded liberalism."[20] Embedded liberalism refers to the idea that Bretton Woods was liberal in the sense of encouraging international economic transactions, but its liberalism was tempered by or "embedded" within a larger social context of goals beyond those of economic efficiency. It stands in contrast to the laissez-faire approach of the nineteenth century, which minimized government intervention and gave primacy to market rationality despite effects on national unemployment and other domestic conditions. This embedded liberalism arrangement, in conjunction with the United States's hegemonic role as stabilizer of the system, was a precondition for multilateral cooperation. The ability to intervene in the domestic economy with the tools of Keynesian macroeconomic management—in other words, monetary policy autonomy—was something national governments were unwilling to sacrifice, even though they sought international monetary stability after World War II.[21] The Bretton Woods arrangement thus "was intended to provide a compromise between the desire to stabilize exchange rates in order to avoid the disorderly markets and competitive depreciations of the 1930s, and the desire to avoid forcing countries to revert to the gold standard 'rules of the game,' under which defence

---

[19] If the gold standard was included in Figure 3, it would be coded in the same way as the EMS case.

[20] John Gerard Ruggie, "International Regimes, Transactions, and Change: Embedded Liberalism in the Postwar Economic Order," in Stephen Krasner, ed., *International Regimes* (Ithaca: Cornell University Press, 1983), 195–232.

[21] This point has been widely acknowledged. See Ronald McKinnon, "The Rules of the Game: International Money in Historical Perspective," *Journal of Economic Literature* 31 (March 1993), 11–15; Benjamin Cohen, *Organizing the World's Money* (New York: Basic Books, 1977), 90–107; and Robert Solomon, *The International Monetary System, 1945–1981* (New York: Harper and Row, 1982).

of the exchange rate overrides the pursuit of domestic full employment policies."[22] But the only way to ensure this intention could be realized was to limit capital movements within the system; indeed capital controls were a major preoccupation of John Maynard Keynes in designing Bretton Woods.[23] Thus, with autonomous monetary policy, fixed rates, and low levels of capital mobility, in Bretton Woods the Holy Trinity conditions were met.

The resurgence in international capital mobility in the late 1960s and early 1970s had serious consequences for European governments' efforts to sustain a fixed exchange rate regime. Although it was not well understood by policymakers at the time, when the Snake was created in the wake of a sinking Bretton Woods system, the rising level and mobility of capital flows was beginning to make the pursuit of fixed exchange rates conditional upon the surrender of monetary policy autonomy. In other words, the compromise of embedded liberalism, which allowed states to expand and contract the national money supply in the quest for full employment and economic growth, could no longer form a basis for multilateral monetary cooperation within a fixed exchange rate regime. Capital flows were simply becoming too high to continue to coexist with fixed rates and policy autonomy.

Many European governments did continue to use autonomous, Keynesian macroeconomic policies oriented to the particular needs of their domestic polities after Bretton Woods and throughout the Snake period, making the maintenance of fixed exchange rates extremely difficult. By the time of the creation of the EMS, however, key European governments, and most importantly France, had begun to eschew domestic policy autonomy. This shift formed the basis for the achievement of fixed exchange rates in the EMS.

Mundell's framework helps make sense of what David Andrews has called "the capital constraint" on national monetary policymaking that

---

[22] John Williamson, *The Failure of World Monetary Reform* (New York: New York University Press, 1977), 3.

[23] See Alexandre Lamfalussy, "Changing Attitudes towards Capital Movements," in Frances Cairncross, ed., *Changing Perceptions of Economic Policy* (London: Methuen, 1981), 194–231; on the construction of the Bretton Woods regime, see G. John Ikenberry, "The Political Origins of Bretton Woods," in Michael D. Bordo and Barry Eichengreen, eds., *A Retrospective on the Bretton Woods System* (Chicago: University of Chicago Press, 1993).

European governments faced in trying to achieve fixed rates.[24] Yet it only sets the structural conditions under which governments decide on policy. It does not tell us what choice governments will make when faced with these three incompatible goals of capital mobility, policy autonomy, and fixed rates. Although costly, governments may choose to limit capital mobility to regain some policy autonomy and stabilize exchange rates, particularly through multilateral policy coordination. Governments may also choose to float their rates rather than keep them fixed, as in the case of the governments that left the Snake. Indeed, many former Bretton Woods members moved to floating rates after that system's collapse and have never gone back. Why were the European states willing to forgo the autonomous conduct of monetary policy to achieve exchange rate stability under the EMS but not in the Snake?

IDEAS AND POLICY CONSENSUS IN MONETARY COOPERATION

This question can be answered by complementing the analysis of international economic structures and the trade-offs they present with an examination of how states' interests in monetary cooperation have been constructed and transformed over the postwar period. This focus on interest definition is critically important, for a new convergence in interests brought about cooperation in the EMS, in contrast to the Snake. National elites' ideas about the nature of the domestic economy and the goals and instruments of monetary policy directly informed their positions on European monetary integration. Although the international economic environment is important, as Emanuel Adler has pointed out, "the environment does not 'instruct' policymakers, it challenges them."[25] In the macroeconomic realm, the responses policymakers formulate to address those challenges cannot be understood without attention to ideational factors, in particular, policymakers' shared beliefs about the nature of monetary policy.

[24] Andrews, "Capital Mobility and State Autonomy."

[25] Emanuel Adler, "Cognitive Evolution: A Dynamic Approach for the Study of International Relations and Their Progress," in Adler and Beverly Crawford, eds., *Progress in Postwar International Relations* (New York: Columbia University Press, 1991), 53.

Ideas and Uncertainty

Much of the political science literature tends to assume that interests can be determined from an actor's position in the economy or within the prevailing political order. State or societal actors simply know or recognize what is in their interest and act on that knowledge; in many accounts, interests are given or exogenous. Some theorists have argued, however, that interpretations of the external world, be it market structures or power politics, are problematic. Actors must rely on conceptual frameworks to make sense of the world and their place within it. The most fundamental critique of the "rationalist" approach comes from the social constructivist school.[26] Others have elected to critique the rationalist approach from within, by using social science methodology to study the role of ideas.[27] That is the approach taken here.

Ideas are critical in the monetary realm because of continuing uncertainty over the basic workings of the macroeconomy, the difficulties of collecting and interpreting signals from macroeconomic data about the effects of policy, and the lack of agreement over what constitutes "correct" macroeconomic policy. In other words, economic structure alone is indeterminant in its effects and meaning for policymaking. Shared beliefs are thus fundamental to monetary politics.[28] These be-

[26] On constructivism see Alexander Wendt, "Anarchy Is What States Make of It: The Social Construction of Power Politics," *International Organization* 46 (Spring 1992), 391–425.

[27] Notably Kathryn Sikkink, *Ideas and Institutions: Developmentalism in Brazil and Argentina* (Ithaca: Cornell University Press, 1991); Judith Goldstein, *Ideas, Interests, and American Trade Policy* (Ithaca: Cornell University Press, 1993); and others to be cited below. For an astute critique of this ambition, see Mark Laffey and Jutta Weldes, "Beyond Belief: Ideas and Symbolic Technologies in the Study of International Relations," *European Journal of International Relations* 3 June, 193–238; and Mark W. Blyth, "Any More Bright Ideas? The Ideational Turn of Comparative Political Economy," *Comparative Politics* 29 (January 1997), 229–50. A promising approach addressing these critiques is Peter J. Katzenstein, ed., *The Culture of National Security: Norms and Identity in World Politics* (New York: Columbia University Press, 1996). The volume's authors draw on sociological theory in ways that ground the theoretical insights in empirical analysis and provide a valuable alternative to existing approaches.

[28] Peter Hall, "Policy Paradigms, Social Learning, and the State," *Comparative Politics* 25 (April 1993), 275–96, and Hall, "The Movement from Keynesianism to Monetarism: Institutional Analysis and British Economic Policy in the 1970s," in Sven Steinmo, Kathleen Thelen, and Frank Longstreth, eds., *Structuring Politics: Historical Institutionalism in Comparative Analysis* (New York: Cambridge University Press, 1992). On ideas as focal points for policy coordination in the EU, see Geoffry Garrett and Barry Weingast, "Ideas, Interests, and Institutions: Constructing the European Community's Internal Market,"

liefs serve as a crucial guide for government officials attempting to analyze the complex technical relationships that make up the macro-economy, providing them with a means-end knowledge that allows for the development of economic policies. In other words, these policy ideas can function like flashlights, guiding policymakers by illuminating a specific path through the darkness of crisis and confusion, and providing policymakers with strategies for governance. The choice of path or strategy is not politically neutral, however, but involves political contests over which paradigm is authoritative. These shared beliefs also have important normative implications, as they have profound effects on the substantive content of monetary cooperation, most importantly, the balance between the state and the market.

Conceptual uncertainty about cause-and-effect relationships in the macroeconomy includes ambiguity over the microlevel distributional effects of exchange rate and monetary cooperation. As Alberto Giovannini has argued, there is little agreement within the economics profession on a "benchmark" model for analyzing the distributional effects of alternative monetary regimes. His analysis of three existing models leads him to conclude that "economic interests in favor of a fixed currency versus flexible exchange rates are not easily identifiable" and that the economic effects of a monetary regime are highly contextual—that is, they change depending on what the specific institutional setting and economic conditions are at a particular time. In a more comprehensive critique of the limitations of the field, Paul Krugman points out that the microeconomic foundations of international monetary affairs compose one of the weakest areas in economics. Even though we have some "suggestive" notions, Krugman asserts that "what we do not have, however, is anything we can properly call a model of the benefits of fixed rates and common currencies."[29]

---

in Judith Goldstein and Robert O. Keohane, eds., *Ideas and Foreign Policy* (Ithaca: Cornell University Press, 1993).

[29] Alberto Giovannini, "Economic and Monetary Union: What Happened? Exploring the Political Dimension of Optimum Currency Areas," in *The Future of Monetary Integration* (London: 1993), Centre for Economic Policy Research, 22; Krugman, "What Do We Need to Know about the International Monetary System?" *Essays in International Finance*, no. 190 (Princeton: Princeton University, July 1993), 3, 4. The literature on "model uncertainty" and international macroeconomic policy coordination makes a similar analytic point but does not address the domestic implications or sources of differing ideas about economic policy. See Richard Cooper, "Prolegomena to the Choice of an

This uncertainty translates into inaction on the part of domestic interest groups in contrast to other areas of sectoral and firm activity, such as trade policy, lending more space to the role of interpretation by elite policymakers. Industrial interests in the majority of the European states have expressed a constant preference throughout the postwar years for exchange rate stability because of the high level of openness of EU economies and their significant trade integration (see Table 4). Yet beyond this general policy preference, national policymakers are not subject to significant lobbying on exchange rate or monetary issues. Uncertainty and the dilemmas of collective action it produces tend to keep interest group activity to a minimum on monetary issues, as does the relative institutional insulation of the national treasury and central bank officials from direct societal pressures.

The importance of ideas in explaining the dynamics of monetary cooperation is evident, although usually only implicitly, in the literature on international monetary regimes. Policymakers' perceptions of the costs and benefits of domestic policy autonomy versus international monetary cooperation and the importance of common beliefs—or alternatively, conflicting interpretations about the role of monetary policy, both within and among states—are key themes in the literature. For example, Joanne Gowa points to "shared images" among administration officials about the need for a reassertion of domestic policy priorities as a crucial determinant of the U.S. decision to abandon Bretton Woods, an account congruent with John Odell's evidence about the importance of ideas in explaining U.S. international monetary policies more broadly. Barry Eichengreen has argued that an appropriate and effective international macroeconomic response to the severe worldwide depression of the 1930s did not occur primarily because national policymakers had strongly divergent views "derived from the different historical experiences of the nations involved" on what type of action should be taken. Kenneth Oye's examination of the pattern of monetary conflict and cooperation during the interwar era likewise

International Monetary System," *International Organization* 29 (1975), 63–97; Jeffrey Frankel and Katharine E. Rockett, "International Macroeconomic Policy Coordination When Policymakers Do Not Agree on the True Model," *American Economic Review* 78 (June 1988), 318–40; and Atish Ghosh and Paul Masson, *Economic Cooperation in an Uncertain World* (Cambridge: Blackwell, 1994).

relies heavily on the role of "changing economic beliefs" in altering "perceptions of interest in international monetary arrangements."[30]

Despite recognition of ideational factors by political scientists, their role in producing policy outcomes has not been studied fully. Of the authors mentioned above who discuss ideas in their accounts of international monetary politics, only John Odell explicitly explores their role in producing outcomes. In the area of European integration more generally, ideas have also been pointed to as important to outcomes but have not been evaluated systematically.[31]

Three challenges confront those scholars studying ideas. First, the causal effect of ideas should be delineated clearly and demonstrated empirically. An important contribution of the articles in Judith Goldstein and Robert O. Keohane's edited volume on ideas, in contrast to other works, is its close attention to the causal force of ideas.[32] Second, the study of ideas would be furthered by attempts to trace the source of ideas that significantly shape outcomes as well as explain why other ideas are abandoned. This attempt has rarely been made in previous accounts of ideas and foreign economic policymaking.

Finally, the importance of ideas in shaping states' interests can be appreciated better if alternative explanations derived from the litera-

[30] Joanne Gowa, *Closing the Gold Window* (Ithaca: Cornell University Press, 1983); John Odell, *U.S. International Monetary Policy* (Princeton: Princeton University Press, 1982); and Odell, "From London to Bretton Woods: Sources of Change in Bargaining Strategies and Outcomes," *Journal of Public Policy* 8 (July-December 1988), 287–316. Barry Eichengreen, "Relaxing the External Constraint: Europe in the 1930s," in George Alogoskoufis, Lucas Papademos, and Richard Portes, eds., *External Constraints on Macroeconomic Policy: The European Experience* (New York: Cambridge University Press, 1991), 150. Swings between "monetary orthodoxy and inflationist hearsay" are important in Oye's analysis. Kenneth Oye, "The Sterling-Dollar-Franc Triangle: Monetary Diplomacy, 1929–1937," in Oye, ed., *Cooperation under Anarchy,* (Princeton: Princeton University Press, 1986), 175.
[31] Exceptions are Garrett and Weingast, "Ideas, Interests, and Institutions," and Amy Verdun, "Europe's Struggle with the Global Political Economy: A Study of How EMU Is Perceived by Actors in the Policy-Making Process in Britain, France and Germany" (Ph.D. diss., European University Institute, 1995); also both Andrew Moravcsik, "Negotiating the Single Act: National Interests and Conventional Statecraft in the European Community," *International Organization* 45 (Winter 1991), 19–56, and Wayne Sandholtz and John Zysman, "1992: Recasting the European Bargain," *World Politics* 42 (October 1989), 95–128, emphasize the convergence of preferences and mention ideas but do not provide detailed analyses.
[32] See Judith Goldstein and Robert O. Keohane, "Ideas and Foreign Policy: An Analytical Framework," in Goldstein and Keohane, eds., *Ideas and Foreign Policy,* 13–17; for investigations along these lines, see the contributions by G. John Ikenberry, Nina P. Halpern, Robert Jackson, and Kathryn Sikkink in that volume.

ture on international cooperation are evaluated. Care must be taken, however, in doing so. For example, uncertainty about the costs and benefits of monetary cooperation makes it difficult to formulate what Goldstein and Keohane call the "null hypothesis," against which any study positing a causal role for ideas should, in their view, be tested.[33] They argue that "the materialistically egocentric maximizer of modern economic theory" in the context of power relations should be used to generate a hypothesis where "variations of interests are not accounted for by variations in the character of the ideas that people have."[34] If "modern economic theory" cannot agree on a fixed definition of what states' interests or sectoral interests within states should be in exchange rate or monetary cooperation, it is difficult to create a convincing null hypothesis. This exercise shows how limiting such a standard may be, given the prior importance ideas may have in constructing interests. As Thomas Risse-Kappen has pointed out in his study of the end of the cold war, a null hypothesis based on rational principles may be consistent with the evidence *after* the event, but "a power-based analysis using the model of egotistic utility maximizers is underdetermining in the sense that it leaves various options as to how actors may define their interests in response to underlying structural conditions."[35]

Creation of Neoliberal Consensus

The broad outlines of the evolution of policy consensus that produced cooperation in the EMS, despite the challenge of rising capital mobility, are the following.[36] In the years between the birth of the

[33] See Goldstein and Keohane, "Ideas and Foreign Policy," in Goldstein and Keohane, eds., *Ideas and Foreign Policy*, 6, 26.

[34] Ibid., 27.

[35] Thomas Risse-Kappen, "Ideas Do Not Float Freely: Transnational Coalitions, Domestic Structures, and the End of the Cold War," *International Organization* 48 (Spring 1994), 214.

[36] Others have pointed to the role of policy consensus in European monetary integration, but there has been little systematic investigation of its development or implications; see Louis Pauly, "The Politics of European Monetary Union: National Strategies, International Implications," *International Journal* 47 (Winter 1991–92), 96; Wayne Sandholtz, "Choosing Union: Monetary Politics and Maastricht," *International Organization* 47 (Winter 1993), 5–6. The role that changing attitudes about inflation played in creating exchange rate stability has been assessed quantitatively by Susan G. Collins and Francisco Giavazzi in "Attitudes toward Inflation and the Viability of Fixed Exchange Rates: Evidence from the EMS," in Michael D. Bordo and Barry Eichengreen, eds., *A Retrospective*

Snake and the creation of the EMS, the majority of EC states ceased following domestically oriented, Keynesian monetary policies. The neoliberal policy consensus at the core of this shift was critically important to the maintenance of the EMS, given the increasingly high level of capital mobility; it also formed an important basis for the subsequent revival of the EMU project.

The beliefs underlying the neoliberal consensus center on the importance of price stability above all other goals.[37] The specific contentions can be characterized as follows: first, expansionary monetary policies used in the hope of stimulating demand and employment instead produce inflation and inflationary expectations and are thus counterproductive. Such policies also drive down the exchange rate, further worsening inflation and creating balance of payments problems because of inflationary expectations on the part of financial markets.

Second, high and varying rates of inflation are incompatible with growth and employment, in contrast to the assumptions of the Phillips Curve, which posits an inverse relationship between inflation and unemployment. Instead, the neoliberal consensus posits that inflation creates uncertainty over future price levels, high nominal interest rates, and falling financial asset values, all of which dampen business and spending activity, thus producing low levels of economic growth. Growth, and therefore employment, can come about only if inflation and inflationary expectations are brought under strict control. The larger implication is that price stability is most readily achieved if governments commit themselves *not* to intervene in the economy with expansionary policies but take a passive role in macroeconomic management instead, setting low money-supply growth targets and keeping the exchange rate fixed.

A convergence in policy beliefs or a policy consensus is not the same as a convergence in policy outcomes. Although the commitment to

---

on the Bretton Woods System: Lessons for Monetary Reform (Chicago: University of Chicago Press, 1993), 547–86. Collins and Giavazzi use data on consumer expectations about the economy to conclude that there was a significant increase in concerns about inflation relative to unemployment among the EC states from 1974 to 1990. This conclusion is in line with the polling data contained in Richard C. Eichenberg and Russell J. Dalton, "Europeans and the European Community: The Dynamics of Public Support for European Integration," *International Organization* 47 (Autumn 1993), 507–34.

[37] This assessment draws on Andrea Boltho, "Economic Policy and Performance in

monetary rigor began in some countries, such as France, in 1976 and hardened throughout the EMS states in the 1980s, the policies of increased commitment to price and exchange rate stability took time to pay off in terms of overall economic performance. The reason is simple: there is a lag between policy actions and policy outcomes. Although policy beliefs and economic strategies began to converge in Europe in the late 1970s, economic convergence itself took longer.[38] Nonetheless, this convergent quest for price stability made possible the achievement of exchange rate stability in the EMS, as per Mundell's Holy Trinity conditions.

The new European neoliberal policy consensus differed from the embedded liberalism of the Bretton Wood system in two key ways: it entailed a much higher level of conformity among nations in the goals and instruments of monetary policy; and it was based on more orthodox liberal or conservative principles than its predecessor. Yet the policy shift was not driven by a purely ideological commitment to these orthodox principles but was instead a politically and historically contingent response by government leaders concerned about the deteriorating position of their economies in an increasingly open and competitive world economy. For this reason, I term this new normative approach "the consensus of competitive liberalism."[39]

The evolution of European macroeconomic policymaking strategies is evident in Figure 4, which depicts the degree of divergence and

---

Europe since the Second Oil Shock," in Michael Emerson, ed., *Europe's Stagflation* (Oxford: Clarendon Press, 1984), 24.

[38] In general terms, it takes time for societal expectations about the path of inflation—and, hence, actual price levels—to change. Despite the efforts of governments to project a hard line, anti-inflationary policy stance, price levels will not stabilize until economic actors believe these policies to be credible and likely to endure. Therefore, it was not surprising that the restrictive monetary policies and institutional reforms aimed at lowering inflationary expectations only began to have noticeable effects on economic indicators by the second half of the 1980s.

[39] It thus cannot be equated with the classical liberalism of the gold standard era, because of the extent of both democratic participation and government intervention in the present era. On the orthodoxy of the gold standard, see Karl Polanyi, *The Great Transformation* (Boston: Beacon Press, 1957); more generally, see Barry Eichengreen, ed., *The Gold Standard in Theory and History* (London: Methuen, 1985). Philip Cerny has made a somewhat similar argument beyond the European case. He calls this policy consensus "embedded financial orthodoxy." Philip Cerny, "The Infrastructure of the Infrastructure? Towards 'Embedded Financial Orthodoxy' in the International Political Economy," in Ronan C. Palen and Barry Gills, eds., *Transcending the State-Global Divide* (Boulder, Colo.: Lynne Rienner, 1994).

convergence, respectively, in the core EC states' responses to the first and second oil crises.

Figure 4. Macroeconomic policy in Europe: Responses to OPEC I and II

OPEC I—Oil shock of 1973

More expansionary   More restrictive

<———————————————————————————————————————>

Italy   France   Germany
Britain

OPEC II—Oil shock of 1979

More expansionary   More restrictive

<———————————————————————————————————————>

                                             Germany
                                             Britain
                                             France
                                             Italy

SOURCE: Based on data on fiscal and monetary policies provided in Andrea Boltho, "Economic Policy and Performance in Europe," in Michael Emerson, ed., *Europe's Stagflation* (Oxford: Clarendon Press, 1984), Table 1.1, p. 14.

The source of this new consensus is found in three key elements, which, when translated through the domestic political arena, produced this policy change throughout the majority of the EC. They are the failure of Keynesianism in the wake of the first oil crisis, the existence of an alternative policy paradigm—monetarism—to frame and legitimize the new macroeconomic policy, and finally, Germany's success with restrictive, monetarist policies.

First, European governments' experience with macroeconomic policy failure in the aftermath of the first oil crisis spurred officials to search for alternatives to their traditional Keynesian policies. The sense of crisis that accompanied the policy failures weakened postwar political and societal arrangements, creating the space for a new conception of the role of government in the macroeconomy. Second, monetarist theory, whose advocates made a compelling case for curing the ills of stagflation, provided a template and legitimizing framework for a new economic strategy of neoliberal, anti-inflationary policies. This policy

64

paradigm provided an alternative policy prescription at a time of great uncertainty about the workings of the global and domestic economies. Third and finally, Germany's success with monetarist policies and a strong currency stance gave policymakers a powerful example to emulate. The willingness of the other European governments to follow Germany's example increased the chance that the EMS would hold together because of the weight the German mark carried in the system.

These three sources of neoliberal change—policy failure, the monetarist policy paradigm, and policy emulation—are detailed in the empirical discussion of the years surrounding the creation of the EMS in chapter 6. Here, I provide an overview of the three factors.

Stagflation and the Political Effects of Policy Failure

The experience of policy failure was the crucial first step in the process of interest redefinition among the EC states.[40] During the four years following the first oil crisis in 1973, policymakers and their publics gradually came to believe that the expansionist, activist policies that had worked so well throughout the Bretton Woods years could no longer achieve national employment and growth goals. The advent of stagflation (simultaneous inflation and recession) and the puzzling breakdown of the historical Phillips Curve relationship between unemployment and inflation were central to this experience. Gradually, through a process of trial and error reflected most clearly in the erratic path of policymaking of the European states during this period, the new contours of their economies were interpreted and absorbed by policymakers.

This timing of this process varied among the EC states. Countries such as Germany and the Benelux states, where Keynesianism was the

---

[40] On the importance of policy failure and preference convergence in Europe, see also Moravcsik, "Negotiating the Single Act," 19–56. On learning from failure more broadly, see Jack S. Levy, "Learning and Foreign Policy: Sweeping a Conceptual Minefield," *International Organization* 48 (Spring 1994), 279–312; George W. Breslauer and Philip E. Tetlock, eds., *Learning in U.S. and Soviet Foreign Policy* (Boulder, Colo.: Westview Press, 1991); Charles Herman, "Changing Courses: When Governments Choose to Redirect Foreign Policy," *International Studies Quarterly* 34, no. 2 (1990), 3–21; Sarah E. Mendelson, "Internal Battles and External Wars: Politics, Learning, and the Soviet Withdrawal from Afghanistan," *World Politics* 45 (April 1993), 327–60; and Hall, "From Keynesianism to Monetarism," in Steinmo, Thelen, and Longstreth, eds., *Structuring Politics,* 90–113.

least entrenched, were the first to respond to stagflation with more restrictive policies within a year of the first oil crisis; Italy and France did not set aside Keynesian reflationary strategies until several years of unsuccessful attempts at demand management.[41]

Common across the European continent, however, was the effect that the crises had on domestic political debates. The widespread perception of crisis allowed political leaders to implement reforms without eliciting significant opposition from groups in society, such as labor, that traditionally opposed austerity measures. According to Kenneth Dyson, this experience of "great strains, of frequent puzzlement amongst economic policymakers and occasionally of anger and resentment" reopened the debate on the workings of the economy, while at the same time taking the wind out of the traditional labor and union strategies of reflation and full-employment strategies.[42] The inability of the left to come up with effective alternatives to monetary rigor meant orthodox views of the primacy of price stability took hold more easily. This experience of policy failure gave greater salience to the next crucial step in the process that produced the neoliberal consensus: monetarist theory.

Monetarism and Policy Paradigm Innovation

In this context of crisis, monetarism provided an alternative policy paradigm to Keynesianism, and its prescriptions appealed to policymakers by addressing both the changed economic environment and their political needs.[43] Monetarism offered policymakers a coherent lens through which to view their experiences with macroeconomic policy while offering a legitimizing framework that made austerity reforms viable politically. In particular, monetarists could posit an explanation for stagflation and the deterioration of the Phillips Curve relationship,

[41] See Niels Thygesen, "Monetary Policy," in Boltho, ed., *The European Economy* for an overview of this policy history.

[42] Kenneth Dyson, "The Politics of Economic Recession in Germany," in Andrew Cox, ed., *Politics, Policy, and the European Recession* (New York: St. Martin's, 1982), 33. See also Peter Lange, et al., Unions, Change, and Crisis (London: Allen and Unwin, 1982).

[43] The classic monetarist statement is Milton Friedman and Anna Schwartz, *A Monetary History of the United States, 1866–1945* (Princeton: Princeton University Press, 1963). See also Thomas Mayer, *The Structure of Monetarism* (New York: W. W. Norton, 1978); Philip Cagan, "Monetarism," *The New Palgrave* (London: Macmillan, 1991).

which implied that less—not more—government intervention was the cure for what ills the economy.

The monetarists view rejected the Phillips curve relationship and argued that rapid economic expansion would lead directly to inflation without an increase in economic activity and employment. Counter to the Keynesians, monetarists argued that each economy has a nonaccelerating inflation rate of unemployment (NAIRU) that is structurally determined and that any efforts to "buy" more employment by stimulating the economy and allowing for inflation cannot affect this rate. Indeed, such "fine-tuning" policies would only bring on more stagflation, and governments should cease actively trying to shape the economy by using the levers of monetary expansion and contraction.

Setting goals or monetary targets for a stable, predictable annual increase in the aggregate money supply, monetarists argued, would be the best way to avoid inflation and provide an environment conducive to economic growth. The widespread adoption of monetary targeting as a policy tool by the majority of continental European governments by the mid-1970s indicated the influence of the monetarist framework on policymaking.[44]

It is important to note, however, that the governments of Europe followed a *pragmatic*, not ideologically purist, type of monetarism. This course is evident in the fact that monetary targets, though widely adopted among the European governments after the first oil crisis, were only one of many tools used to achieve national economic goals. Whereas monetarist theory would argue that exchange rates should be allowed to float because the only appropriate policy target is the money supply, European governments viewed the fixing of their exchange rates in the EMS as a way to reinforce the attempt to reduce inflation.[45] The exception to this pragmatic monetarist stance in Eu-

[44] For details of the transition to targeting in Europe, see Organization for Economic Cooperation and Development (hereinafter cited as OECD), "Monetary Targets and Inflation Control," *Monetary Studies Series* (Paris: OECD, 1979).

[45] For a discussion of the difference in these approaches, see Johnson, "Unpopular Measures: Translating Monetarism into Monetary Policy in the Federal Republic of Germany and the United States, 1970–1985" (Ph.D. diss., Cornell University, 1991), chap. 1. For an overview of the differences in monetary practices, see U.S. Congress, Joint Economic Committee, "Monetary Policy, Selective Credit Controls, and Industrial Policy in France, Britain, West Germany, and Sweden," *Staff Study, Joint Economic Committee, U.S. Congress* (Washington, D.C.: U.S. Government Printing Office, June 26, 1981).

rope was Britain, which most particularly in the first years of Margaret Thatcher's government did adhere to the purist view of monetarism, as did the U.S. Federal Reserve under Paul Volcker. Throughout the early 1980s, Thatcher's government targeted only the money supply and let exchange rates float. This purist orientation, combined with Britain's different trade structure, helps make sense of "British exceptionalism" when it comes to exchange rate cooperation in Europe.[46]

The pragmatic—not purist—monetarism practiced by continental European governments indicates the contributions and limits of an explanation for European monetary cooperation that centers on the epistemic communities approach. Peter Haas, for example, has argued that groups of experts who share consensual scientific knowledge can exert strong influence over the outcomes of international agreements and international regimes. Some elements of epistemic communities do seem to be present in the European case, such as the role that more frequent and congenial meetings among the Committee of Central Bank Governors has played in promoting stability in the EMS by encouraging a shared vision of monetary policy goals.[47] Monetarism had been propounded by certain academics for decades, however, before its principles were taken up by European governments. Also, although the role of monetary policy is certainly a technical issue, it has a broader social purview than the scientific knowledge bases that are the typical focus of epistemic community theory, for example, in its normative implications regarding the appropriate role for government in society.

[46] This is borne out in Mark D. Harmon, "'If I Can't Change the Rules, I Won't Play Your Game': Britain in and out of the Exchange Rate Mechanism of the European Monetary System," paper prepared for the 9th Annual International Conference of Europeanists, Chicago, March 31–April 2, 1994. Harmon finds that growing disillusionment in the mid-1980s with pure targeting of the money supply to reduce inflation led senior British officials to begin to advocate joining the EMS. The British decision not to enter the fixed exchange rate agreement also has been characterized as "la folie du grandeur" by one senior British government official. In his view, the British did not want to reduce the pound's symbolic sovereignty by linking it to the other European currencies (interview, Brussels, October 1993). On the pound's historic role, see Stephen Blank, "Britain: The Politics of Foreign Economic Policy, the Domestic Economy, and the Problem of Pluralistic Stagnation," in Peter J. Katzenstein, ed., *Between Power and Plenty: Foreign Economic Policies of Advanced Industrial States* (Madison: University of Wisconsin Press, 1978), 89–138.

[47] Peter Haas, "Do Regimes Matter? Epistemic Communities and Mediterranean Pollution Control," *International Organization* 43 (Summer 1989), 377, and Peter Haas, ed., "Knowledge, Power, and International Policy Coordination," special issue of *International*

In sum, pragmatic monetarist ideas were critical to the success of the EMS. The substantive constant of the monetarist paradigm lent itself very well to the type of policy convergence needed to make exchange rate stability possible under conditions of high capital mobility. By stressing price stability before all other goals and delegitimizing the use of independent, activist monetary policies, the policy prescriptions of monetarism dovetailed with the requirements spelled out in Mundell's Holy Trinity framework.

Policy Emulation and the German Model

The third key factor producing the policy consensus across Europe was Germany's policy success. The experience of the German government with restrictive, anti-inflationary policies offered a powerful and persuasive example of the merits of pragmatic monetarism for other European governments to emulate and strengthened the role of the mark as the anchor currency of the EMS. When most of Europe was struggling with stagflation after the first oil crisis, West Germany stood out as successful in managing its economy, particularly in terms of inflation and employment. German officials were not hesitant to make known their views on the importance of price stability, proselytizing the merits of restrictive monetary policy to their neighbors. These efforts were aided by the increasing importance of institutionalized interactions among national economic policymakers in the EC, which aided the transnational learning process.

Germany was most clearly a preoccupation of France under President Valéry Giscard d'Estaing, but similar emulation processes were underway in the other EC countries (see chapter 6). Giscard was highly motivated to find a way for France to match the economic performance of Germany, both because of his desire to improve the performance of the French economy for domestic reasons and because he wished to see France have equal weight to Germany in the EC. In his speeches and writings promoting the virtues of austerity programs after 1976, Giscard continually held Germany up as an example France should

Organization 46 (Winter 1992); interviews, EC officials from Directorate General II and the Committee of Central Bank Governors, Brussels (October 1991 and May 1994).

emulate, extolling the virtues of price stability policies and warning of the need for France to stay competitive with the German powerhouse.

This focus on Germany brings up the question of what sort of power Germany exerts on the rest of the EU and how this power has influenced the path of conflict and cooperation. In chapter 2, the argument that the role of Germany in European monetary cooperation can be characterized in terms of standard theories of hegemonic stability was refuted. A more convincing account might, however, be made by theorists who have referred to the role of nonmaterial aspects of hegemonic rule—the "component of power that is not reducible to the coercive capacities of the hegemonic state."[48] Unfortunately, there has been relatively little explicit study of the process by which shared beliefs support hegemonic orders. John Ikenberry and Charles Kupchan have suggested focusing on the socialization of policymaking elites in the secondary states of a hegemonic system. They conceptualize socialization "as the process through which national leaders internalize the norms and value orientation espoused by the hegemon and, as a consequence, become socialized into the community formed by the hegemon and other nations accepting its leadership position, . . . In this way, socialization can lead to the consolidation of the hegemon's position's and to acquiescence among the states participating within the system."[49]

Two of the three mechanisms they propose to explain how such socialization occurs, however—external inducements and international reconstruction—seem inapplicable to European monetary integration. Only normative persuasion (where the hegemon relies on ideological persuasion and transnational learning, particularly in times of crisis) is appropriate, given the empirical evidence that I present in the case studies.

The other account of hegemony related most closely to the EMS experience is John Ruggie's attention to both the "power and the purpose" underlying hegemony. Ruggie argues that it is necessary to

---

[48] G. John Ikenberry and Charles Kupchan, "Socialization and Hegemonic Power," *International Organization* 44 (Summer 1990), 283–315; quote on p. 289.

[49] Ibid., 290. See also Paul J. DiMaggio and Walter W. Powell, "The Iron Cage Revisited: Institutional Isomorphism and Collective Rationality," in Powell and DiMaggio, eds., *The New Institutionalism in Organizational Analysis* (Chicago: University of Chicago, 1991), 63–82.

look beyond power alone to see how "power and legitimate social purpose become fused to project political authority into the international system."[50] Social purpose is the normative framework or guiding principles and norms for the cooperative regime. In Ruggie's view, political power is important in establishing a regime, but the legitimacy of social purpose is also crucial in bringing about cooperation; without a preponderant, hegemonic power, purpose alone can be enough. This conceptualization seems to fit the European experience with emulation of the German example, as we will see.

In sum, a process of policy failure, policy paradigm innovation, and policy emulation transformed European policymakers' ideas about the workings of their political economies and thus their interests at both the domestic level—to eschew independent, activist monetary policies—and at the level of EC regimes—to participate in the EMS.[51]

---

[50] Ruggie, "International Regimes, Transactions, and Change," in Krasner, ed., *International Regimes,* 198.

[51] Chapter 4 also highlights both the experience of policy failure (with interwar financial orthodoxy) and policy paradigm innovation (Keynesianism) as important determinants of cooperation in the Bretton Woods system, suggesting that this process of interest redefinition is more universal than the EMS case.

CHAPTER FOUR

Capital Control, Keynesianism, and Bretton Woods

The European Union's efforts at monetary cooperation cannot be understood fully without examining the Bretton Woods system. The same features crucial to the later EU regimes—the interaction of ideas and economic structure—also proved decisive in the rise and demise of the Bretton Woods system. In Bretton Woods, the decision to limit capital mobility after World War II allowed for the achievement of exchange rate cooperation with the preservation of monetary autonomy, in contrast to the constraint created when capital mobility began to rise in the late 1960s and 1970s. Policy experience and economic ideas, particularly policy failure in the interwar period and the existence of a potent alternative policy paradigm, Keynesianism, strongly influenced governments' decisions regarding international monetary cooperation. In one major aspect, however, Bretton Woods differed from the subsequent efforts at European monetary cooperation—the hegemonic leadership of the United States. Tracing the process by which cooperation was achieved in Bretton Woods and the role the United States played in the creation and dissolution of the system therefore provides an instructive comparison to the role Germany has played in the European-only cases.

STABILITY IN THE BRETTON WOODS SYSTEM, 1944–1968

The decades following the end of World War II were marked by unprecedented economic growth and prosperity, due in no small part to the international agreement forged in 1944 at Bretton Woods, New Hampshire.[1] The agreement established the institutional foundations of an international monetary system that was to encompass the majority of the noncommunist world and, with U.S. leadership, provide a basis for the expansion of international trade and investment.

The eminent British economist John Maynard Keynes and his U.S. colleague Harry Dexter White spent much of World War II hammering out a plan for reconstructing the world economy once the war finally came to an end.[2] Although the specifics of the British and the American plans differed, the respective Treasury departments shared the goal of designing a monetary system that would provide for a relatively open, liberal international economy while at the same time effectively cushioning the domestic economies of participating states from the most stringent effects of that openness. The challenge was formidable for two reasons: first, the recent history of international monetary cooperation had been marked by conflict and closure, as evidenced by the prevalence of regional blocs and competitive devaluations during the interwar period.[3] Second, unlike the fixed exchange rate regime established in the previous international monetary system, the nineteenth-century gold standard, the new postwar system would have to coexist with an entirely unprecedented level of national macroeconomic policy intervention. As will be discussed more fully, the influence

[1] More precisely, the International Monetary and Financial Conference of the United and Associated Nations, in July 1944. Forty-four nations signed the constitution, the Articles of Agreement of the new International Monetary Fund, and the Articles of Agreement of the International Bank for Reconstruction and Development (World Bank).

[2] The history of the founding of the Bretton Woods system is told by Richard Gardner in *Sterling Dollar Diplomacy in Current Perspective* (New York: Columbia University Press, 1980); see also Robert Solomon, *The International Monetary System, 1945–1981* (New York: Harper and Row, 1982).

[3] This point of view was expressed in Ragnar Nurske, *International Currency Experience: Lessons of the Inter-War Period* (Geneva: League of Nations, 1944); see Michael D. Bordo, "The Bretton Woods International Monetary System: A Historical Overview," in Bordo and Barry Eichengreen, eds., *A Retrospective on the Bretton Woods System* (Chicago: University of Chicago Press, 1993), 28–31. On the interwar experience, see Barry Eichengreen, *Golden Fetters: The Gold Standard and the Great Depression, 1919–1939* (New York: Oxford University Press, 1992), and *Elusive Stability: Essays in the History of International Finance, 1919–1939* (New York: Cambridge University Press, 1990); Benjamin Rowland, ed., *Balance of Power or Hegemony* (New York: New York University Press, 1976); and Beth Simmons, *Who Adjusts? Domestic Sources of Foreign Economic Policy during the Interwar Years* (Princeton: Princeton University Press, 1994).

of Keynes's theories of demand management meant that for any international monetary agreement to be successful, it had to allow for full employment and economic stabilization programs by participating governments.[4]

The compromise arrangement finally agreed to at Bretton Woods created a series of new international organizations that were to provide for the goal of international liberalism—but within the context of significant domestic intervention in the economy. The result was an entirely unprecedented level of institutionalization of international monetary cooperation and the explicit development of global rules and norms to guide states' actions in the monetary realm.[5] The pivot of the system was to be the International Monetary Fund (IMF), which was designed to provide both an institutional forum for multilateral monetary coordination and the financial resources for countries facing temporary balance of payments difficulties.

Monetary coordination in Bretton Woods system centered on the construction of a new fixed exchange rate regime. In consultation with the IMF, member states agreed to set the value of their currencies at predetermined rates and promised to act to keep their currencies trading in international markets within a band of 2 percent (thus plus or minus 1 percent of the predetermined central rate) at all times. In practice, their dislike of exchange rate variability led the European countries to stay within a smaller margin of three-fourths of 1 percent (.75) on either side of the dollar.[6] Though not originally designed to do so, the Bretton Woods system soon evolved into a fixed exchange rate system pegged to the dollar, which was in turn pegged to gold at the fixed rate of $35 an ounce.

The participating states were given little leeway in realigning the declared value of their currency without the approval of the IMF. To assist governments seeking to redress balance of payments difficulties, the IMF designers created a fund made up of the pooled contributions of member states from which states could draw for short-term financing

[4] The spread of Keynesianism is detailed in the national case studies found in Peter Hall, ed., *The Political Power of Economic Ideas: Keynesianism across Nations* (Princeton: Princeton University Press, 1989).
[5] The following discussion draws on Solomon, *The International Monetary System*, 12–13.
[6] See chapter 3 for a discussion of the preference for exchange rate stability among the European states.

of their deficits in lieu of exchange rate adjustments.[7] The assumption was that the IMF fund would be used only to tide governments over while they undertook the internal domestic policy changes to bring their balance of payments back into line. Finally, the Bretton Woods agreement dictated that even though currencies would be freely convertible into one another after a transition period following the agreement's implementation, Article VI allowed members to place capital controls on currency transactions if such capital flows threatened to overwhelm a nation's balance of payments or exchange rate stability.

The goal of these attempts at cooperative management was to preserve the stability of the international monetary system, particularly exchange rate stability, in order to keep international trade and economic growth from being jeopardized by the same forces that had been unleashed in the interwar period. Exchange rates were indeed very stable throughout the first years of the Bretton Woods system. The Bretton Woods system also succeeded in providing the three elements essential to a functioning international monetary system, namely, liquidity, adjustment, and confidence.[8] Briefly stated, the system could only function effectively if there was adequate financing or liquidity in the system to support global investment and trade; if some mechanism existed to allow states in balance of payments difficulties to adjust and redress their problems without undue hardships; and if there was adequate confidence in the durability and stability of the system itself, so as to avoid destabilizing speculation and runs on key currencies.

The United States and Hegemonic Power

The institutions of the Bretton Woods system were designed to meet these systemic requirements, but the powerful leadership of the United States ended up providing the key underpinnings for stability. Robert

[7] A lucid explanation of the relationships between these policy choices is Richard Cooper, *The Economics of Interdependence* (New York: Columbia University Press, 1968; rev. ed. 1980), especially chap. 1.

[8] Benjamin Cohen, *Organizing the World's Money* (New York: Basic Books, 1977), chap. 1, after Fritz Machlup and Burton Malkiel, eds., *International Monetary Arrangements: The Problem of Choice* (Princeton: International Finance Section, 1964). On the effort to solve these challenges in Bretton Woods, see Bordo, "The Bretton Woods International Monetary System," in Bordo and Eichengreen, eds., *A Retrospective on the Bretton Woods System*, 50.

Gilpin has noted that "the United States assumed primary responsibility for the management of the world monetary system beginning with the Marshall Plan and partially under the guise of the IMF. The Federal Reserve became the world's banker, and the dollar became the basis of the international monetary system."[9] It is worthwhile to consider exactly what role the United States played in the Bretton Woods system and how theorists have written about that role, so that we can understand the later cases of European monetary cooperation in light of the thesis that stability and cooperation can come about only in the context of hegemony or leadership.

Charles Kindleberger has offered some guidelines for understanding why leadership is important to the functioning of the international economy. As was discussed in chapter 2, he argues that the United States provided for stability by offering a large, open market for foreign goods, even in times of economic distress; a steady and countercyclical flow of capital to smooth out the effects of economic downturns; and enough liquidity to keep the monetary system afloat. The United States willingly provided all of these things in the years following the Bretton Woods agreement. It was the only state capable of doing so, as both its military and economic strength vastly overshadowed that of all other states in the system.

For Robert Gilpin, the role of the United States in providing for liquidity, adjustment, and confidence is best interpreted in terms of power politics in the international system.[10] Gilpin explores the political implications of the fact that the U.S. dollar and the character of U.S. economic policymaking determined the nature of the Western world's economic interactions. Because Bretton Woods was centered on the dollar, international liquidity was dependent on American macroeconomic policies, placing the United States in a position where it could enjoy the ability to run large, liquidity-producing deficits without correcting its balance of payments. The vital role of the dollar also meant

---

[9] Robert Gilpin, *The Political Economy of International Relations* (Princeton: Princeton University Press, 1987), 133; cf. 131–42.

[10] Charles Kindleberger, *The World in Depression, 1929–1939* (Berkeley: University of California Press, 1973); Gilpin, *The Political Economy of International Relations,* 131–42.

that confidence in the system rested in large part on the continuation of the political and economic power of the United States.

Thus, the political power and leadership of the United States ended up being central to the functioning of the Bretton Woods system and the achievement of exchange rate stability, albeit in ways not intended by the original designers of the system. This reliance on U.S. power and management capabilities contained critical flaws that would eventually bring about its downfall. But for almost two decades after its founding, U.S. leadership and political power, combined with the institutional resources and cooperative framework of the IMF, gave the Bretton Woods member states a historically unique position. It allowed them to address their own domestic economic stability needs, most often through the use of Keynesian-type policies, without jeopardizing their participation in the exchange rate regime, in contrast to both the gold standard and the later European monetary regimes.

International Capital Flows and Monetary Cooperation

An additional factor was critical to the operation of the early postwar Bretton Woods system, one not adequately highlighted in the literature on international monetary cooperation. Although the role of the United States was certainly crucial to explaining the character of Bretton Woods, when interpreting the postwar experience, it is important to also examine the overall structure of the international economy, namely, the level of international capital flows. It is particularly important to understand this aspect in any comparison of the Bretton Woods system and contemporary efforts at exchange rate cooperation in Europe.

According to macroeconomic theory, if capital mobility is low, states can have both fixed exchange rates and domestic policy autonomy, at least in the short to medium term. Countries in the Bretton Woods system were thus more able to formulate their monetary policies unilaterally, that is, without a high degree of attention to the policies of other states or external systemic constraints. During the early Bretton Woods years, the low level of capital mobility placed only minimal pressure on governments to follow similar policies, as interest rate changes and other policy differences were not immediately counter-acted by the effects of large flows of financial assets. This level of capital mobility in the early postwar period was historically low in comparison to both the era preceding Bretton Woods—that of the nineteenth-century gold standard, and the era following Bretton Woods, when the Snake and the EMS were operational.[11]

One key reason for the relative insularity of national economies during the early Bretton Woods years was the slow pace of reconstruc-tion of international banking after World War II. One account states that "for more than thirty years, from the Great Depression until the late 1950s, international banking was in a state of hibernation."[12] There were several reasons for this "hibernation." First, international financial transactions were hampered by widespread capital controls, which governments used to regulate the flow of capital in and out of their countries. In addition, limited international reserves and the develop-ment of a dollar shortage by definition kept international capital flows to a minimum after the war. Indeed, only through the large-scale aid program of the Marshall Plan was enough liquidity injected into the system to allow for the financing of reconstruction. The Japanese yen and the European currencies were not freely convertible for at least a decade after the war, and this lack of convertibility also slowed the expansion of international banking. Obviously, the ability of private actors to freely exchange national currency for other currencies is crucial to the development of international financial markets. When the Western European countries began to post current account sur-pluses, however, they finally moved to currency convertibility in Decem-ber 1958.[13]

By the late 1950s international banking began to revive. Around this time, a new mechanism for international financing was created.

---

[11] Daniel Gros and Niels Thygesen, *European Monetary Integration* (London: Longman, 1992), 15; a similar theme is found in Cohen, *Organizing the World's Money*. See also the data in Philip Turner, "Capital Flows in the 1980s: A Survey of Major Trends," *BIS Economic Papers* 30 (April 1991), 13–20. For a discussion of the measurement and growth of capital flows, see "Fear of Finance," special survey, *Economist*, September 19, 1992, 5.

[12] Yoon S. Park and Jack Zwick, *International Banking in Theory and Practice* (Reading, Mass.: Addison-Wesley, 1985), 7.

[13] The Europeans created a temporary system to overcome the difficulties of noncon-vertibility, the European Payments Union, which lasted from 1950 to 1958 and acted as a clearinghouse for intra-European settlements of surpluses and deficits incurred

This was the Eurodollar market, which was later to become a key vehicle for increased international capital mobility (see chapter 5). The volume of international banking in general, and the offshore market activity and the new financial instruments (such as Eurobonds and Eurocredits) that arose from these markets, did not reach a significant magnitude until the 1970s and 1980s, however. International banking was virtually nonexistent before 1964, the years of greatest exchange rate stability in the Bretton Woods system (see Figure 5).

Figure 5. The growth of international banking, 1964–1994

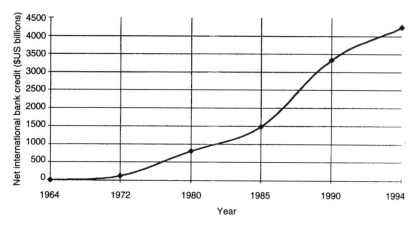

SOURCE: Bank for International Settlements, *Annual Reports* (Basel: BIS, various years). This series does not count interbank redeposits and includes only the BIS reporting area, which is made up of the largest industrial countries.

A further indicator of the extent of international finance is the growth of overseas bank branches. Foreign-owned banks have been particularly important in the expansion of international finance, according to the Bank for International Settlements, for these banks "as a rule carry out a higher proportion of their business in foreign cur-

through trade. See Jacob Kaplan and Gunther Schleiminger, *The European Payments Union* (Oxford: Clarendon Press, 1989).

rency with non-residents or multilateral companies than do domestic-owned banks."[14] Again, data on foreign bank branch offices, shown in Table 5, indicate that the level of international bank activity was low during the early Bretton Woods period in comparison with the late 1960s.

Table 5. Foreign banking presence in selected countries (December 1960–June 1985)

Host country	1960	1970	1980	1985
	Number of institutions[a]			
Belgium	14[b]	26	51	57
Italy	1	4	26	36
Netherlands	N/A	23	39	40
Switzerland	8	97	99	119
United Kingdom	51[c]	95	214	293
	Number of banking offices[d]			
France	33	58	122	147
Germany	24	77	213	287
Japan	34	38	85	112
Luxembourg	3	23	96	106
United States	N/A	50[e]	579	783

SOURCE: Based on Bank for International Settlements, *Recent Innovations in International Banking* (Basle: BIS, 1986), Table 7.1, 151.

[a]Number of foreign banking institutions ("families") operating in the country through branches or majority-owned subsidiaries, unless otherwise specified. An institution is counted only once, regardless of the number of branch offices in the country.

[b]1958.

[c]1962.

[d]Foreign banking organizations represented by more than one entity are double counted.

[e]Estimated number in the early 1970s.

Another related indicator of international banking activity over the Bretton Woods years is the rising relative importance of foreign assets in national banking markets, shown in Table 6. These data illustrate the degree to which a nation's financial sector is penetrated by multinational banking institutions.

---

[14] Bank for International Settlements, *Recent Innovations in International Banking* (Basle: Bank for International Settlements, 1986), 150.

Table 6. Foreign banks' assets in selected countries (in percent of total assets of all banks operating in selected countries)

Host country	1960	1970	1980	1985 (end-June)
Belgium	8.2[a]	22.5	41.5	51.0
France	7.2	12.3	15.0	18.2[b]
Germany	0.5	1.4	1.9	2.4
Italy	N/A	N/A	0.9	2.4
Japan	N/A	1.3	3.4	3.6
Luxembourg	8.0	57.8	85.4	85.4
Netherlands	N/A	N/A	17.4[c]	23.6
Switzerland	N/A	10.3	11.1	12.2
United Kingdom	6.7	37.5	55.6	62.6
United States	N/A	5.8[d]	8.7	12.0

SOURCE: Based on Bank for International Settlements, *Recent Innovations in International Banking* (Basle: BIS, 1986), Table 7.2, 152.

[a]1958.
[b]1984.
[c]1983.
[d]1976.

Finally, it is useful to compare the level of capital flows as a proportion of GNP in the Bretton Woods era in contrast to the gold standard era (1881–1913). Unfortunately, there was no precursor to the BIS reporting system for international banks begun in the 1960s, so proxy indicators must be used to assess the level of financial flows. The data that do exist indicate that the levels of capital mobility seen in the nineteenth century far outstripped those of the Bretton Woods years, which did not reach comparable levels until the 1980s. One BIS study has concluded that "current account imbalances—and the associated capital flows—in the years before 1914 were actually larger, measured in relation to GNP, than in the 1980s."[15] It further surveys both short- and long-term interest rate differentials across national markets (another proxy measure of the extent of capital mobility) during the gold standard years. The low differentials recorded indicates the ability of international investors to move their monies in and out of national financial markets under the gold standard, despite what we now view as a relatively low level of communications technology.[16]

[15] See the data provided in Turner, "Capital Flows in the 1980s," 13–20.
[16] See ibid., 16. Low interest rate differentials also reflect the very low expectations of

The data on capital flows are congruent with the historical record of OECD government policies on capital controls in the early Bretton Woods years.[17] Although Bretton Woods was constructed to encourage openness in the international economy, under its rules countries were allowed, for an indefinite transition period, to both limit currency convertibility and to use exchange controls, as specified in Articles XIV and VI, respectively, of the Bretton Woods agreement. Bretton Woods did not begin to function as a true open and liberal international monetary system until after 1958, because currencies remained inconvertible within Europe while a temporary system for intraregional payments among trading partners ensured that trade could go on.[18] Yet capital controls continued beyond this first decade, their use fostered by the experience of the interwar period, when large flows of speculative capital disrupted the already tenuous economic situation of many nation states.

DOMESTIC POLICIES AND EMBEDDED LIBERALISM

How did the domestic imperatives of the participating countries shape cooperation in the Bretton Woods system? As we have seen, the central compromise that guided Keynes and White in creating the institutions and rules of the Bretton Woods system was simple, though revolutionary in terms of the gold standard, the previous monetary system. Bretton Woods was designed so that the terms of international cooperation would not supersede national political authority over macroeconomic management. As noted earlier, this historic mediation

---

exchange rate changes during the gold standard and the strong convergence in prices across countries. Neither of these conditions have held in the postwar era.

[17] For a survey of the use of capital controls in the early postwar era, see Alexandre Lamfalussy, "Changing Attitudes towards Capital Movements," in Frances Cairncross, ed., *Changing Perceptions of Economic Policy* (London: Methuen, 1981), 194–231; for a period after 1980, see Turner, "Capital Flows in the 1980s."

[18] Nonconvertibility and exchange controls mean that currencies cannot freely flow across borders, even if required for trade payments. Controls were deemed necessary because of a shortage of international reserves after the devastation of World War II, and it was thought that capital needed to be carefully apportioned to the most important uses. Bordo, "The Bretton Woods International Monetary System," in Bordo and Eichengreen, eds., *A Retrospective on the Bretton Woods System*, 38; see also n. 17.

between international regime and domestic political concerns has been summed up by John Ruggie as the compromise of embedded liberalism.[19]

The term *embedded liberalism* derives from Karl Polanyi's distinction between economic orders that are "embedded" in the larger social context of human relations and those that are "disembedded," where economic motives and logic are viewed as separate from the broader concerns of society.[20] Polanyi argued that throughout most of history, the rules and overall functioning of economies have been subordinated to political and social goals, as in the case of tribal, feudal, and mercantilist societies. The nineteenth-century gold standard and its free-trade regime departed from this norm of embeddedness, because it elevated and legitimated market rationality above domestic political authority. Under the gold standard, this shift in the state's role "fundamentally transformed state-society relations, by redefining the legitimate social purposes in pursuit of which state power was expected to be employed in the domestic economy. The role of the state became to institute and safeguard the self-regulating market."[21] The market rationality of orthodox liberalism was the normative consensus that underlay the gold standard. The agreement reached at Bretton Woods, in contrast, shifted the balance in international monetary cooperation back to domestic political authority by allowing for deviations from the liberal orthodoxy of the gold standard.

Why did the balance between state and market shift? Ruggie points to the role of economists like Harry Dexter White and John Maynard Keynes in proposing policy solutions to the demands for social protection coming from "all sides of the political spectrum and from all ranks of the social hierarchy (with the possible exception of orthodox financial circles)."[22] The shared beliefs of policymakers were a central determinant of the response to these societal demands.[23] Particularly

[19] John Gerard Ruggie, "International Regimes, Transactions, and Change: Embedded Liberalism in the Postwar Economic Order," in Stephen Krasner, ed., *International Regimes* (Ithaca: Cornell University Press, 1983), 195–231.

[20] My comments follow Ruggie, ibid., 201. See also Karl Polanyi, *The Great Transformation* (Boston: Beacon Press, 1944), and Karl Polanyi et al., *Trade and Markets in the Early Empires* (Glencoe, Ill.: Free Press, 1957).

[21] Ruggie, "International Regimes, Transactions, and Changes," 202.

[22] Ibid., 204.

[23] This is examined in G. John Ikenberry, "A World Economy Restored: Expert Consen-

important is how policymakers viewed the relationship among unemployment, inflation, and external stabilization. Although an in-depth assessment is beyond the scope of this discussion, two factors can be mentioned that were crucial in bringing about monetary cooperation in Bretton Woods, just as they would later be crucial in the EMS. As Peter Gourevitch has noted, the first factor is the devastating experience of policy failure in the interwar period:

> The Great Crash of 1929 was the greatest economic catastrophe since the industrial economy's beginnings in the mid-eighteenth century. . . . As the Depression rippled around the world, most countries responded with the same economic policy—deflation, the response prescribed by orthodox analysis of the market economy. It did not work. After some two to four years of failure most countries abandoned deflation and broke with orthodoxy. Initially, most of them turned to familiar deviations from the classical rules: tariffs, devaluation of the currency, leaving the gold standard, and some corporatist regulations of domestic markets.[24]

Governments, Gourevitch goes on to say, experimented with newer models of governance, among them deficit spending, social welfare systems, and public ownership. But whereas "during the thirties these departures from orthodoxy were experimental and uneven both within and across countries," after the war the debates coalesced into agreement on the need for regulation and intervention in the national economy, as well as for the constraining of market forces at the level of the international system.

The immediate postwar response was also decisively and dramatically shaped by the Keynesian paradigm (and by Keynes himself), which radically changed the domestic political environment of the advanced industrialized economies. Keynes's theoretical framework, elaborated in his 1936 work *The General Theory of Employment, Interest, and Money*, established an historically unprecedented, activist role for government

---

sus and the Anglo-American Postwar Settlement," *International Organization* 46 (Winter 1992), 289–322; see also a revised version of his argument in "The Political Origins of Bretton Woods," in Bordo and Eichengreen, eds., *A Retrospective on the Bretton Woods System,* 155–200. John Odell has also contributed to this line of argumentation; see John Odell, "From London to Bretton Woods: Sources of Change in Bargaining Strategies and Outcomes," *Journal of Public Policy* 8 (July–December 1988), 287–316.

[24] Peter Gourevitch, *Politics in Hard Times* (Ithaca: Cornell University Press, 1986), 124.

in the economy through the use of countercyclical demand management techniques.[25] The term *Keynesianism* is used to describe a broad spectrum of policies, some of which have little to do with Keynes's original writings and formulations. For this analysis of international monetary cooperation, it is most useful to focus on three general implications of Keynes's work.[26]

First, Keynes rejected the canonical view, Say's Law, that supply creates its own demand and that markets will automatically clear at an equilibrium level.[27] Instead of assuming that, left to themselves, markets will generate an efficient and productive level of economic activity, Keynes argued that markets were inherently unstable, at least in the short and medium term. Market rigidities, in his view, are prevalent enough to produce unnecessarily high unemployment levels; it is the proper role of government to act to stimulate economic activity and employment to overcome market imperfections.[28]

The second implication follows from the first: Keynes's analysis promoted a new role for government in the economy through the use of countercyclical demand management. His rejection of Say's Law in favor of demand stimulus legitimized policies of deficit spending financed by public borrowing during economic recessions and posited that states would run budget surpluses during economic upswings. A balanced government budget was no longer a goal in itself; instead, the budget would be used to smooth out the business cycles of contraction and expansion that Keynes viewed as an inevitable component of imperfect markets.

The final and most important implication of Keynes's analysis for the development of the international monetary order was the idea

---

[25] J. M. Keynes, *The General Theory of Employment, Interest, and Money* (London: Macmillan, 1936).

[26] I am drawing here on Peter Hall's introduction to Hall, ed., *The Political Power of Economic Ideas*. This volume is the most comprehensive comparative assessment of the role of Keynesian ideas in interwar and postwar policymaking.

[27] As Walter Salant states, Keynes's "attack on Say's Law was important in undermining the view that aggregate demand could not be insufficient, and in explaining that during depression or when economic activity was threatening to decline, government action to increase or sustain demand was desirable, not useless, let alone destructive, as the neoclassical theory expounded by Hayek and others of the 'Austrian' school held." Salant, "The Spread of Keynesian Doctrines and Practices in the United States," in Hall, ed., *The Political Power of Economic Ideas*, 29.

[28] See Elizabeth Johnson, Donald Moggridge, and Sir Austin Robinson, eds., *The Collected*

that policymakers should direct their attention to the particular situations they face in their domestic economies and act to improve economic performance at home. Although this seems somewhat obvious a half century later, at the time it represented a clear departure from the modus operandi of the gold standard. Instead of passively allowing the domestic economy to contract in response to the balance of payments and exchange rate situations, governments in the Bretton Woods era focused on domestic imperatives like employment and growth. The international monetary system was to be designed so that exchange rate stability would be achieved without sacrificing national political control over the domestic economy. The economic crises of the interwar years had discredited prevailing economic theories and created barriers to cooperation during that time, but as Odell states, by 1944 "many of the world's economists had converged on elements of a new monetary consensus, as indicated by the League of Nations 1944 report, *International Currency Experience: Lessons of the Inter-War Period.* This statement recognized that many governments now rejected the traditional gold standard rule of maintaining external payments balances even at the price of high unemployment at home."[29]

Related to this concern was the view that it was necessary for states to control capital movements to preserve this policy autonomy.[30] In a 1944 speech about the design of the IMF, Keynes stated his intentions:

> We intend to retain control of our domestic rate of interest, so that we can keep it as low as suits our purposes, without interference from the ebb and flow of international capital movements or flights of hot money. . . . Not merely as a feature of the transition, but as a permanent arrangement, the plan accords to every member government the explicit right to control all capital movements. What used to be hearsay is now endorsed as orthodox. . . . Our right to control the domestic capital market is secured on firmer foundations than ever before, and is formally accepted as a proper part of agreed international arrangements.[31]

Writings of John Maynard Keynes (London: Macmillan, 1973); Lawrence Klein, *The Keynesian Revolution* (New York: Macmillan, 1947).

[29] Odell, "From London to Bretton Woods," 309.

[30] A comprehensive history is provided in Eric Heillener, *States and the Reemergence of Global Finance* (Ithaca: Cornell University Press, 1994).

[31] John Maynard Keynes, *Collected Writings*, vol. 26, 16–17, quoted in Ralph Bryant, *International Financial Intermediation* (Washington, D.C.: Brookings Institution, 1987), 59–60.

The result of this conviction was the allowance for capital controls built into the Bretton Woods agreement in the form of Article VI, with the goal of easing the ability of governments to pursue domestically oriented macroeconomic policies.[32] International capital flows were to be regulated so as to insulate domestic polities from a replication of the crises of the interwar period. As was to be the case in the EMS some forty years later, these interwar crises and policy failures made possible the development of a new view on the need for balance between external and internal stability.

AGREEING TO DISAGREE: A SURVEY OF DOMESTIC POLICIES

The policies followed by the major European states in the years following the Bretton Woods agreement show the influence of Keynesian thought on national policymaking. They also provide evidence for the claim that the major countries of Europe were able to follow relatively independent macroeconomic policies with varying degrees of emphasis on employment, growth, and inflation, while remaining within the fixed exchange rate agreement of the Bretton Woods system.

It is appropriate to begin this survey of domestic politics with France, for in France certain principles of Keynesianism demand management ultimately became established the most firmly.[33] French macroeconomic strategy during the period following World War II focused on the stimulation of investment to promote industrial growth in the wake of the war's vast destruction. Expansionary monetary policy was the major force behind the stimulation of demand, with fiscal policy also playing a role. For example, during the 1960s, France's money supply grew at an average rate of 14 percent per year, because the French let monetary aggregates increase at a much faster rate than in Germany or Britain.[34]

---

[32] Of course, the control over capital movements and low levels of capital mobility that Bretton Woods allowed for did not last indefinitely; it was to erode over the course of the late 1960s and 1970s (see chap. 5).

[33] Pierre Rosanvallon, "The Development of Keynesianism in France," in Hall, ed., *The Political Power of Economic Ideas,* chap. 7.

[34] Peter Hall, *Governing the Economy* (New York: Oxford University Press, 1986), 244–46. See also John Zysman, "The French State in the International Economy," in Peter

French industrial growth was also pursued through national policies of credit subsidization, which funded investment and served to increase demand as well. The elaborate government system of credit allocation and subsidization was effective in rebuilding French industry after the war, but it also fueled the expansion of what Michael Loriaux has termed the French "overdraft economy," characterized by overly indebted industrial enterprises.[35] Although the demand management policies promoted growth, they were also highly inflationary: in 1950–75, "the French cost of living rose by 6 percent more than the British and by 42 percent more than the German." When faced with the inflationary consequences of expansionary policies, however, such as the weakening of the franc, France tended to choose to devalue its currency instead of pursuing deflationary policies.[36]

Overall, French macroeconomic policy during the Bretton Woods era has been characterized as mobilizing domestic resources to neutralize or counter international constraints rather than promoting internal adjustment to international markets.[37] In its emphasis on buffering the national economy from the negative effects of out-and-out liberalism, the French experience in the early postwar period embodies embedded liberalism.

In contrast to the insulation provided French industry, West German policy was marked by the pursuit of economic stability in conjunction with policies to promote industrial adjustment to international economic conditions. Keynesian policies were used only sparingly in Germany during the Bretton Woods years. This exceptionalism was partly due to the fundamentally different way that German policymakers and the German public viewed the functioning of the economy. Instead of considering inflation as something that might be traded off for growth or employment gains, Germans consistently regarded inflation as a

---

Katzenstein, ed., *Between Power and Plenty: Foreign Economic Policies of Advanced Industrial States* (Madison: University of Wisconsin Press, 1978), chap. 8.

[35] Loriaux, *France after Hegemony* (Ithaca: Cornell University Press, 1991). Loriaux argues that this overdraft economy was allowed to take root because of the permissive nature of American hegemony during the postwar era, which enabled states to escape the pressures of adjustment to the international market economy.

[36] Hall, *Governing the Economy*, 245.

[37] Zysman, "The French State in the International Economy," in Katzenstein, ed., *Between Power and Plenty*, chap. 8. See also Rosanvallon, "The Development of Keynesian Ideas in France," in Hall, ed., *The Political Power of Economic Ideas*, chap. 7.

unmitigated evil. Although this view was to become the consensus across the EC by the 1980s, during the Bretton Woods years only Belgium and the Netherlands came to share this view with Germany.[38]

Peter Hall has noted that Germany's macroeconomic policy was unusual in Europe because of "the presence of bias in favor of deflationary macroeconomic policies consistent enough to constitute a repudiation of Keynesian anti-cyclical policy and severe enough to culminate in the artificial creation of recession from time to time."[39] He traces this policy stance to two factors: the anti-Keynesian doctrines of policymakers in the years immediately after the war and the institutional independence of the Bundesbank. German policymakers' distaste for Keynesianism sprang in part from perceptions that it might serve to reignite the inflation of the interwar years, as well as from a feeling that the close cooperative relations among industry, the state, and labor were incompatible with the structure of Keynesian policies.[40] Corporatism made German economic policymaking a much more consensual process than that found elsewhere (with the exception of Belgium and the Netherlands); hence, many of the goals of Keynesian policies could be achieved through negotiation. Christopher Allen has stated that in Germany, the Keynesian emphasis on countercyclical demand policies was "effectively preempted by another set of policies, oriented toward the supply side and the social market economy."[41] The second factor, Bundesbank independence, certainly was important, since it allowed German central bankers to use contractionary monetary policies to counteract the effects of fiscal stimulation, often effectively thwarting the government's attempts at anticyclical policy.[42]

The period from 1967 to 1972 was an exception to the relatively minimal influence of Keynesian ideas in Germany. Although some officials, most notably one of the top government economists, Karl

[38] See Erik Jones, "Economic Adjustment in Belgium and the Netherlands within a Changing Political Formula" (Ph.D. diss., School of Advanced International Studies, Johns Hopkins University, 1995), chaps. 2 and 3.

[39] Hall, *Governing the Economy*, 237.

[40] These points are made in Christopher Allen, "The Underdevelopment of Keynesianism in the Federal Republic of Germany," in Hall, ed., *The Political Power of Economic Ideas*, 268 and passim.

[41] Ibid., 263.

[42] Ellen Kennedy, *The Bundesbank: Germany's Central Bank in the International Monetary System*, Chatham House Papers (New York: Council on Foreign Relations Press, 1991).

Schiller, had been advocating reflation for some time, it took the election of the Social Democrats in 1966 to bring about a change in strategy. The shift was embodied in the subsequent passing of a new law, the Stability and Growth Law, in 1967, which directed the federal government to be responsible for employment and economic growth, as well as the traditional German concerns of price stability and balanced trade. Keynesian countercyclical policies during this time were tempered by the independent Bundesbank, however, and by the relative weakness of the left's coalition. As chapter 5 shows, this experiment with countercyclical demand policies in Germany was to end abruptly in the wake of the stagflation of the first oil crisis.

British economic policy both strongly diverged from both the German focus on price stability and export-led growth and from the French concern with growth and industrial development. British governments of both parties made full employment their primary goal during the Bretton Woods years and used demand management in pursuit of that goal, achieving a certain degree of success throughout the 1950s and 1960s. Although Labour had won a decisive victory at the end of the war with a program that included widespread nationalization plans and a commitment to full employment, by the early 1950s Keynesian strategies had taken prominence as the route to achieving Labour's goals. Direct intervention and nationalization were set aside in favor of macroeconomic management, which effectively dampened the conflict between the upper classes, who wanted the state out of the private sector, and the lower classes, whose primary concern was unemployment.[43]

The use of Keynesian fiscal and monetary policies was complicated, however, by the unwillingness of the British to devalue the pound sterling. In fact, the most distinctive element of British macroeconomic policy during the 1950s to the mid-1960s was its reliance on "stop-go" policies of reflation and deflation: periods of expansion were followed by restrictive macroeconomic policies in an attempt to defend a falling pound and avoid devaluation.[44] The stop-go policies were driven in

---

[43] Hall, *Governing the Economy,* 72. See also Adam Przeworski and Michael Wallerstein, "The Structure of Class Conflict in Democratic Capitalist Societies," *American Political Science Review* 76 (1982), 215–38.

[44] Hall, *Governing the Economy,* 250–51. A detailed analysis of the stop-go policy is also

part by the historical and institutional primacy given to a strong pound, but they also sprang from the desire of the important British financial sector for a strong and stable currency. This contrasts with the comparative willingness of the French, when faced with similar circumstances, to seek depreciation during the Bretton Woods era in order to protect industrial growth.

In the latter years of the Bretton Woods era, the poor performance of the British economy, particularly in terms of growth and export competitiveness, spurred policymakers to attempt policy reforms. These reforms included the introduction of incomes policies and eventually a move away from a strong pound after the balance of payments crises of the late 1960s.[45] During most of the Bretton Woods period, however, unemployment dominated British macroeconomic policymaking.

Finally, Italian policy during the Bretton Woods era can be generally characterized as a compromise between Keynesian demand management and more laissez-faire neoclassical economics.[46] Keynesian policies were viewed with suspicion by some Italian leaders, who equated government management of the economy with the high level of state direction under Fascism. Orthodox neoclassical economics were advocated by those who wished to divorce themselves from any previous Fascist leanings.[47] The technical innovations offered by Keynesianism, however, were taken up by Italian policymakers and economists, and countercyclical stabilization policies were indeed followed in the postwar years. Yet a high level of tax evasion, inefficient administration of

---

found in Michael Surrey, "United Kingdom," in Andrea Boltho, ed., *The European Economy: Growth and Crisis* (Oxford: Oxford University Press, 1982), 531–37.

[45] Growth was consistently below that of the other industrialized economies, averaging 3 percent per year over 1950–64, lower even than other countries like France (5 percent) and the Scandinavian nations (4 percent on average) that were playing catch-up after the war, as were Germany and Italy. Figures from Surrey, "United Kingdom," in Boltho, ed., *The European Economy*, 538.

[46] Marcello de Cecco, "Keynes and Italian Economics," in Hall, ed., *The Political Power of Economic Ideas*, 195–230.

[47] De Cecco asserts that most of the academic supporters of corporatist fascism initially "had in fact, with great aplomb, moved back into the camp of neoclassical orthodoxy. In order to bleach their black shirts, or because of the sincere realization of their intellectual errors, they swung in the other direction and could not stop at the half-way house of Keynesianism." Ibid., 222–23.

the national budget, and a patronage-based system of public spending impeded the effective exercise of demand management in Italy.[48]

The main concern of Italian policymakers during this period was the rebuilding of the Italian economy through economic growth and industrial development.[49] Inflation, however, was not a primary concern: the 1950s and 1960s were marked by relatively stable prices, in contrast to the later Italian experience.[50]

Two points can be drawn from this survey of macroeconomic policy-making in Europe. Both reinforce the contention that European governments exercised a substantial degree of economic policy autonomy in the Bretton Woods years and that the prevailing Keynesian paradigm in fact produced a strong divergence in the goals and the instruments of macroeconomic policy. First, although the majority of countries held to the basic principles of Keynesianism, each government modified the approach to fit its particular national circumstances. Overall, the European nations pursued countercyclical strategies tailored to their institutions and needs, and with varying degrees of enthusiasm, resulting in a lack of conformity in macroeconomic policies.

Second, the very nature of Keynesian policy prescriptions meant that countries did not necessarily follow the same policies at the same time. In fact, the idea of domestic demand management was predicated on the notion that policymakers would respond to their own internal economic needs with either expansionary or contractionary policies, depending on the domestic business cycle and the direction of such national economic indicators as employment, growth, and inflation rates. Thus, policymakers used an array of monetary policy instruments in ways that often diverged from other countries; at any one time, a country might try to stimulate its economy with an increase in the money supply while another country attempted to contract the money supply to dampen inflation.

---

[48] Alan Posner, "Italy: Dependence and Political Fragmentation," in Katzenstein, ed., *Between Power and Plenty*, 225–54. See also Guido M. Rey, "Italy," in Boltho, ed., *The European Economy*, 516.

[49] Regional policies to lessen the large differences between the industrialized and relatively prosperous north of Italy and the depressed south were also a major concern of policymakers.

[50] Michele Salvati, "The Italian Inflation," in Leon Lindberg and Charles Maier, eds., *The Politics of Inflation and Economic Stagnation* (Washington, D.C.: Brookings Institution, 1985), 509–63.

This observation is important for understanding the nature of the compromise of embedded liberalism: it did not constitute an agreement on the specific timing and use of monetary policy among countries to support an international monetary regime. It was instead an "agreement to disagree" that allowed countries to respond to their own internal needs, without the pressure of having to conform to the strictures of an international monetary standard, as was to be the case in the Snake and the EMS in the context of rising capital mobility.

The second point of this historical overview is that during the Bretton Woods years, European governments largely viewed the primary role of macroeconomic policymaking as one of smoothing out fluctuations in demand to promote growth and employment, with much less attention to inflation control.[51] An OECD study surveying monetary policy across the major industrial countries concluded that until 1972, "the main internal task of monetary policy was seen as one of stabilizing real demand at a level commensurate with current productive capacity. The longer run linkages from monetary variables to price developments and the role of monetary policy in dampening cost inflation were not nearly as much in the forefront of policy debates" as they were to become in the mid-1970s.[52] This ranking of priorities was congruent with the assumptions of Keynesian analysis. The key exception, of course, was Germany, which flirted only briefly with Keynesian-type policies, concentrating instead on price stability and export competitiveness.

THE END OF BRETTON WOODS, 1968–1973

The combination of low capital mobility and U.S. leadership made the Bretton Woods system a success through its first two decades. Yet the undermining of the factors that had made it successful finally conspired to bring on its de facto end in 1971 and, finally, its de jure end in 1973. The system began to crumble in the fall of 1968, when an exchange rate crisis erupted that was so severe, it closed financial

---

[51] This observation is also made in OECD, *The Role of Monetary Policy in Demand Management* (Paris: OECD, 1975), 9.

[52] Ibid., 131.

markets in France, Britain, and Germany.[53] Currency realignments, previously relatively rare, began in earnest in 1969: in August, the French government devalued the franc by 12.5 percent, and in September, the German government briefly floated the mark, then came back into the system after revaluing the mark by 9.29 percent in October. The Bretton Woods system struggled through two more years. But confidence in U.S. leadership and economic strength waned as short-term dollar liabilities held by foreigners increased and U.S. gold stocks continued to be drawn down. Once again, in May 1971, the German government decided to float the mark and was joined by the Dutch guilder. The collapse of the Bretton Woods system finally came in August 1971, when President Nixon suspended convertibility of the dollar into gold, imposed price controls, and levied 10 percent surcharge on imports.

After a period of floating rates, the Group of Ten, an informal association of leading industrialized countries, met in Washington in December 1971 to repair the international monetary system. The Smithsonian Agreement they signed there called for the signatories to keep their currencies within slightly wider bands of fluctuation in an effort to reconstitute a fixed exchange rate system. The Smithsonian Agreement affirmed that the U.S. dollar, now worth $38 vis-à-vis an ounce of gold, was no longer convertible into gold, and the United States made no commitment to defend the value of the dollar. Despite the new agreement, by June 1972 the British pound was floating against the dollar, and by March 1973, after a final devaluation of the dollar, the international system of fixed rates collapsed.

The closing of the gold window signaled the end of the formal role of the United States as the international manager of the world's monetary affairs. As Joanne Gowa has argued, the decision to abandon the Bretton Woods regime was prompted by a consensus view in the Nixon administration that the constraints Bretton Woods set on U.S. policy autonomy had become too costly to maintain U.S. participation in the international regime.[54] The comparatively closed nature of the

---

[53] For a chronology of realignments and negotiations in the Bretton Woods system, see Peter M. Garber, "The Collapse of the Bretton Woods Fixed Exchange Rate System," in Bordo and Eichengreen, eds., *A Retrospective on the Bretton Woods System*, 465–66.

[54] Joanne Gowa, *Closing the Gold Window* (Ithaca: Cornell University Press, 1983), 30–32, and chap. 3.

U.S. economy (which made exchange rate stability less of a priority) and the belief that both capital controls or reform of the international monetary system were unworkable alternatives fed the decision to end U.S. support of the system. In essence, the costs of cooperation were raised to the point that they outweighed the benefits for the United States, resulting in the decision to let the dollar float, thus signaling the regime's demise.

Although the collapse of the Bretton Woods system is one of the most overdetermined events in the history of international political economy, an understanding of the reasons behind this collapse is instructive for the later European cases. A series of critical factors can be identified, but it is virtually impossible to definitively weigh the causal influence of each one.[55] The breakdown can be traced to the three factors examined earlier in this chapter: the institutional structure of the Bretton Woods agreement, the role of the United States as its anchor, and capital mobility.

Although, as I have argued, the Bretton Woods planners institutionalized monetary cooperation in ways that brought stability and prosperity to the industrialized world's nations, the structure of the system had at least one critical problem. This was the "Triffin Dilemma," so named after the economist Robert Triffin, who first described its consequences.[56] The dilemma was rooted in the way that the requirements of a functioning international monetary system were met in Bretton Woods. As we have seen, both liquidity and confidence had to be provided for the monetary system to work.[57] The problem, Triffin argued, was that the Bretton Woods system had become reliant on the United States for both these functions even though the U.S. balance of payments deficits increased the supply of U.S. dollars and created liquidity, thereby the deficits themselves eroded confidence in the system. Second, the technical contradictions in the Bretton Woods system were amplified by U.S. economic policies.[58] The budget deficits

[55] For an example of the debate about the end of Bretton Woods, see the disagreement among prominent economists evidenced in "General Discussion," in Bordo and Eichengreen, eds., *A Retrospective on the Bretton Woods System,* 107–08.

[56] Robert Triffin, *Gold and the Dollar Crisis: The Future of Convertibility* (New Haven: Yale University Press, 1960).

[57] A balance of payment adjustment mechanism constituted the third element needed for the system to function effectively.

[58] Two excellent accounts of U.S. policies during this time are Gowa, *Closing the Gold*

and expansionary effects of President Johnson's war on poverty, as well as the spending required to fight the war in Vietnam, increased worldwide liquidity to inflationary heights and called into question the ability of the United States to back its dollars with gold. The important repercussions of this shift in the role of the United States from stabilizer of the system to spoiler has been pointed to by hegemonic theorists as evidence that international monetary cooperation is reliant upon the strength and the leadership of the strongest state in the system.[59]

The final development that played a part in the demise of the Bretton Woods regime was the rising tide of capital mobility. Richard Cooper has written that the "resiliency of the Bretton Woods system was low by 1970, largely owing to greatly increased mobility of private capital." It is difficult, however, to determine at what point capital mobility began to seriously undermine the workings of the system. As I have indicated, international banking activity and new financial instruments took on increasing importance in the late 1960s and 1970s, fraying a system that had been designed with the intention of keeping capital mobility low to avoid a repeat of the destabilizing speculation of the interwar years. Indeed, government controls on capital movements persisted throughout this period but with varying degrees of effectiveness.[60]

The oil crisis of 1973 was the final blow to the Bretton Woods system. The quadrupling of OPEC oil prices in the early 1970s contributed much to worldwide inflation and to the increase in international financial flows, bringing the international exchange rate cooperation of the Bretton Woods era to a end.[61]

The Bretton Woods system operated as a true international monetary system for only thirteen years, from the advent of currency convertibility in Europe in 1958 to the devaluation of the U.S. dollar and the

---

Window, and John Odell, *U.S. International Monetary Policy* (Princeton: Princeton University Press, 1982).

[59] See Robert Gilpin, *The Political Economy of International Relations,* 134–42.

[60] Richard Cooper, "Comment," in Bordo and Eichengreen, eds., *A Retrospective on the Bretton Woods System,* 106; John Williamson, *The Failure of World Monetary Reform, 1971–1974* (New York: New York University Press, 1977), 3.

[61] See Garber, "Fixed Exchange Rate System," in Bordo and Eichengreen, eds., *A Retrospective on the Bretton Woods System,* 461–94.

closing of the gold window in 1971. Yet it provided an essential forum for the reconstruction of international trade and investment after two immensely destructive wars. The unraveling of the system can be traced to the reversal of its underpinnings: namely, new level of capital mobility that created constraints on states' policymaking capabilities and the changing position of the United States in the system. Nevertheless, two of the system's accomplishments endured throughout the following decades: the full convertibility of currencies among the industrialized economies, and the assumption that cooperative management of the international economic system is a valuable goal. Internationally fixed exchange rates, however, were a casualty of Bretton Woods's demise, and fixed rates would only be revived on a regional basis.

The conditions that allowed the Bretton Woods system to function effectively were in some ways historically unique. In contrast to both the nineteenth-century gold standard and its European successors, the Snake and European Monetary System, countries could have fixed rates and domestic policy autonomy because of the low levels of capital mobility and the allowances for domestic policy independence built into the system by its creators. European governments attempted to recover exchange rate stability in the aftermath of Bretton Woods by establishing the first solely European exchange rate regime, the currency Snake. But rising capital mobility, combined with a continued commitment to Keynesian policies and the norm of embedded liberalism, conspired against the achievement of exchange rate stability.

CHAPTER FIVE

Capital Mobility, Policy Crisis, and the Snake

European governments have historically placed a great value on exchange rate stability. The Bretton Woods international monetary system lent them this stability, but when the system began to break down in the early 1970s, European governments decided to create their own exchange rate regime—the currency "Snake," to establish fixed rates within Europe and begin moving toward an eventual monetary union. This chapter investigates the creation and shaky path of exchange rate cooperation in the Snake and argues that rising capital flows combined with divergent national ideas about the goals and instruments of monetary policy created insurmountable barriers to its success.

TRADE AND THE CAP: THE PURSUIT OF EXCHANGE RATE STABILITY

When the Bretton Woods system began to falter in the late 1960s, European Community governments started to look for ways to create a regional, European exchange rate regime.[1] Europeans feared that

---

[1] The six original members of the EC were Germany, France, Belgium, the Netherlands, Luxembourg, and Italy; Britain, Ireland, and Denmark entered in 1972. The Snake included these states; Norway and Sweden were also associate members at times.

exchange rate instability would disrupt trade in their highly open economies, for uncertainty over currency values makes it harder for buyers and sellers in different countries to calculate appropriate prices and negotiate contracts. Despite the mixed results of scholarly tests of the effect of exchange rate changes on trade, the perception of negative trade effects has long made the limiting of currency fluctuations a salient interest for EC governments. Currency fluctuations were also viewed negatively for a second trade reason: the difficulties currency instability wrought in the administration and financing the EC's Common Agricultural Policy. The relationship between exchange rates and the agricultural programs of the EC is a complex one, but outlining the dynamics of how currency fluctuations complicate the workings of the CAP helps show why European governments were interested in exchange rate stability.[2]

The Common Agricultural Policy was developed in the early 1960s as a European customs union in agricultural products.[3] The centerpiece of the CAP was the standardization of prices for agricultural products across the EC and mechanisms to support those prices, such as internal price subsidies, export subsidies, and external third-country tariffs. These mechanisms were financed out of the EC budget, to which all the members contributed. The stakes were high for the success of the CAP, for it was one of the only areas of integration that all members could agree to pursue, despite the differences in their reasons for supporting it.[4]

---

[2] I am drawing here on the more detailed account of this relationship provided in Kathleen R. McNamara, "Common Markets, Uncommon Currencies," in Jack Snyder and Robert Jervis, eds., *Coping with Complexity in the International System* (Boulder, Colo.: Westview Press, 1992), 303–27. Sections of this article are reprinted with permission from the publisher.

[3] The architects of the EC had recognized agriculture as an area of common concern in the Treaty of Rome, the EC's constitution. Indeed, the CAP was a priority among European governments, spurred by memories of food shortages in the wake of two world wars, a growing European farm lobby, and the view that agriculture was the best candidate for progress toward European integration. Because agriculture was one area in which there already was widespread national intervention, it seemed both natural and necessary that the national programs be replaced by EC-level programs if a unified Common Market was to operate effectively.

[4] Joan Pearce notes that "France would have refused to join a Community that provided for free trade in industrial goods but not in agricultural goods, since this would have meant opening its market to German industrial goods without obtaining an adequate compensating benefit." The Germans, who were not competitive in agricultural products,

A basic problem, however, with the workings of the CAP was the incompatibility of a collective pricing system with sovereign national economies, each with its own currency. CAP prices could be set initially to be equal across all currencies, but once the value of one currency moved up or down, prices in that currency would no longer be in line with the others, defeating the purpose of the collective program. To achieve a common pricing system among countries with different currencies, all the members needed to have fixed exchange rates relative to one another, denominated in some common unit, to limit pricing fluctuations. Thus, when drawing up the CAP, European Commission officials created a new instrument, called the "agricultural unit of account," to fill this need; the values assigned to the national currencies in this account were called "green monies." Green money was not real currency but an accounting device, a separate exchange rate for agricultural purposes.[5]

At its founding in the early 1960s, the CAP pricing system operated within the Bretton Woods fixed exchange rate regime, and the European Commission simply set the accounting value of the agricultural unit of account equal to the value of one U.S. dollar.[6] Since the dollar was the basis for the Bretton Woods system, the green exchange rates would be equal to the regular, nonagricultural rates pegged to the dollar within Bretton Woods.

Indeed, for the first few years of the CAP, the green money exchange rate system worked smoothly and thus so did the Community-wide agricultural price support scheme; as long as the larger monetary

---

went along so as to achieve their goal of political rehabilitation and to assure a free market for their competitive products. See Pearce, "The Common Agricultural Policy: The Accumulation of Special Interest," in *Policy-Making in the European Community*, 2nd ed. (London: John Wiley, 1983), 143–75; quote is on p. 143. For a general overview of the economics of the CAP, see *The Common Agricultural Policy and the European Community*, IMF Occasional Paper no. 62 (Washington, D.C.: International Monetary Fund, 1988).

[5] The price of each agricultural product, fixed in terms of the unit of account, is decided by the national agricultural ministers at annual meetings. Initially, cereals were the only products covered, but the CAP was later expanded to include a large variety of farm products.

[6] R. W. Irving and H. A. Fearn, *Green Money and the CAP*, Centre for European Agricultural Studies, Occasional Paper no. 2 (Kent, Eng.: Wye College, 1975), 3. Much of my discussion of the early years of the CAP follows this account. For a more analytic overview of the issues, see Francesco Giavazzi and Alberto Giovannini, *Limiting Exchange Rate Flexibility: The European Monetary System* (Cambridge: MIT Press, 1989), chap. 1.

system remained stable, the agricultural programs functioned without any serious difficulties. The devaluation of the French franc by 12.5 percent in 1969, however, created a problematic gap between the new Bretton Woods value of the franc and the green rate of the franc. If the EC devalued the "green franc" by the same amount, the common price of all agricultural commodities covered by the CAP agreement would automatically rise by 12.5 percent in terms of French francs.[7] But a large rise in food prices threatened to worsen an already undesirable level of inflation in France, and the French government received permission from the Council of Ministers to phase in the new, higher price level over two season, despite the French farm lobby's desire for a shorter transition to higher prices. In effect, agricultural products were exempted from the overall economic policy changes the French government had put into effect with its devaluation.

The special status of French agricultural prices created unwanted effects throughout the EC. The gradual upward adjustment of French prices had the unintended result of giving the French an artificial trade advantage over the other CAP members during the time that French prices rested below the common CAP price. The example of French sugar exports to Germany after the French devaluation is instructive:

The intervention price [the price guaranteed by the CAP agreement] of sugar in Germany was 849.20 DM and the effective intervention price in France was 1048.14 FF, i.e. the pre-devaluation level. If, however, a French trader exported sugar to Germany and sold it there at the intervention price, he would receive 849.20 DM, for which his bank would give him 1179.15 FF (at the new market rate of exchange of 1 DM = 1.388548 FF)—some 131 FF more than he would have received from the French Intervention Agency.[8]

---

[7] Irving and Fearn, *Green Money and the CAP,* 6. Generally, a currency devaluation makes imports more expensive to domestic buyers while making the devaluing country's exports cheaper in overseas markets. But, the EC-wide operation of the CAP made all agricultural products, even those produced in France, act like imported goods and rise in price, because food prices are set on a uniform, external basis. Thus, a devaluation of a country's green rate causes domestic agricultural prices to rise, whereas a revaluation causes them to fall.

[8] Ibid., 8–9.

French traders quickly realized that this disparity gave them a strong incentive to export their sugar in return for a higher price, and they began to do so. The reverse effects were also true: German sugar exports to France cost 131 FF more than comparable French sugar, making German agricultural products uncompetitive with the French. French speculation in sugar exports and the frustration of other countries' farmers over their disadvantaged position quickly brought these unintended effects to the attention of politicians and EC policymakers.

To adjust for the trade effects of the diverging green money rates, agricultural experts in the European Commission devised monetary compensatory amounts (MCAs) as a temporary measure to help smooth the systemic effects caused by the French desire to phase in gradually green money changes and higher food prices. MCAs were an elaborate program of border levies and subsidies, paid out of the Community budget, that would bring French export prices up to the Community-level prices (the levies) and lower the price of Community food imports into France (the subsidies). They also were used to standardize the prices of agricultural goods from third countries. In effect, MCAs were border controls that insulated the French agricultural market from the rest of the EC, keeping prices lower than they would have been in the wake of the devaluation of the franc.[9]

MCAs solved the immediate problem of speculation and arbitrage across European agricultural markets. But the MCAs reintroduced the very levies and subsidies that the European Common Market had been set up to do away with. The French MCAs set a precedent of allowing the suspension of free trade among EC members when nominal exchange rates changed—a step that ran counter to the basic assumptions of European integration. They also set a precedent of allowing two sets of agricultural prices (one at the national level and one at the common price level) instead of forcing an immediate adjustment on the part of farmers and consumers when an overall exchange rate change was made.[10]

Within a few months, the CAP system was again challenged, this time by the upward revaluation of the German mark by 9.29 percent in

[9] For a concise history of MCAs, see Joan Pearce, *The Common Agricultural Policy*, Chatham House Papers, no. 13 (London: RIIA/Routledge and Kegan Paul, 1981), 37–45.
[10] Irving and Fearn, *Green Money and the CAP*, 10.

October 1969. The potential domestic price effects were the opposite of the French devaluation: CAP prices in terms of marks would fall, reducing the intervention prices paid to German farmers. Heeding the protest of its farm sector, Germany asked for a gradual lowering of the intervention prices until they reflected the new exchange rate, with the EC-funded MCAs again compensating for the trade effects.

The disjuncture between the agricultural pricing programs and exchange rate instability was worsened by the move to a floating rate in 1971 by Germany, Italy, Belgium, the Netherlands, and Luxembourg, as Bretton Woods was collapsing. Green money exchange rates remained at their prefloating levels while the general exchange rates fluctuated, once more opening a gap between the two types of exchange rates. MCAs were again used by the Community to offset the trade-distorting effects of the different rates. The variability of the floating rates introduced a new degree of complexity into the program, however, for MCAs had to move along with exchange rates to be effective, instead of being adjusted only when a realignment took place. To deal with the floating rates, European Commission experts created a system for calculating the degree of divergence between exchange rates and the values of the necessary MCAs, still based on European currency values in terms of the U.S. dollar. Under this system, the Community assigned MCA levies and subsidies out of its budget any time a floating currency moved by more than 1 percent, no matter how frequent that might be. The burden on the Community's budget was not inconsiderable.

The efforts to reestablish an international fixed exchange rate regime that culminated in the Smithsonian Agreement of December 1971 promised to stabilize the currency situation. Yet the widening of exchange rate bands under this agreement to plus or minus 2.25 percent against the U.S. dollar, creating allowable fluctuation bands of 4.5 percent, meant that the potential variation or net change over a period of time in a bilateral EC exchange rate was now 9 percent.[11]

---

[11] This was a function of the European currencies not being pegged to one another but to a third currency—the dollar. For example, in the most extreme case, assume the mark is at the top of its band against the dollar and the lira is at the bottom of its value against the dollar. Then the two currencies change in value against the dollar by 4.5 percent, such that their positions are reversed, with the lira at its top value and the mark at its lowest within the allowed bands. The maximum fluctuation between the two

The possibility of such swings in the value of the EC currencies was viewed widely as a threat to the CAP pricing system, for it would require large and continual MCA adjustments. These pressures, combined with the more general concern that exchange rate instability would harm trade, contributed to the decision to set up a new monetary system within Europe.

THE WERNER REPORT AND THE "SNAKE IN THE TUNNEL"

Monetary integration had been an interest on the part of some EC and national government leaders long dissatisfied with reliance on an international monetary framework.[12] The Treaty of Rome, the "constitution" establishing the European Community in the late 1950s, did not specify the creation of a monetary regime or monetary union as an objective; it did, however, advocate the coordination of monetary policies through the newly created Monetary Committee. The treaty also stated that exchange rates were to be of common interest and suggested the potential for mutual aid in the case of balance of payments difficulties.[13] Much like the language of the Bretton Woods agreement, the Treaty of Rome called for the progressive abolishment of restrictions on the movement of capital "to the extent necessary to ensure the proper functioning of the common market," but it also allowed national governments to "take protective measures" to restrict capital movements if they "lead to disturbances" in that state's markets.[14]

Dissatisfaction with the shakiness of the Bretton Woods system in the late 1960s also prompted the EC states to endorse the goal of a European monetary union in the Werner Plan of 1970, a program for monetary integration drawn up by a study group of high-ranking EC and national officials, and chaired by the prime minister of Luxembourg, Pierre Werner. The Werner Report set forth a timetable for

---

European currencies over time would be 9 percent, even though the allowed fluctuation in regard to the dollar is only 4.5 percent.

[12] A definitive political history of the creation of the Snake is provided in Loukas Tsoukalis, *The Politics and Economics of European Monetary Integration* (London: Allen and Unwin, 1977).

[13] See "Treaty Establishing the European Economic Community," in *Treaties Establishing the European Communities: Treaties Amending These Treaties* (Luxembourg: European Communities, 1987), Articles 105, 107, and 108 in particular.

[14] Ibid., Articles 67 and 73, respectively.

the EC to achieve a European economic and monetary union by 1980. The EMU initiative had originally been launched at the EC's Hague Summit of 1969 by German chancellor Willy Brandt, who was seeking to match his party's *ostpolitik* with a deepened commitment to the EC to assuage any political concerns about German motives. The EMU project envisioned in 1970 also was prompted by a growing concern over what many Europeans viewed as the American mismanagement of the international monetary system.[15] In this second concern, Brandt was joined by French president Pompidou, who, in his advocacy of a European presence in international monetary affairs through the creation of a solely European monetary regime, was continuing in De Gaulle's footsteps.

The Werner Report began with a discussion of the need for economic harmonization in an increasingly interdependent Europe, most notably in reference to the establishment of the CAP and the customs union. The report advised creating a monetary union with complete convertibility of currencies, irrevocably fixed exchange rates, and free capital movements. Although the report gave a timetable for EMU, it was vague on its specific institutional characteristics and lacked enforcement measures to insure compliance with the economic coordination procedures needed to move EC member states closer to monetary union.[16] Although endorsed on March 22, 1971, by the EC's national political leaders, the report was never implemented fully. Various technical and administrative loose ends made its realization unlikely, as did the "implicit reliance on the Bretton Woods system which was collapsing at exactly the time the first stages of the Werner plan were

---

[15] Pierre Werner et al., *Report to the Council and the Commission on the Realisation by Stages of Economic and Monetary Union in the Community* (Werner Report), Supplement to Bulletin II-1970 of the European Communities (Brussels: European Communities, 1970); Tsoukalis, *Politics and Economics of European Monetary Integration,* 85.

[16] This may have been the consequence of competing national views of how to best bring about monetary union. The Germans held the "economist" view that economic convergence should come before EMU; the French and Italians held to the "monetarist" view that monetary union should be attempted quickly, as it could itself bring about convergence. This debate has continued through to the present day in the form of German insistence on strict economic criteria for membership in the EMU contained within the Maastricht Treaty and French and Italian efforts to relax the criteria. On the Snake, see Tsoukalis, *Politics and Economics of European Monetary Integration,* 90–98.

supposed to be implemented."[17] Most important, as will be argued below, was the lack of agreement among the European governments on the basic goals and instruments of monetary policy.

The only aspect of the Werner Plan to be implemented was the creation of an intra-EC exchange rate regime, the Snake.[18] Yet even this initiative was subject to numerous delays and negotiations before it got underway. The governors of EC central banks had planned to reduce intra-EC fluctuations against the dollar starting in June 1971, but instability in the international currency markets infinitely complicated this task. A joint float of the European currencies against the dollar, which would retain currency stability among the European countries, was proposed by the German government at an emergency meeting of EC finance ministers.[19] The plan was rejected by the other governments because they did not want their currencies to appreciate along with the mark, which was being bought in large quantities by investors fleeing the U.S. dollar. No agreement was reached, and the German government chose to float its currency; the others introduced new capital controls in an effort to stave off the currency instability surrounding the closing of the gold window in the summer of 1971.

The debate over what the collective European response should be to the demise of the world monetary regime continued for several months. The French, Belgian, and Luxembourg governments advocated capital controls and fixed rates; Germany and the Netherlands, with support from Italy and Britain, favored a joint European float and no capital controls. These positions reflected the diverging views among national officials on the viability of using capital controls as buffers against the instability of the international economy.

A compromise of sorts was finally reached in February 1972 in a meeting between Pompidou and Brandt a month after the Smithsonian

[17] Daniel Gros and Niels Thygesen, *European Monetary Integration* (London: Longman, 1992), 15.
[18] The report went through several drafts before a compromise version was adopted. See Jocelyn Statler, "EMS: Cul-de-Sac or Signpost to EMU?" in Michael Hodges and William Wallace, eds., *Economic Divergence in the European Community* (London: Allen and Unwin, 1981) 103–05; also Gunter D. Baer and Tommaso Padoa-Schioppa, "The Werner Report Revisited," in Committee for the Study of Economic and Monetary Union, *Report on Economic and Monetary Union in the European Community* (The Delors Report) (Luxembourg: European Communities, 1989).
[19] Tsoukalis, *Politics and Economics of European Monetary Integration,* 112–13.

Agreement was negotiated. The two leaders agreed to implement the Snake by narrowing the bands of fluctuation among the EC currencies; capital controls were to be used during crisis periods (as desired by the French); and they also agreed to create a steering committee to coordinate economic policies among the states—a key goal of the Germans. This compromise resulted in the Snake officially beginning on April 24, 1972, with the participation of all EC members: Belgium, France, German, Italy, Luxembourg, and the Netherlands. Britain, Ireland, and Denmark, which were scheduled to become EC members as of January 1, 1973, entered into the agreement on May 1; later that month, Norway began participating in the agreement. Exchange rate fluctuations among the European currencies were to be limited to plus or minus 1.123 percent relative to one another, thus setting up a purely European exchange rate system, the European Common Margins Agreement. The "snake in the tunnel" moniker came from the image of the smaller band of 2.25 percent for the European currencies (the Snake) within the larger 4.5 percent total allowable band of the Smithsonian Agreement (the tunnel), which held for the rest of the Bretton Woods countries. The European currencies would continue to fluctuate against the U.S. dollar and other non-European currencies within the wider Smithsonian Agreement band, but their intra-European fluctuations would be constrained more narrowly.

Instability and Crisis in the Snake, 1972–1974

The first twelve months of the Snake's existence were fraught with currency crises. The first was against the British pound, brought on by three factors: fears of industrial strife in Britain; fears about inflation exacerbated by an expansive national budget; and the British balance of payments problem.[20] The costs of currency intervention to keep the pound within its band were deemed too high by the Bank of England, and the other EC central bankers' lack of enthusiasm for coordinated intervention indicated a belief that floating was the most feasible path for the British. The British left the Snake and the broader Smithsonian band in June 1972. Denmark quickly withdrew from the Snake in Britain's wake but returned in October 1972.

---

[20] Ibid., 122. The sterling crisis coincided with a run on the dollar.

A European summit meeting in Paris in October 1972 reaffirmed a commitment to achieving EMU by 1980, largely because of French pressure, although strains in the Snake were already making this goal seem questionable. Continued speculation against the dollar was putting upward pressure on the German mark as investors looked for a place to put their money in lieu of greenbacks. In the meantime, speculation against the Italian lira was mounting, prompted in part by fears of political instability in Italy and questions about the health of the economy more generally.

In February 1973, a series of meetings among the German, French, and British finance ministers, who were joined in later sessions by the Italian and U.S. finance ministers, coincided with the devaluation of the U.S. dollar and the floating of the lira outside the Snake. The meetings brought on dissension among the Snake members, however, because the Benelux countries and Denmark resented what they saw as their marginalization in the monetary negotiation process. The United States devalued its currency for a second time, announcing that it would no longer defend the dollar and would eliminate capital controls by the end of 1974. In an attempt to shore up the Snake, the European Commission proposed a deal whereby Britain, Ireland, and Italy would return to the Snake, and all would maintain the fixed rates vis-à-vis each other but would float jointly against the dollar. The Commission also advocated an increased institutional basis for the Snake, with financial support for members and a pool of funds for currency intervention, as well as more effective capital controls. Both the British and Italian finance ministers came back with requests for other concessions, none of which were viewed favorably by the other EC states, although they were pressuring the two defectors to reenter the Snake.[21]

In March 1973, the Snake countries severed their link to the dollar. The costs of trying to maintain fixed rates against the dollar in the face of U.S. policies of "malign neglect" were too high, particularly given the squabbling going on among the EC countries. They agreed

[21] The British asked for unlimited financial support to keep the pound within its margins, the Italians for the creation of a regional fund to equalize the economic disparities across and within the EC countries. Both were seen as unacceptable by the other states. See ibid., 128.

to establish the European Monetary Cooperation Fund to coordinate policymaking, although the fund would not have any real institutional authority. Despite these actions, a series of revaluations occurred throughout the year, leading up to the coup de grace for the Snake—the decision by the Pompidou government in January 1974 to exit the Snake and float the franc independently. Although France eventually came back into the Snake some eighteen months later, on the second go-around the French remained in less than a year. France's exit in 1974 signalled the end of the pretense that the Snake was an EC-wide, successfully functioning independent monetary regime. Instead, the Snake continued as a "D-mark zone," consisting of Germany, the Netherlands, Belgium, and sometimes Denmark, with only the Netherlands able to keep a close link to the stable German currency.

In sum, a high level of discord plagued the entire Snake experience. As Daniel Gros and Niels Thygesen have noted, "The mid-1970s marked the low point in European monetary integration." They cite a 1975 report prepared by EC experts and policymakers that described the efforts toward monetary cooperation as a failure and stated that "national economic and monetary policies have never in 25 years been more discordant, more divergent, than they are today."[22]

THE RISE OF INTERNATIONAL CAPITAL FLOWS

What explains the Snake's short and checkered history? I began this discussion by describing the strong desire of the EC governments to find a way to continue to stabilize exchange rates as Bretton Woods crumbled around them. The growth of intra-EC trade and the complications of running the CAP made exchange rate stability preferable to floating rates. But fixed exchange rates cannot be achieved without sacrificing one of two other policy options: capital mobility or independent macroeconomic policies. The bumpy path of cooperation in the Snake was largely due to European governments' attempts to follow all three policy options simultaneously. By the Snake's inception, capital

[22] Gros and Thygesen, *European Monetary Integration*, 20. The quote is in Robert Marjolin et al., *Report of the Study Group, Economic and Monetary Union 1980* (Marjolin Report) (Brussels: Commission of the European Community, 1975).

flows were rising precipitously, while the oil crisis increased the economic policy divergence that was readily apparent in the EC: a strong currency core of countries (Germany, the Netherlands) followed price stability policies, whereas weak currency countries (France, Denmark) continued to practice Keynesian policies, with Belgium balancing in the middle.

The rapid growth of capital mobility in the 1970s can be traced to a remarkable confluence of events, all of which acted to expand the scope and domain of international banking. R. M. Pecchioli states that this expansion "is to be ascribed to a number of profound modifications in the world economic and financial environment."[23] The first important factors in this "profound modification" was the expansion of foreign exchange markets. This expansion was initially brought on by uncertainty over the future of the Bretton Woods fixed rate regime, as doubts over U.S. leadership capabilities created strong incentives for currency speculation. The financial environment further changed with the international move to floating rates in 1973, which created a whole new world of currency trading, much of it centered on the U.S. dollar.

The increase in foreign exchange speculation is indicated by Table 7 which shows changes in the Bundesbank's level of foreign exchange holdings over the postwar years. A high weekly change is indicative of the level of central bank intervention required to fight off foreign exchange market pressures on the currency.

John Williamson, an IMF official during the early 1970s, points out why these data clearly indicate an increase in the level of capital mobility: "What is particularly significant is the 20-fold increase in the size of the maximum weekly inflow between the late 1950s and the end of the adjustable peg era [1971–73] (over which period German trade increased less than 5-fold). Since both were periods of intense speculation on a DM revaluation, the increase must be a reflection of the increase in capital mobility."[24]

---

[23] R. M. Pecchioli, *The Internationalisation of Banking: The Policy Issues* (Paris: OECD, 1983), 20.
[24] John Williamson, *The Failure of World Monetary Reform* (New York: New York University Press, 1977), 48.

Table 7. Weekly changes in Bundesbank holdings of foreign exchange, 1949–1973 (in millions of DM)

Year	Average absolute weekly change	Maximum weekly increase
1949	35	104
1952	73	184
1955	56	146
1958	129	774
1960	204	514
1963	127	369
1966	150	1089
1967	147	570
1968	477	3036
1969	1310	11482
1970	567	3270
1971	1230	8040
1972	581	6261
1973	3735	16064

SOURCE: John Williamson, *The Failure of World Monetary Reform* (New York: New York University Press, 1977), 48; based on Deutsche Bundesbank *Annual Reports,* Appendix 4, "Weekly Returns of the Deutsche Bundesbank."

This increase was beginning to garner notice, although the implications were not well understood. When the German mark floated in May 1971, the *Economist* noted that the time in which speculation forced the German government to break off its commitments to the crumbling Bretton Woods agreement "has been radically shortened. In 1968 and 1969 it took nearly eighteen months. This time it took a few weeks" until the pressure for a revaluation of the mark reached unsustainable proportions. While the German currency came under particularly heavy market pressure, an increase in the level of intervention was typical across all the European central banks that were attempting to maintain fixed rates. For example, Robert Russell notes that in March 1961, a currency crisis in the Bretton Woods system generated the conversion of $300 million into Swiss francs over a four-day period, whereas a similar crisis in February and March of 1973 caused $3 billion to be converted in one day alone.[25]

[25] "Up Goes the Mark?" *Economist,* May 8, 1971, 67; Robert Russell, "Crisis Management in the International Monetary System, 1960–73," paper prepared for delivery at the International Studies Association Convention, New York City, March 1973, cited in Peter

Innovations in international banking were also contributing to the increase in capital mobility. Although some of the new banking arrangements, such as the Eurodollar market, had existed previously, they did not reach substantial size until the 1970s. A contributing factor was the balance of payments surpluses of the OPEC countries brought on by the 1973 oil crisis that created a huge demand for the recycling of OPEC funds through international banks, which in turn financed the deficits of the oil-importing countries.[26]

The growth of "offshore" banking, that is, national banks taking deposits and lending in currencies other than their own domestic money (in the case of Eurodollars, deposits of dollars in banks located outside the United States), opened up a range of new opportunities for investors and lenders.[27] The attraction was in part based on these new markets being largely free of national regulation.[28] Freedom from regulation became increasingly attractive because of new U.S. regulations on foreign investment and banking activity. Imposed in an effort to improve the shaky U.S. balance of payments situation, the regulations created new demands for offshore banking facilities. In the end, they had the perverse effect of increasing international capital mobility, to the dismay of policymakers.[29] The volume of market activity and the new financial instruments (such as Eurobonds and Eurocredits) that were to arise from this innovation did not reach a significant magnitude until the 1970s and 1980s, however (see Figure 6).[30]

J. Katzenstein, *Between Power and Plenty: Foreign Economic Policies of Advanced Industrial States* (Madison: University of Wisconsin Press, 1978), 13.

[26] Figures showing the large imbalances can be found in Pecchioli, *Policy Issues,* 23.

[27] See chap. 4 for more data on international banking.

[28] One version of the development of eurocurrency markets is that the British government's restrictions in 1957 on the use of pounds for trade financing among nonresidents led to the use of U.S. dollars for trade credits and the development of dollar deposits in banks located in Europe. See Yoon S. Park and Jack Zwick, *International Banking in Theory and Practice* (Reading, Mass.: Addison-Wesley, 1985), 9–14, for an excellent overview of the development of the Eurocurrency markets.

[29] For details on how the U.S. policy measures created incentives for the development of offshore banking, see Neil Coulbeck, *The Multinational Banking Industry* (New York: New York University Press, 1984), 56–57; see also Park and Zwick, *International Banking,* 26–31.

[30] An invaluable guide to the interpretation of various statistical series that attempt to measure the Eurocurrency market is Geoffrey E. J. Dennis, *International Financial Flows: A Statistical Handbook* (London: Graham and Trotman, 1984); see especially chap. 6.

Figure 6. Estimated size of the eurocurrency market, 1964–1981

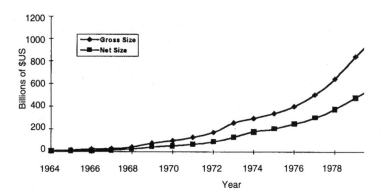

SOURCE: BIS Annual reports, cited in R. M. Pecchioli, *The Internationalisation of Banking* (Paris: OECD, 1983), 133.
NOTE: Gross size equals external foreign liabilities of reporting European banks plus foreign currency liabilities to residents. Data prior to 1974 are partly estimated. Net size is an estimated adjustment of the gross number to exclude interbank transfers of funds that do not add to the volume of credit.

Finally, international financial flows were also increased by the establishment of a new market for international lending—that of developing nations (see Table 8).

Table 8. Private and official lending to developing countries, 1956–1980 (in billions of $US at current prices)

Type of lending	1956	1964	1970	1975	1980
Official	3.2	6.3	13.05	32.82	62.13
Private	2.5	2.3	6.99	23.78	33.92
Total	5.7	8.6	20.04	56.60	96.05

SOURCE: Draws on figures cited in Joan Spero, *The Politics of International Economic Relations* (New York: St. Martin's Press, 1990), 168, from OECD, *Development Co-operation* (Paris: OECD, various years).
NOTE: Official lending equals official development assistance, grants by private voluntary agencies, officially supported export credits, and other flows. Private lending is private flows including bank sector, bond lending, and direct investment.

The reemergence of international capital mobility occurred with the support of the key financial states in the international system—the

United States and Britain, whose international investors and multinational businesses benefited from an open international economy.[31] Once integrated into the global capital market, however, states found it increasingly difficult to control capital movements. Without coordinated regulation, capital controls are difficult to impose unilaterally, and powerful domestic interests may keep states from attempting to regulate international financial flows, thereby giving capital mobility self-reinforcing tendencies. Capital controls were used throughout the postwar era to reinstate some degree of policy autonomy by preventing or slowing down the adjustment that would occur if financial transactions were free from controls. As capital mobility increased, however, capital controls started to become less effective in all but the very short term, because of the increased volume and responsiveness of capital.[32]

THE STRUGGLE TO MAINTAIN EMBEDDED LIBERALISM

The economic turbulence surrounding the end of the Bretton Woods era and the first oil crisis severely tested European governments' ability to provide for economic stability and prosperity. For the most part, their initial response was to continue to adhere to the policies of Keynesian demand management. The key exception was Germany, whose government ended its 1968–72 experiment with expansionary policies and turned to deflationary monetary strategies to combat the economic crisis. The Netherlands, Denmark, and Belgium gradually and sometimes haltingly followed suit.

That many of the European governments continued to follow Keynesian-type policies, even as their divergent strategies produced instability in the new European Snake, indicates the continued relevance of the compromise of embedded liberalism as the norm guiding the behavior of the European governments.[33] That norm, established

[31] This argument is made in Eric Helleiner, *States and the Reemergence of Global Finance* (Ithaca: Cornell University Press, 1994).

[32] See Daniel Gros, "The Effectiveness of Capital Controls: Implications for Monetary Autonomy in the Presence of Incomplete Market Separation," *Staff Papers of the International Monetary Fund,* vol. 34/4 (December 1987), 621–42; and "Fear of Finance: A Survey of the World Economy," *Economist,* September 19, 1992, 12. This survey provides an excellent overview of the growth of capital flows.

[33] John Gerard Ruggie, "International Regimes, Transactions, and Change: Embedded

in the Bretton Woods agreement, made domestic policy autonomy a priority not to be subordinated to the demands of international monetary cooperation. European leaders largely chose to follow economic policies oriented toward what they perceived to be the needs of their domestic polities—the resumption of growth and the decrease of unemployment—even as those policies conflicted with their external goals of exchange rate stability. They were soon to decide however, that these Keynesian strategies were no longer effective in achieving the goals of growth and employment but instead seemed only to feed inflation and worsen the domestic situation.

Domestic Policy Responses to the First Oil Shock

The two-year period before the first oil shock of 1973 was marked by expansionary policies on the part of most European countries, which some economists later pointed to as worsening the effects of the oil shock.[34] The policies were pursued in an effort to stimulate growth in the face of a slowdown in economic activity and ameliorate the economic situation before major elections in France, Italy, and Germany.[35] When the OPEC states quadrupled the price of oil in 1973, national responses to the crisis diverged sharply particularly in the area of macroeconomic policymaking.[36] As Peter Katzenstein describes it, "At no time since the late 1950s did the advanced industrial states jointly

---

Liberalism in the Postwar Economic Order," in Stephen Krasner, ed., *International Regimes* (Ithaca: Cornell University Press, 1983). See chap. 4 for a discussion of the sources and implications of the norm of embedded liberalism in the Bretton Woods system.

[34] See, for example, Lucio Izzo and Luigi Spaventa, "Macroeconomic Policies in Western European Countries, 1973–1977" in Herbert Giersch, ed., *Macroeconomic Policies for Growth and Stability: A European Perspective* (From a 1979 symposium of the Institut für Weltwirtschaft an der Universität Kiel) (Tübingen: Mohr, 1981), 89.

[35] See Paul McCracken et al., *Towards Full Employment and Price Stability* (Paris: OECD, 1977) (hereinafter cited as the McCracken Report), 53, for a schema of the electoral cycle during this period.

[36] Andrea Boltho's edited volume, *The European Economy: Growth and Crisis* (Oxford: Oxford University Press, 1982), contains both analytic surveys of the economic issues discussed here and empirical chapters on each major European country's macroeconomic experience during this period. Individual policy histories for the major European countries can also be found in two volumes: Katzenstein, ed., *Between Power and Plenty,* and Peter Hall, ed., *The Political Power of Economic Ideas: Keynesianism across Nations* (Princeton: Princeton University Press, 1989). See also Peter Hall, *Governing the Economy* (New York: Oxford University Press, 1986), and Michael Loriaux, *France after Hegemony* (Ithaca: Cornell University Press, 1991).

confront a threat as serious as the one in October 1973. The oil embargo and the ensuing price increases aimed at the core of their industrial economies and endangered the stability of their societies. However, even this common crisis led them to pursue divergent strategies of foreign economic policy. . . . All major advanced industrial states developed different strategies to manage the terms of interdependence."[37]

In this essay, Katzenstein surveys the objectives and instruments of macroeconomic policy among the advanced industrial states, and concludes that the divergence in strategies pursued in the 1970s was mainly due to differences in domestic structures. He argues that governments were largely acting in ways congruent with historical trends in national policymaking that arose from longstanding patterns of interaction between governments and their societies.

In monetary policy, the divergence centered on two camps, surveyed below: one that was connected to Germany and price stability, and one that continued to embrace various versions of Keynesian policies. The experience of Germany and the mini-Snake countries shows the importance of domestic policy consensus in bringing about multilateral exchange rate cooperation, for this group of like-minded governments did manage to keep their exchange rates somewhat in line throughout the upheavals of the 1970s. In contrast, the extent of policy divergence that existed among the majority of the EC states made the achievement of exchange rate cooperation in the larger, EC-wide Snake highly unlikely.

Germany and the Mini-Snake

Of all the European nations, Germany's experience with stagflation in the wake of the oil crisis was the least severe. Although Willy Brandt's government had been following somewhat expansionary policies during Germany's short-lived experiment with Keynesianism from 1968 to 1972, the creeping rise in inflation and the burden of increased oil prices reoriented German policy firmly back toward restrictive policies aimed at price stability, even at the expense of high unemployment

[37] Katzenstein, "Conclusion: Domestic Structures and Strategies of Foreign Economic Policy," in Katzenstein, ed., *Between Power and Plenty*, 295–96.

and slow growth. Evidence of a hardening in the government's attitude toward inflation came in late 1973 and early 1974, during wage negotiations with the public-sector trade unions.[38] German officials, particularly in the finance ministry and the Bundesbank, had been attempting to limit wage increases by repeatedly offering predictions of the 1974 inflation rate that were below what many outside observers, such as EC officials, were predicting. The Bundesbank, not surprisingly, had been advocating restrictive monetary policies to try to regain price stability, while the unions were favoring the relaxation of macroeconomic policy to combat unemployment.

The debate was fierce, and the conflict between the unions and the federal government "escalated dramatically."[39] Strikes by workers in such key services as mass transit and garbage collection forced the government's negotiators to concede to wage increases of 15 percent and presented the government with a vexing trade-off. Should the Bundesbank continue to use monetary policy to fend off inflation, even if it meant severe unemployment, because the wages negotiated would be much higher than the general rate of price increases in the economy? Or should the government allow inflation to rise at the same rate as the wage settlements, thus avoiding the squeeze on employers that the higher wage settlement would produce?

The Bundesbank's independence and the historic political adherence to policies of stability played a part in the government's ultimate decision. Announced jointly by Finance Minister Karl Schiller and Bundesbank president Karl Klasen, the decision was to continue the Bundesbank's restrictive policies, despite the potential for large increases in unemployment. This prescription was backed by all the major German economic research institutes, but was deplored by the German trade union federation. It constituted a decisive return to the primacy of inflation reduction as the key German policy goal in the

---

[38] This account follows that of Norbert Kloten, Karl-Heinz Ketterer, and Rainer Vollmer, "West Germany's Stabilization Performance," in Leon Lindberg and Charles S. Maier, eds., *The Politics of Inflation and Economic Stagnation: Theoretical Approaches and International Case Studies* (Washington, D.C.: Brookings Institution, 1985), especially 386–90. See also Fritz Scharpf, *Crisis and Choice in European Social Democracy*, trans. Ruth Crowley and Fred Thompson (Ithaca: Cornell University Press, 1991; German edition first published in 1987), 128–31.

[39] Kloten et al., "West Germany's Stabilization Performance," in Lindberg and Maier, eds., *Politics of Inflation*, 388.

face of the first oil crisis. It also ensured that the German mark would be viewed as the safest haven in the currency Snake and thus would appreciate in value only against its Snake partners.

The Dutch, Belgian, and Danish governments maintained a relatively tight monetary stance and were able to keep their exchange rates fairly stable vis-à-vis one another and Germany during the 1970s. A commitment to restrictive monetary policies and careful control of domestic liquidity helped keep exchange rates in line by containing inflation. For example, prices in the Benelux countries over the period 1973–79 rose by about 20 percent less than prices in the other EC states.[40] In the Netherlands, currency stability and inflation control were achieved through the use of a "liquidity ratio" rule.[41] The tradition of monetary policy conservatism and Dutch energy self-sufficiency cushioned the impact of the first oil crisis and enabled the guilder to stay closely linked to the German mark. This policy stance hardened in the post-1976 period, becoming increasingly monetarist as the perception of economic crisis mounted.[42] As was the case in Germany, the results were relatively good compared to those in other European states and paid off in a stable currency.[43]

Belgium's economic situation historically has closely resembled that of the Netherlands because of its trade openness and integration within the EC, but with some crucial differences. First, and most important for the argument being made here, the Belgian franc, although linked to the German mark throughout the 1970s within the mini-Snake, has never been as hard a currency as the guilder. Like the Dutch, the

[40] Willy van Rijckeghem, "Benelux," in Boltho, ed., *The European Economy,* 598.

[41] See Niels Thygesen, "Monetary Policy," in Boltho, ed., *The European Economy.* For an assessment of the relationship among openness, economic policy constraints, and political decision making in the Netherlands, see Erik Jones, "Economic Adjustment in Belgium and the Netherlands within a Changing Political Formula" (Ph.D. diss., School of Advanced International Studies, Johns Hopkins University, 1995), especially chap. 7; and Paulette Kurzer, *Business and Banking: Political Change and Economic Integration in Western Europe* (Ithaca: Cornell University Press, 1993), chap. 2.

[42] J. Wil Foppen, "The Netherlands and the Crisis as a Policy Challenge: Integration or Ideological Manoeuvres?" in E. Damgaard, P. Gerlich, and J. J. Richardson, eds., *The Politics of Economic Crisis* (Aldershot, Eng.: Avebury, 1989), 103.

[43] In addition, unlike other countries facing the repercussions of the first oil shock, the Dutch trade unions had not pushed for wage indexation in the 1970s but had gone along with the government's efforts to keep inflation contained by keeping wage agreements in line.

Belgians were relatively successful at containing inflation after the first oil shock, thanks to a conservative monetary policy and the pegging of their currency to the German mark.[44]

Denmark also has a history of using a "monetary rule" that does not allow for the accommodation of external imbalances but strives instead for low inflation and adjustment to external constraints.[45] Denmark's historical commitment to low inflation contributed to the government's willingness to keep trying to peg to the German mark throughout the 1970s, but the overvaluation of the krone and the deteriorating relative cost position of the Danish economy in the late 1970s forced a series of large depreciations and the krone's temporary exit from the Snake in its early years.[46] Although this Snake link improved the stability of the exchange rate, unemployment remained high and public expenditures increased, which put pressures on the Benelux countries and Denmark to attempt fiscal reforms in the 1980s (see chapter 6).

The Keynesian Core

In contrast to Germany and the mini-Snake countries, France's policy response to the oil crisis was largely Keynesian: periods of restrictive policies followed by expansionary programs when domestic conditions deteriorated and growth and employment lagged. Despite President Giscard d'Estaing's "high priority on anchoring the franc to the joint European currency float and thus on aligning French policies on German policies," Prime Minister Jacques Chirac's arguments that a more rigorous, restrictive policy would give the Socialists a victory in local elections swayed Giscard from adherence to the Snake.[47] Instead, the *relance Chirac,* the prime minister's expansionary plan launched in 1975, reinstated expansionary policies and elevated growth and employment over the struggle to contain inflation. The "stop-go" macro-

[44] See the analysis in van Rijckeghem, "Benelux," in Boltho, ed., *The European Economy;* see also Erik Jones, "Economic Adjustment in Belgium and the Netherlands," chap. 7.

[45] Thygesen, "Monetary Policy," in Boltho, ed., *The European Economy.*

[46] For more on the Danish case, see Lars Calmfors, "Stabilization Policy and Wage Formation," in Michael Emerson, ed., *Europe's Stagflation* (Oxford: Clarendon Press, 1984).

[47] Michael Loriaux, *France after Hegemony* (Ithaca: Cornell University Press, 1991), 201.

economic policies the French followed were reflected in their record of participation in the Snake: they exited the regime in 1974 and returned again in 1975, only to leave for good in 1976.

Italy's initial response to the oil crisis was a tightening of the money supply which had expanded rapidly in the year preceding the oil shock.[48] In 1975, however, Italy again turned to a reflationary policy because economic activity had fallen so severely that an expansion seemed warranted, despite the balance of payments troubles brought on by the country's 80 percent dependence on high-priced imported oil.[49] During this time, the lira had been under constant pressure because of the government's seeming inability to put its fiscal and monetary house in order. Italy's decision to withdraw from the Snake in 1973 ended up being final, despite the Italian government's desire to find some way to participate in the agreement.[50]

Economic disarray in tandem with the continuation of the stop-go macroeconomic policies of the Bretton Woods years made Britain the first country to leave the Snake agreement; unlike France, it never returned.[51] An initial effort at expansionary stimulus in 1972 had quickly worsened inflation while increasing imports. A deterioration in the balance of payments brought on a run against the pound, and within a month of its initial joining Britain had left the Snake.

The Werner Report's first stage of monetary union, the currency Snake, was a bold European experiment in establishing a cooperative regime to replace the U.S.-based Bretton Woods system. The Bretton Woods arrangement "was intended to provide a compromise between the desire to stabilize exchange rates in order to avoid the disorderly markets and competitive depreciations of the 1930s, and the desire to avoid forcing countries to revert to the gold standard 'rules of the

[48] See the policy history provided in Izzo and Spaventa, "Macroeconomic Policies in Western European Countries," in Giersch, eds., *Macroeconomic Policies,* 73–136. See also John Goodman, *Monetary Sovereignty* (Ithaca: Cornell University Press, 1992), 144–58.

[49] Paul Furlong, "Political Underdevelopment and Economic Recession in Italy," in Andrew Cox, ed., *Politics, Policy, and the European Recession* (New York: St. Martin's, 1982), 177.

[50] See OECD, *Why Policies Change Course* (Paris; OECD, 1988), chap. 7; see also Guido M. Rey, "Italy," in Boltho, ed., *The European Economy,* chap. 17 for more on this period.

[51] On British economic strategy during the 1970s, see Hall, *Governing the Economy,* 93–99.

game', under which defence of the exchange rate override the pursuit of domestic full employment policies."[52] The Snake was created in the hopes that exchange rate stability—uniquely important to Europeans because of their highly open economies and their EC-wide agricultural pricing system—could be achieved with the same compromise in mind, but this was no longer possible. I have argued rising capital mobility was significant enough by the early 1970s to make the achievement of exchange rate stability impossible unless governments were willing to forgo the autonomous use of monetary policy. The legacy of the Bretton Woods years made domestic macroeconomic policies incongruent with exchange rate cooperation. This incongruence made the Snake a still-born experiment in EC monetary cooperation. The development of a new policy consensus across the European states in the years following the demise of the Snake made the next European effort at cooperation in 1979 a very different proposition.

---

[52] Williamson, *Failure of World Monetary Reform*, 3.

CHAPTER SIX

Neoliberal Policy Consensus and the European Monetary System

The European Community had little success in establishing a fixed exchange regime after the collapse of the Bretton Woods system in the early 1970s. A combination of increasing capital mobility and divergent national macroeconomic policies broke the European currency Snake apart within a few years of its founding. Despite this inauspicious record, the European states once again decided to try to establish an EC-wide exchange rate agreement. In March 1979, the European Monetary System (EMS) and its exchange rate mechanism (ERM) officially came into being, with Germany, the Benelux countries, Denmark, France, Ireland, and Italy participating; Britain was the only EC member to join the EMS but not the ERM.

Initially, the EMS was viewed with almost universal skepticism.[1] Its institutions were very similar to those of the Snake's; moreover, it was established at a time of deep pessimism about Europe's ability to act collectively on any issue, much less one as complex and difficult as multilateral monetary cooperation. In this chapter I investigate how the EMS confounded many observers by evolving into a stable cooperative regime despite the pressures of increasing international capital mobility.

I begin with the creation of the EMS. Two factors were decisive in the revival of this first step toward European monetary integration. First, intra-European trade-related concerns fueled European leaders'

---

[1] I follow the convention of using EMS and ERM interchangeably.

construction of the EMS, as they did in the Snake. Second, on a geopolitical level, French president Valéry Giscard d'Estaing and German chancellor Helmut Schmidt sought to strengthen European institutions to compensate for what they saw as U.S. mismanagement of the Western world's affairs. Yet neither factor wholly accounts for the fundamentally different degree of monetary cooperation maintained in the following decade of EMS operations. A deeper causal understanding must draw on the interaction between changing international economic structures and domestically held ideas about monetary policy that produced a redefinition of interests among the European states.

THE CREATION OF THE EUROPEAN MONETARY SYSTEM

The European Monetary System was constructed in a series of negotiations held throughout 1978.[2] The idea of reviving the effort to stabilize exchange rates and eventually create an economic and monetary union had never completely left the European agenda, despite the Snake debacle.[3] The first significant boost to the project came from the president of the European Commission, Roy Jenkins. His decision to support the creation of a new Community-wide exchange rate regime was prompted by his feeling that the EC was "bogged down" and that a major new initiative "was therefore manifestly necessary."[4] In summer 1977, he "came firmly to the conclusion that the most open axis of advance for the Community in the circumstances of 1977 lay in reproclaiming the goal of monetary union," as it was at once a bold offensive and one that could build on the EC's historical interest in monetary integration.[5]

[2] The definitive political history of the founding of the EMS is Peter Ludlow, *The Making of the European Monetary System* (London: Butterworth, 1982).

[3] For example, in 1975 a group of economists and policymakers had published in the *Economist* the so-called "All Saint's Day Manifesto," a plea for monetary stabilization in Europe through the creation of a European currency. *Economist*, November 1, 1975, 33.

[4] Roy Jenkins, *A Life at the Centre* (London: Macmillan, 1991), 463. Jenkins also acknowledges a more personal impetus: his decision to launch the EMS was spurred by reading a negative review in the *Economist* of his first six months as European Commission president.

[5] Ibid. Jenkins's public launching of the EMS initiative took place in October 1977 in his Monnet Lecture at the European University Institute in Florence.

Yet the most important impetus for the EMS originated not with the European Commission but rather in the personal determination of President Giscard D'Estaing and Chancellor Schmidt to see the EMS come to life. There were several interests at stake : some were common to all the EC member states, but some were peculiar to the French and German heads of state. The basic reasons for the creation of the EMS were essentially the same as those that underlay the Snake agreement. First was the Europe-wide belief that exchange rate instability impedes trade and investment activity within the European common market. Giscard summed up the longstanding postwar interest in exchange rate stability in Europe as "obvious": "We could not hope to maintain stable trade flows within the common market with prices that fluctuate as much as the currencies."[6]

The second trade-related reason for the pursuit of exchange rate stability within the EC is the Common Agricultural Policy (CAP).[7] A myriad of technical problems made administering the CAP system extremely difficult if national currencies fluctuated widely.[8] With the creation of an EC-wide currency regime, these fluctuations would be limited, and the program would become less complex and less costly. These two trade-related interests in exchange rate cooperation were essentially constant over the two periods, and held for all of the EC states except Britain, which had a trade structure less dependent on EC markets than had the other large states. Since the Snake's demise, however, changes in the international geopolitical environment made the idea of exchange rate stabilization, with the potential for further

[6] "L'intérêt de cet effort était évident: on ne pouvait espérer maintenir des courants d'échanges stables à l'intérieur du Marché commun avec des prix qui auraient flotté autant que les monnaies." Giscard d'Estaing, *La pouvoir et la vie* (Paris: Compagnie Douze, 1988), 137.

[7] For example, Jean-Jacques Rey, a senior Bank of Belgium official, cites three reasons for the creation of the EMS: the high degree of openness of the member states and its implication for exchange rate policy; "various facets" of the linkages among the EC states, such as the CAP and broader political concerns; and the negative experience of floating exchange rate arrangements. Rey, "Discussion," in Francesco Giavazzi, Stefanio Micozzi, and Marcus Miller, *The European Monetary System* (New York: Cambridge University Press, 1988), 138.

[8] This is covered in detail at the start of chap. 5; see also Kathleen McNamara, "Common Markets, Uncommon Currencies: System Effects and the European Community," in Jack Snyder and Robert Jervis, eds., *Coping with Complexity in the International System* (Boulder, Colo.: Westview Press, 1993).

monetary integration and a heightened profile for Europe in international affairs, more attractive. This incentive played a large part in Schmidt and Giscard's interest in resurrecting the EMS initiative.

In 1978 the immediate concern of the German leader was the decline of the value of the U.S. dollar, which had fallen by 23.5 percent against the German mark in the previous year. Schmidt viewed the dollar's depreciation as going far beyond what was warranted by "economic fundamentals" and worried that it placed excessive upward pressure on the German currency. Schmidt feared that this appreciation would make Germany's exports uncompetitive, squeeze profits, and increase unemployment that was already high by German standards.[9]

More fundamentally, both Giscard and Schmidt viewed the economic and political leadership of U.S. president Carter as inadequate. Roy Jenkins has commented that the depreciation of the dollar caused "Schmidt to add monetary slovenliness to the long list of sins by which he saw Carter devaluing his great *ex officio* position as captain of the West."[10] Giscard has written that Schmidt's "loss of confidence in the Carter administration was definitive. . . . This psychological attitude created a new willingness for the next two stages of European union that we were to tackle together: money and defense."[11]

Jonathan Story argues that Giscard and Schmidt had "similar assessments of a deterioration in the international environment, and from a shared aspiration to preserve the Community as an island of stability in a fragmenting world."[12] The EMS initiative developed from Germany's recognition of the need to look beyond the American military umbrella and from France's recognition of the economic decline it faced unless something drastic was done.

The personal amity between Giscard and Schmidt and the dovetailing of their desires for increased European monetary coherence were

[9] See Daniel Gros and Niels Thygesen, *European Monetary Integration* (London: Longman, 1992), 36–37.

[10] Jenkins, *A Life at the Centre*, 475.

[11] "La perte de confiance d'Helmut Schmidt dans l'administration Carter a été définitive . . . cette attitude psychologique créait une disponibilité nouvelle pour les deux prochaines étapes de l'union Européenne que nous devions aborder ensemble: la monnaie et la Défense." Valéry Giscard d'Estaing, *Le pouvoir et la vie*, 136.

[12] Jonathan Story, "Convergence at the Core? The Franco-German Relationship and Its Implications for the Community," in Michael Hodges and William Wallace, eds., *Economic Divergence in the European Community* (London: Allen and Unwin, 1981), 177.

critical in bringing the EMS to fruition.[13] Indeed, in his memoirs Giscard takes the credit for the EMS initiative, stating that "it was above all my idea," whereas Schmidt proposed moving forward in the area of defense.[14] But it seems likely that public and private lobbying by Jenkins in the European Commission also was helpful in placing the project at the top of the agenda in 1978.

The EMS negotiations began with a Schmidt-Giscard presentation to the EC heads of state at the Copenhagen Summit of April 1978. The two convinced the other EC leaders to study the possibility of establishing a new European exchange rate system, one that would have routine policy coordination, foreign exchange intervention obligations, and a new institution, the European Monetary Fund, to manage a pool of foreign exchange reserves and provide balance of payments assistance.[15] The importance of Giscard and Schmidt's commitment to the creation of the EMS is evident in the way its basic outlines were negotiated in the months following the initial discussion at Copenhagen.[16] The French and German leaders, joined by British prime minister James Callahan, called for official study of the various plans while at the same time delegating responsibility for developing a plan of their own to a few close aides. The initial proposal was constructed entirely outside and in secret from the normal channels of national and EC policymaking. The German Bundesbank found this particularly egregious, as it was entirely excluded from the discussions.[17]

Another summit meeting in Bremen in July 1978 was held on the way to hammering out the contentious details of how the system would

[13] Story points to a key bilateral summit in February 1977, where Giscard announced that "the Franco-German entente constitutes the cornerstone of all progress in the constitution of Europe" and stated that he hoped that the EC would renew its movement toward economic and monetary union. Maurice Delarue, "Paris et Bonn resserrent leur coopération," *Le Monde,* February 5, 1977, quoted in Jonathan Story, ibid. Jenkins notes the importance of the Giscard-Schmidt friendship and recalls that European Council meetings would see Schmidt changing seats "with his foreign minister so that he and Giscard could always be next to each other, like two 'best friends' who insisted on sharing the same double school desk." Jenkins, *A Life at the Centre,* 460.

[14] Giscard, *Le pouvoir et la vie,* 136.

[15] Gros and Thygesen, *European Monetary Integration,* 42.

[16] A detailed historical reconstruction of the policymaking process from the early stages to the implementation of the EMS is found in Ludlow, *The Making of the European Monetary System.*

[17] Giscard's representative to the secret meetings was the governor of the Bank of France, but Schmidt had chosen an economist from the chancellor's office.

work. I will not recount the specifics of the negotiations here.[18] In short, the broad lines of national disagreement over the working of the system divided the strong currency countries, namely Germany and the Netherlands, from the weak currency countries, primarily France and Italy. The disagreement centered on whether the EMS could be designed so that there was no asymmetry among the participants in terms of national currency intervention obligations. Throughout the history of exchange rate regimes, for technical reasons weaker currency countries have had to pay a higher price foreign exchange reserves to stay within fixed rate regimes. The failure of the Snake had made the weaker currency governments particularly wary on this point, while the strong currency states feared that a symmetrical system of obligations would be inflationary. Much of the negotiations therefore focused on the attempt to find a solution that would reassure the weak currency countries about their position in the system and address the fears of the strong currency countries. A solution was finally reached with the creation of a "divergence indicator" that was supposed to signal to both the weak and strong countries the need for intervention when exchange rates started moving away from a central rate, the European Currency Unit.[19]

The agreement establishing the EMS was signed at the Brussels Summit of December 1978. Its implementation was delayed, however, for a few months by byzantine squabbles between Giscard and French farming interests. Finally, in March 1978, the EMS was inaugurated, albeit under a cloud of skepticism.[20] Despite the bargaining that went

[18] See Andrew Moravcsik, "Why the European Community Strengthens the State: Domestic Politics and International Cooperation," paper presented at the 9th Annual Conference of Europeanists, Chicago, March 31–April 2, 1994.

[19] The issue was essentially whether the interventions should be based on the series of bilateral exchange rate relationships or whether they should be based on each currency's relationship with a multilateral average. See the summary discussion in David Begg and Charles Wyplosz, "The European Monetary System: Recent Intellectual History," in *The Monetary Future of Europe* (London: Centre for Economic Policy Research, 1993), 11–20.

[20] See "European Monetary System: Texts of the European Council of 4 and 5 December 1978," in *European Economy* (Luxembourg: Commission of the European Communities, March 1979). The Bundesbank warned repeatedly that it would cease to uphold its EMS commitments if German domestic price stability was threatened, and it was understood that this was no idle threat. Chancellor Schmidt's minister of economics, Count Otto Lambsdorff, stated publicly that the chancellor had promised that the Bundesbank would not be bound by the EMS obligation should this be the case. Bundestag report, December 6, 1978, reported in Ludlow, *The Making of the European Monetary System*, 240.

on at the EMS negotiations, within a year it was obvious that the new system would be more like the Snake than not. The divergence indicator turned out to have mathematical properties that rendered it ineffective, and the proposed European Monetary Fund soon sunk without a trace. Despite the efforts of the EC governments, the EMS ended up close to the Bundesbank's vision of a system that did not threaten German price stability but instead required the other states to follow German policies.[21] This asymmetry begs the question of why the other governments continued to participate in the EMS, when it did not reflect their wishes for a more symmetrical, balanced system.

Monetary cooperation of the type achieved in the EMS reaches deep into the domestic realm of the state: unless the cooperative agreement is congruent with prevailing domestic political preferences, a state cannot maintain its commitments, even if it is motivated by the geopolitical concerns that preoccupied Schmidt and Giscard in 1978. By the time the EMS was created, rising capital mobility meant that the maintenance of fixed exchange rates would require extensive domestic economic adjustments; these adjustments would not have been acceptable to a society that still valued Keynesian strategies.[22] It is extremely unlikely that the desire for an integrated Europe on the part of national elites could by itself have turned the domestic economy around to the extent necessary to hold the EMS together. Instead, as we will see, the recognition that independent monetary policies of the Keynesian, full-employment kind were diminishing in their effectiveness made governments willing to subordinate national monetary policy to the constraints of exchange rate cooperation.

---

[21] This is a version of the n-1 phenomena. Technically, the easiest way for an exchange rate system to hold together is for one country to act as an anchor for the system, setting the monetary policies for the other states to follow. In theory, an alternative is for the participating countries to establish a policy "rule." For example, this rule could be that every member will expand the money supply by 2 percent a year. In practice, however, it is extremely hard to design a rule that will keep rates together, because the same monetary actions will have different effects in each country. It is easier for the strongest state in the system to set policies to which other states adjust their stances. For further discussion, see Alberto Giovannini, "How Do Fixed-Exchange Rate Regimes Work? Evidence from the Gold Standard, Bretton Woods, and the EMS," in Marcus Miller, Barry Eichengreen, and Richard Portes, eds., *Blueprints for Exchange Rate Management* (London: Academic Press, 1989), 13–35.

[22] See the data on capital mobility in chap. 4 and 5.

To understand why governments made the difficult policy choices to stay within the EMS—to understand the maintenance of the regime—one must go beyond the bargaining that accompanied the establishment of the EMS. My argument is that the EMS's asymmetry was tenable because it coincided with a transformation within the member states in domestic macroeconomic policymaking that made the operation of a system based on German price stability newly possible. An ideational shift toward neoliberal monetary orthodoxy drove political leaders to change their calculation of the costs of this trade-off, choosing exchange rate stability while fundamentally redefining the role of the state in the economy away from the postwar Keynesian norm.

The Creation of a European Policy Consensus

The first major factor in the creation of the new neoliberal European policy consensus was the experience the majority of European governments had in the early 1970s with policy failure. Governments found that standard Keynesian demand management tools were inadequate for coping with the slow growth, high unemployment, and high inflation of the 1970s. As Peter Haas has observed, "Failed policies, crises, and unanticipated events that call into question [decision makers'] understanding of an issue-area are likely to precipitate searches for new information, as are the increasing complexity and technical nature of problems."[23] Broadly speaking, the experience of crisis and failure forced policymakers to adjust their policies to the changed international environment—in essence, to learn from their mistakes. The learning did not take place immediately, however, nor would it have occurred in the same way without the existence of an alternative paradigm—monetarism—and an example—Germany—to guide adjustment.

The major policy programs of the major EMS member states can be grouped into two waves of policy reforms that moved the European governments toward what I call the policies of competitive liberalism.

---

[23] Peter Haas, "Introduction: Epistemic Communities and International Policy Coordination," *International Organization* 46 (Winter 1992), 29.

Pre-EMS Reforms in France and Italy

The neoliberal policy shifts of France and Italy in 1976 were the most critical to the success of the EMS. Although their commitment wavered somewhat throughout the first years of the EMS, the initial change in the goals and instruments of monetary policy that occurred created the foundation for cooperation. This policy shift brought these governments closer to the policy of price stability pursued by Germany and the Benelux states, which still participated in the joint float that remained in the aftermath of the Snake debacle (the mini-Snake or D-mark zone).

It is appropriate to consider France first, since the evolution of French macroeconomic policy is arguably the most important for the eventual success of the EMS. Simply put, for the EMS to be a truly European project, it had to have France's participation. Most immediately, the political entrepreneurship of Giscard d'Estaing was key in bringing about the agreement that created the EMS. This participation by France was dependent, however, on a change of policies from those that had forced it to exit the Snake twice before.[24]

The change in French policy occurred after the failed economic expansion undertaken by Prime Minister Jacques Chirac in 1975–76. Under a plan devised in 1976 by the new prime minister, Raymond Barre, France radically shifted its policy toward monetary rigor.[25] Barre put forward a comprehensive reform plan centered on restrictive monetary policy and the use of monetary targets. The eventual goal of the Barre Plan was to stabilize the franc and to reinforce domestic austerity reforms by joining the new European exchange rate system.[26] In its content and presentation, the Barre Plan was modeled explicitly on the German policy position.[27]

---

[24] The shift is strikingly evident in the vastly different assessments of French macroeconomic policy offered in the 1972 and the 1979 versions of the OECD's *Country Survey: France.*

[25] Barre also acted as his own economic and finance minister.

[26] Jack Hayward, "France: The Strategic Management of Impending Impoverishment," in Andrew Cox, ed., *Politics, Policy, and the European Recession* (New York: St. Martin's Press, 1982), 111–40.

[27] See *Rapport économique et financier: Comptes prévisionnels pour l'année 1978* (Paris: Ministère de l'Economie, July–August, 1978).

In an article reviewing his government's record from 1976–80, Barre discusses the four key policies his government attempted to implement in 1976 to carry out the inflation fight: first, control of the money supply through published targets; second, restrictive budgetary policies; third, wage restraint by the social partners; and fourth, stabilization of the franc as a cornerstone of government policy.[28] Barre blamed France's exit from the Snake in 1976 on the Chirac *rélance* and claimed that it brought more inflation and depreciation. These policies "must be avoided," Barre insisted, because inflation constituted the most severe threat to employment and growth.[29]

The basic stance of the Giscard-Barre years was marked by a "willingness to 'take' unemployment in the hope of an exchange for greater international competitiveness and relatively low inflation; its determination to hold claims for social equality in abeyance better to foster the ability of capital to invest; and its enthusiastic efforts to reduce direct social controls over the economy by turning more and more decision-making authority back to the market."[30] This policy reversal was startling in its overt rejection of the previously sacred notion of full employment. In contrast to public officials' statements in earlier periods, "by 1978 it was possible openly and officially to assert that for the foreseeable future mass unemployment would endure in France," primarily because of external constraints.[31] This position was driven by the view that France "must adapt to irreversible changes in the world economy" if it was to survive, and it was reflected in the changing emphasis of the macroeconomic stance in the official five-year "Plan Nationale" and in the interim updates published by the Commissariat du Plan during 1971–84.[32]

---

[28] Raymond Barre, "L'économie française quatre ans après," *Revue des Deux Mondes* (September 1980), 513–32.

[29] Ibid, 523. Oddly enough, Chirac claimed later that the Barre Plan had closely followed an economic policy initiative contained in a memo he left for the new prime minister, but this was denied by Barre. Recounted in Henri Amouroux, *Monsieur Barre* (Paris: Editions Robert Laffont, 1986), 263–64.

[30] Stephen Cohen and Peter Gourevitch, "Postscript: The Socialists—Major Movements in a Narrow Space," in Cohen and Gourevitch, eds., *France in the Troubled World Economy* (London: Butterworth, 1982), 181. A detailed account of the political formulation of the Barre Plan is found in Amouroux, *Monsieur Barre,* chap. 8.

[31] Hayward, "France," in Cox, ed., *European Recession,* 113.

[32] Barre, "L'économie française quatre ans après," 517.

Despite the potentially high costs of this austerity strategy, the domestic political situation in France was conducive to this project and allowed Barre's government to sustain adequate electoral support in the 1978 elections to stay the austerity course. In part, these favorable conditions reflected the declining importance of the labor movement in France, whose membership had dropped to 20 percent by the mid-1970s.[33] But the lack of serious opposition also reflected the failure of traditional expansionary policies, which had made it difficult for the French Left, or the Gaullist Right for that matter, to develop a counter strategy.[34] The Communists and the Socialists were also split on broader foreign policy issues such as the Soviet Union and cooperation in the European Community. As Jonathan Story noted, "Unable to overcome the incompatibility between their policies of domestic reforms and continued support for the European Community, the Socialist left the way open for M. Barre to announce his version of Modell Deutschland for France in Europe."[35]

By late 1976, a similar program of reform was being attempted in the second crucial EMS member state, Italy.[36] The Italian government had charted an erratic macroeconomic course since the first oil shock: expansionary policies leading into the oil shock of 1973, followed by very restrictive policies in response to the shock and in line with the terms dictated by 1974 IMF loan.[37] This restrictive course was then

[33] Volkmar Lauber, "France and the Economic Crisis," in Erick Damgaard, Peter Gerlich, and J. J. Richardson, eds., *The Politics of Economic Crisis* (Aldershot, Eng.: Avebury, 1989), 107–24.

[34] The French Left was divided in its assessment of the experience of Chirac's 1975–76 reflation. The two major trade unions each proposed their own conflicting versions of "maximalist" approaches to the economic crisis. The maximalist course essentially offered a new model of industrialization oriented toward stimulating domestic growth in lieu of international trade and investment. See George Ross, "French Labor and Economic Change," in Cohen and Gourevitch, ed., *France in the Troubled World Economy*, 158–59.

[35] Story, "Convergence at the Core?" in Hodges and Wallace, eds., *Economic Divergence in the European Community*, 173. Giscard and Barre were also aided by the constitution of the Fifth Republic, which gives considerable power to the executive to govern without serious concern over challenges from the National Assembly. See Lauber, "France and the Economic Crisis, 1974–1987."

[36] A detailed assessment of Italy's macroeconomic policies during this period is found in OECD, *Economic Surveys: Italy* (1977).

[37] Italy was particularly hit by a deterioration in its terms of trade because of its heavy dependence on oil, which was used to meet 70 percent of its energy needs. Guido M. Rey, "Italy," in Andrea Boltho, ed., *The European Economy: Growth and Crisis* (Oxford: Oxford University Press, 1982), 522.

followed by a massive multiyear program of monetary and fiscal reflation in late 1975, adopted in the hopes of stimulating growth and
electoral success for the governing Christian Democrats.[38] The results
were unimpressive as Italy's inflation rate soared, unemployment
worsened, and the country's total indebtedness mounted to $22 billion
while its foreign exchange reserves dwindled.

The drying up of foreign funds in the context of uncertainty over
Italy's financial stability and a series of domestic political crises led to
a dramatic run on the lira at the start of 1976. This crisis forced the
government to close foreign exchange markets and suspend efforts
to stabilize the currency.[39] Fearing the inflationary effects of a large
depreciation, the government tightened monetary policy and imposed
exchange controls. Emergency measures taken while the foreign exchange markets were closed included increasing the discount rate and
raising bank reserve ratios; these measures were later supplemented
by a requirement for prior deposits on imports, further increases in
the discount rate, and the introduction of a ceiling on bank credit.[40]

Only with the creation of a new coalition, which included the Communist Party, and which was formed behind Prime Minister Andreotti in
summer 1976, was the reform package consolidated. Surprisingly,
given the traditional leftist partisan preference for reflationary policies,
the Communists shared the growing consensus view that the situation
was unsustainable and that the austerity conditions attached to the
IMF loan were in fact necessary on their own merits.[41] Indeed, Enrico
Berlinger, a leading official of the Italian Communist Party, PCI, advo-

---

[38] A detailed account of the political infighting that accompanied these policy zigzags
is John Goodman, *Monetary Sovereignty* (Ithaca: Cornell University Press, 1992), 148–61.
See also Lucio Izzo and Luigi Spaventa, "Macroeconomic Policies in Western European
Countries 1973–1977" in Herbert Giersch, ed., *Macroeconomic Policies for Growth and
Stability: A European Perspective* (from a 1979 symposium of the Institut für Weltwirtschaft
an der Universität Kiel) (Tübingen: Mohr, 1981).

[39] OECD, *Why Policies Change Course* (Paris: OECD, 1988), 78–79, recounts "the surprisingly little room for manoeuvre" that the Italian authorities experienced in trying to
halt the lira's decline with dwindling foreign reserves in the face of high capital outflows.
In addition, a rumor began to circulate that an American banking supervisory agency
was going to advise against lending to Italy, which brought private lending to a standstill
and led authorities to close the official Italian exchange markets.

[40] The discount rate—6 percent at the start of 1976—had been raised to the postwar
high of 15 percent (19 percent including certain penalties) by October. OECD, *Economic
Surveys: Italy* (1977), 32.

[41] Goodman, *Monetary Sovereignty*, 161.

cated *austerità* and deflationary policies. He used his association with the government from 1976 to 1979 to promote monetary stabilization and significant wage restraints.[42] One of Berlinger's allies and the head of the CGIL trade union told workers at their annual congress in 1978 to make "substantial sacrifices" to bring Italy's economy back to health.[43]

The Communists helped the government sell further monetary tightening to the unions, advocating the view that the reduction of domestic absorption and the control of the exchange rate and imported inflation should be the key priority, even at the cost of high unemployment and low growth. This position mirrored a longstanding contention of the Bank of Italy. The level of policy consensus made this period seem an unusually harmonious one in the normally highly contentious Italian political setting.[44] Nonetheless, Italy's tight monetary policy stance was continually hindered by the lack of rigor on the fiscal side, where a fragmented budget process and the need for political accommodation fed a growing public deficit.[45] Despite efforts to weaken its impact, the Italian wage indexation system, the *scala mobile*, continued to exacerbate the price-wage inflationary spiral.

The new commitment to monetary stabilization did help strengthen Italy's external position by the end of 1977. The lira, which had depreciated by more than 20 percent in 1976, fell by only 7 percent in 1977, making more credible the decision to participate in the EMS negotiations in 1978. The change in strategy was put to the test with the second oil shock of 1979, but Italy responded with a consistent policy of monetary tightening and high interest rates to defend the

[42] Patrick McCarthy, "France Faces Reality: *Rigueur* and the Germans," in David Calleo and Claudia Morgenstern, eds., *Recasting Europe's Economies: National Strategies in the 1980s* (Lanham, Md.: University Press of America, 1990), 38. Goodman notes that the Communists took this position in part to show that they could be a responsible governing party and to try to increase their legitimacy with non-PCI voters. Goodman, *Monetary Sovereignty*, 159.
[43] Paul Furlong, "Political Underdevelopment and Economic Recession in Italy," in Cox, ed., *European Recession*, 188.
[44] Ibid., 182.
[45] On the institutional roots of this division, see James I. Walsh, "International Constraints and Domestic Choices: Economic Convergence and Exchange Rate Policy in France and Italy," paper presented at the European Community Studies Association biennial meeting, May 27–29, 1993.

exchange rate, instead of allowing the currency to depreciate.[46] This strategy was crucial for the return to surplus of the current account and the relative stability of the lira in 1979–80. Officials stated publicly that they did not wish to "repeat the mistakes" of the first oil crisis and that Italy's interests were no longer served by policies of currency depreciation and demand stimulus, even at the cost of "zero growth in the economy."[47]

In its review of the evolution of Italian monetary policy at the end of the 1970s, the OECD stated that "in the face of the acceleration of inflation in the course of the year, the defense of the exchange rate now seems to have become the priority objective of the Banca D'Italia, in order to prevent the triggering of an inflation-depreciation spiral."[48] The dangers of monetary expansion, currency depreciation, and increased inflation were emphasized by Italian central bankers and economists in the Ministry of Finance. Despite the Banca d'Italia's special weight in Italian political life, however, it took the experience of policy failure and the sense of international constraints on the lira and Italian balance of payments to prepare the ground for this view to gain acceptance beyond the central bank.

Solidifying Reform within the EMS, 1981–1987

Unlike the first wave of neoliberal policy reversals, which started in the mid-1970s, the second wave of reforms took place within the EMS and extended beyond France and Italy to encompass the small northern states of Europe. These reforms solidified the EMS's status as an effective institution during the 1980s. The most dramatic policy episode of the second wave—and centrally important for the functioning of the EMS and the drive to EMU—occurred in France. By attempting one last Keynesian reflation, President François Mitterrand's Socialists in effect showed the rest of the EMS the dangers of divergence from the German low-inflation model. Mitterrand's original expansionary policy was to last only a short while, for the constraints of international interdependence again brought Mitterrand and the French franc into

[46] Niels Thygesen, "Monetary Policy," in Boltho, ed., *The European Economy,* 359.
[47] Goodman, *Monetary Sovereignty,* 165; OECD, *Economic Surveys: Italy* (1980), 39.
[48] OECD, *Economic Surveys: Italy* (1980), 39.

the deflationist fold. By reinvigorating the pre-oil crisis policies of reflation and depreciation, and subsequently repeating the policy failures of the 1975 Chirac *rélance*, the French evolved from the experience as the foremost supporters of the neoliberal policy consensus, epitomized by the *franc fort* policy. The first years of the Mitterrand government have received much analysis; here I will highlight a few points particularly relevant for my argument about the sources of cooperation in the EMS.[49]

An important question must be considered first: if a strong policy consensus had been growing in the years between the Snake and the EMS, as I argue, why did the Socialists initially try to reflate the economy to get out of economic recession? It is important to remember that Mitterrand's party came into office after twenty-three years of political exile, with a platform that had been formed in the years *before* the first oil crisis. As Peter Gourevitch has noted, the Socialist Party "therefore had never confronted the need to manage the tension between the demands of its core constituencies . . . And the constraints of capital flows and investment, profitability and modernization." Further, they were forced to learn how to manage these tensions during a period of "deep economic distress."[50] Because the French Socialists were out of power during the stagflation years of the 1970s, in contrast to the other parties of the left in Europe, they could blame the rightist parties and their policies for the country's economic problems.

The Mitterrand government thus radically shifted the French macroeconomic stance in 1981 back to classical Keynesianism, breaking away "in a spectacular fashion from the orthodox deflationist-monetarist

[49] The literature on the early years of the Mitterrand presidency is extremely rich. A few of the major works are Philippe Bauchard, *La guerre des deux roses* (Paris: Bernard Grasset, 1986); Charles Wyplosz and Jeffrey Sachs, "The Economic Consequences of President Mitterrand," *Economic Policy* 2 (1986), 261–321; David Cameron, *The Colors of a Rose* (Cambridge: Center for European Studies, Harvard University, 1988), and Cameron, "The Franc, the EMS, Rigueur, and l'Autre Politique," manuscript, Yale University, April 1992; Alain Fonteneau and Pierre-Alain Muet, *La gauche face à la crise* (Paris: Fondation Nationale des Sciences Politiques, 1985); Peter Hall, *Governing the Economy* (New York: Oxford University Press, 1986), chap. 8; George Ross, Stanley Hoffmann, and Sylvia Malzacher, eds., *The Mitterrand Experiment* (New York: Oxford, 1987); and Howard Machin and Vincent Wright, eds., *Economic Policy and Policy-Making under the Mitterrand Presidency, 1981–1984* (New York: St. Martin's Press, 1985).

[50] Gourevitch, *Politics in Hard Times* (Ithaca: Cornell University Press, 1986), 185.

mainstream."[51] When the Socialists came to power in 1981, they immediately implemented a mixture of Keynesian reflationary policies designed to increase employment and redistribute wealth to the less affluent. In addition, a program of industrial restructuring through nationalization was quickly implemented.[52]

By 1982, however, a series of exchange rate crises, two devaluations of the franc, and a deterioration in France's economic situation began to call into question the effectiveness of the expansionary policies of the "socialism in one country" strategy. The French leadership had assumed that favorable international conditions would provide a fertile ground for their experiment, but instead they found themselves mired in a global recession, with other governments following contractionary policies. By March 1983, continuous downward pressure on the franc brought on a third devaluation for Mitterrand and a reversal of the Keynesian strategies. In part, this decision rested on the realization that deflationary strategies would be necessary to right the French economy, whether in or out of the EMS.[53] Also critical was the high political cost of exiting the EMS and the view that for the Socialists' policies to be effective, France would have to put up barriers to trade with its European partners—the route advocated by such advisers as Jean Riboud and Pierre Bérégovoy. These factors made Mitterrand willing to listen to the more centrist faction of his advisers, led by Pierre Mauroy and Jacques Delors, that advocated a turn toward *rigueur,* devaluation, and renewed commitment to the EMS.

By 1984 recognition of the seriousness of the external constraints on French economic policy was complete. For example, in a speech entitled "French Economic and External Constraints," Robert Raymond, a senior Bank of France official, stated "that external constraints

[51] Hayward, "France," in Cox, ed., *European Recession,* 138. George Ross writes that the results of the 1981 elections surprised everyone and that the victory of the left sprang from many roots: a "general rejection of the Giscard-Barre approach to economic crisis, fratricidal divisions on the Right between neo-Gaullists and Giscardians, plus the collapse of PCF electoral support, which finally freed Centrist electors to support the Socialist candidate." Ross, "French Labor and Economic Change," in Gourevitch and Cohen, eds., *France in the Troubled World Economy,* 175.

[52] See Peter Hall, "The Evolution of Economic Policy under Mitterrand," in Ross, et al., eds., *The Mitterrand Experiment.*

[53] This is the view taken by Peter Hall, ibid., 56–57. More room for political maneuver is portrayed in David Cameron's detailed assessment of the internal politics of the decision. See Cameron, "The Franc, the EMS, Rigueur, and l'Autre Politique."

exist is something evident from multiple examples of the past 12 years" and in terms of recent events, the balance of payments deficit and continued fragility of the exchange rate confirm it.[54]

The changing view of the costs and benefits of competitive depreciations also reinforced the turn toward *rigueur* and the strong franc. The Socialists, like governments in the other EC states, came to believe that a weak currency could hurt more than it could help because import costs would rise, and French exporters would not be helped because they increasingly compete not on price but on quality and service.[55] The experience of policy failure with expansionist measures, combined with the influence of monetarist analysis and the German example discussed below, brought the French to the consensus view that depreciation leads to a vicious circle of inflation, further depreciation, and an investment-dampening rise in short-term interest rates required to stabilize the exchange rate.

This policy reversal required that the Socialists distance themselves from two groups never dominant in the party—the unions, who were unhappy with the increasing level of layoffs, and the Communists. Prime Minister Pierre Mauroy was replaced by Laurent Fabius, a party leader with closer ties to the elites than to the working class.[56] Mitterrand was able to take these steps because his Socialist electoral basis was much less reliant on the unions and the working class than were other European parties of the left, such as the German SPD (Social Democrats), British Labour, or the Italian PCI.[57] Indeed, after a long decline throughout the 1970s, by the 1980s "trade union division and cacophony reigned," membership had declined, and the unions were left without any coherent economic policy alternative.[58] Also, the centralization of French policymaking and the power of the presidency left space

[54] Robert Raymond, "L'économie française et les contraintes exterieures," speech given at the Banque de France conference held at Grenoble, March 12, 1984.

[55] McCarthy, "France Faces Reality," in Calleo and Morgenstern, eds., *Recasting Europe's Economics*, 56.

[56] Ibid., 36.

[57] See the electoral figures cited in ibid., 38; and in George Ross, "French Labor and Economic Change," in Gourevitch and Cohen, eds., *France in the Troubled World Economy*, 175.

[58] George Ross, "French Labor and Economic Change," in Gourevitch and Cohen, eds., *France in the Troubled World Economy*, 172, 176.

for Fabius to impose policies of *rigueur,* just as they had for Barre in 1976.

The French government's stark reversal of its policies in 1982–83, returning to the highly restrictive monetary stance first proposed by Barre in 1976, illustrates the difficulties governments faced in attempting to follow their own policies while at the same time participating in the European fixed exchange rate system. This reversal also came to be seen by others as a powerful example of the pitfalls of trying to achieve full employment through the use of reflationary policies and the relative lack of penalty in the domestic electoral arena to be had from abandoning such policies. The "policy failure" of the Socialists, in the words of one EU official, "made clear once and for all the futility of trying expansionary policies in today's world."[59]

The subsequent success of the Socialist government in reducing inflation was also taken to heart by other EC states. Luiz Martinez Arévalo, a Spanish banker, stated that Spanish entry into the EMS in 1989 was taken in the hopes of achieving *"la desinflation á la française* [disinflation in the French manner] . . . Following the example of the [French] Fabius Government in the mid eighties, whose motto might well have been 'squeeze them and blame the Bundesbank.'"[60] The Mitterrand experiment in expansionary policies was the only real break in the consensus that underlay the successful years of the EMS, but it was a short-lived experiment, ending in a policy U-turn back to the austerity policies promoted by Giscard and Barre in the late 1970s.

Italy also undertook significant reforms in the early 1980s to reduce inflation and strengthen the lira's precarious position in the EMS. The initial monetary stabilization efforts begun in Italy in 1976 had been set back somewhat by the increase in oil prices in 1979 and the international recession in 1980, as inflationary pressures built up once more despite growing unemployment and limited growth. The first reform

---

[59] Interview with European Commission official, Brussels November 1991. The Mitterrand experience is given this interpretation in macroeconomic policy courses at France's elite policy school, L'École Nationale d'Administration.

[60] Luiz Martinez Arévalo, "A Confident Nation: Spain Boldly Joins the EMS," *European Affairs* 2 (Fall 1989), 22–23, quoted in Mark D. Harmon, "'If I Can't Change the Rules, I Won't Play Your Game': Britain in and out of the Exchange Rate Mechanism of the European Monetary System," paper presented at the 9th Annual Conference of Europeanists, Chicago, March 31–April 1994, 11.

was institutional: the decision to "divorce" the Bank of Italy from the Treasury, thus freeing the central bank from its obligation to purchase unsold public debt at primary auctions. This policy change occurred, according to John Goodman, because of the private sector's declining resistance to monetary restriction and because of the government's willingness to undertake the difficult decisions needed to deal with inflation and the deterioration of the Italian balance of payments. The institutional divorce facilitated a deflationary policy stance by lessening the influence of public deficits on the growth of the money supply and making the use of monetary targets and interest rate policy targets more effective. It also had the effect of increasing the political independence of the bank from both government and societal groups, which could no longer pressure the bank to finance government deficits. The Banca d'Italia, already "the honourable exception" among Italian government agencies in its coherence, expertise, and organization, had its dominance over monetary and exchange rate policy strengthened even more by this move.[61]

In addition, this second wave of efforts at inflation reduction included the 1984 attempts by Bettino Craxi, the Socialist leader, to rein in the *scala mobile*. This unpopular move brought opposition from the PCI and its trade unionist supporters, but it also contributed to the reduction of inflation, the restoration of business confidence, and the strengthening of the lira in the EMS.[62]

The smaller states of Europe, which throughout the 1970s had managed to better control inflation and stay linked with the German mark in the mini-Snake, were not entirely immune to the need for austerity and adjustment during the EMS years. Despite their initial success in the wake of the first oil shock, described in chapter 5, the fast growth of public expenditures in these states eventually forced the need for further fiscal and regulatory reforms if these countries were to stay in the EMS. High unemployment had been addressed by massive

---

[61] Goodman, *Monetary Sovereignty*, 143; Gerald A. Epstein and Juliet B. Schor, "The Divorce of the Banca d'Italia and the Italian Treasury: A Case Study of Central Bank Independence," in Peter Lange and Marino Regini, eds., *State, Market, and Social Regulation: New Perspectives on Italy* (New York: Cambridge University Press, 1989); quote from Furlong, "Economic Recession in Italy," in Cox, ed., *European Recession*, 168.

[62] Giorgio La Malfa, "Italy: New Dimensions and Old Evasions," in Calleo and Morgenstern, eds., *Recasting Europe's Economies;*, 153.

public spending, but the mounting budget deficits that resulted were beginning to shake the confidence of the financial markets, putting pressure on exchange rates.

The wave of fiscal reforms undertaken by the Netherlands, Belgium, and Denmark played a role similar to monetary policy failures among the larger countries in promoting monetary cooperation. A brief review of these policy shifts gives a sense of the degree to which EC member states adjusted to the requirements of the EMS. It also highlights the degree to which the pursuit of these reforms was driven by the domestic perception of crisis and the need for austerity policies. Finally, looking at the experiences of the small, very open countries of Europe can also provide clues as to the likely direction of change in the large countries as economic interdependence increases.

Despite the Netherlands' record of price and exchange rate stability, rising unemployment, increasing real labor costs (blamed in part on the "Dutch disease"), and a deteriorating trade balance had become serious concerns by the early 1980s. The Dutch increasingly monetized their growing budget deficit—a potentially inflationary policy that could not continue without jeopardizing the success of their low inflation, hard currency policies. When, in the two years following the second oil crisis, the Dutch budget deficit ballooned and the unemployment rate nearly doubled, a perception developed across Dutch society that the government had to act decisively to get the economy back on track.[63]

In 1982, a new Christian Democrat-Conservative-Liberal coalition, headed by Ruud Lubbers, capitalized on this support for change by making the reduction of the budget deficit the paramount national goal.[64] Although the austerity efforts brought the government into some conflict with Dutch unions, the rise in unemployment was taken as a signal by the unions that they had no option but to assist in the suppression of real wage growth.[65] The reforms made the Dutch guilder

[63] OECD, "Netherlands, 1975–82: Containing the Public Sector," in *Why Policies Change Course* (Paris: OECD, 1988), 90.

[64] The Lubbers government also used the budget reduction plans to undertake the deregulation and privatization of the Dutch economy.

[65] Erik Jones, "Economic Adjustment in Belgium and the Netherlands within a Changing Political Formula" (Ph.D. diss., School of Advanced International Studies, Johns Hopkins University, 1995). See also Bram Pepper, "The Netherlands: A Permissive Response," in Cox, ed., *European Recession*, 87–110. Pepper argues that Dutch trade unions "are very

the strongest currency in the EMS, after the German mark, throughout the 1980s; unemployment continued to grow, however, despite extremely low inflation throughout the 1980s.

Belgium's economic situation bears a fairly close resemblance to that of the Netherlands because of its trade openness and integration within the EC but with some crucial differences—a weaker currency and a lack of indigenous energy supplies foremost among them. These factors, plus the fiscal effects of the competition between the linguistic regions for state resources left Belgium in a tenuous economic position by the early 1980s.[66] Belgium thus had to undergo significant domestic economic adjustments to maintain its position in the EMS. A series of exchange rate crises, beginning in 1981, resulted in the progressive depreciation of the Belgian franc over the next two years. In 1983, Belgium undertook a final devaluation of 8.5 percent, agreed to by the other EMS members with the condition that the realignment be accompanied by austerity reforms. As the Belgian authorities were themselves seeking to bring inflationary pressures down and promote adjustment through austerity, this external pressure provided a helpful framework for imposing discipline.[67] The steps taken included the temporary freezing of wages and prices, longer-run measures to scale back wage indexation, and a reduction in the corporate tax burden.[68] Although the Belgian deficit continued to grow along with unemployment, the exchange rate stabilized soon after the reforms were imple-

sensitive to macro-economic arguments and since 1975 they have contributed to the fight against inflation by attuning their initial wage demands to what is economically feasible" (101).

[66] Unemployment rose and public sector debt accumulated as large-scale government subsidies and loan guarantees to enterprises were handed out to try to stop the job losses. Willy van Rijckeghem, "Benelux," in Boltho, ed., The European Economy, 606.

[67] Paulette Kurzer, Business and Banking: Political Change and Economic Integration in Western Europe (Ithaca: Cornell University Press, 1993), 226. A brief description of the terms of each EMS realignment during the 1980s is found in Horst Ungerer, et al, The European Monetary System: Developments and Perspectives, Occasional Paper 73 (Washington, D.C.: International Monetary Fund, November 1990), Appendix I, Table 1.

[68] According to one observer, the dramatic austerity program begun in 1981 rested on "an 'enough is enough' acknowledgment that all the traditional solutions and remedies to combat the economic decline had failed miserably." Bert Pijnenburg, "Belgium in Crisis: Political and Policy Responses, 1981–1985," in Damgaard et al., eds., The Politics of Economic Crisis, 30–31.

mented, inflation dropped, and Belgium solidified its position as one of the key "core" members of the EMS.[69]

A third member of the mini-Snake, Denmark, also had to undertake policy reforms in the early 1980s to stay within the exchange rate parities of the EMS. A tumultuous political situation, which saw five minority governments rise and fall in the decade after the first oil crisis, worsened problems similar to those of its small-state neighbors—growing budget deficits and unemployment. The Liberal-Conservative majority elected in October 1982 ended the debate by imposing a series of austerity policies soon after its election.[70] The package aimed at promoting competitiveness by strengthening the krone, lowering inflation, reducing wage increases, and cutting public spending. As in Belgium and the Netherlands, the government was quick to seize the political space created by the perception of crisis, pervasive throughout Danish society, to push through austerity and privatization reforms. In so doing, the government moved ahead with little input or consultation with the major social groups, particularly trade unions. The policies paid off in that inflation fell, interest rates came down, and a host of new private sector jobs were created, but the issue of unemployment and balance of payments problems remained.[71]

This section has shown how the experience of macroeconomic policy failure in the 1970s and early 1980s changed the views of policymakers across the larger nations of Europe about the uses of monetary policy. Most critically, in the cases of Italy and France, this failure led them to reject Keynesian strategies of reflation aimed at simulating growth and employment. The experience of crisis in the 1970s also reinforced the commitment of the small, low-inflation countries to following the German mark and, by the early 1980s, had prompted them to implement their own set of reform policies—fiscal austerity and inflation control. Across the board, European governments in both the large

[69] See Kurzer, *Business and Banking*, chap. 6.

[70] See Erik Damgaard, "Crisis Politics in Denmark, 1974–87," in Damgaard et al., eds., *The Politics of Economic Crisis*, 77.

[71] Ibid. The last of the small states of the EC—Ireland—also underwent a major economic policy shift in 1981 to dampen inflation and strengthen its position in the EMS. The changes resulted in a real appreciation of the Irish punt throughout the early 1980s.

and small states were able to take advantage of the perception of crisis to implement reforms without eliciting significant opposition from those groups in society, such as labor, that traditionally opposed austerity measures.

More generally, the crises of the 1970s laid the groundwork for the EMS by calling into question the power of national monetary policies designed to protect the domestic polity against the changing global economy. Yet, although they created an impetus and political willingness for policy change, crisis and policy failure do not explain why and how these governments chose to follow strongly convergent policies. We must look at how policymakers interpreted their experiences in order to devise a new strategy; specifically, the role that monetarism played in offering a paradigm for explaining the economy and in providing concrete instruments for addressing the crisis.

Policy Paradigms: Consensus and Monetarism

The development of a European consensus regarding the need for monetary rigor would not have occurred without monetarism. Its advocates provided policymakers with a ready-made, alternative, and accessible intellectual framework for guiding the move away from Keynesianism.[72] Given the conditions they faced in the 1970s, it is not difficult to explain why policymakers turned to monetarism. Although monetarist ideas had been promoted as early as the 1930s and were taken up by a cadre of academics in the 1960s, they became politically relevant only after the first oil crisis, when they could provide a means for making sense of policymaking in the turbulent economic environment.

What were the fundamental differences between Keynesianism and monetarism? As was argued in chapter 4, at the most general level, the Keynesian policy paradigm embraced by governments throughout the early postwar years viewed the private sector as fundamentally unstable. Keynesianism emphasized the role of the state in directing the economy, particularly through the use of fiscal and monetary policy designed to influence growth rates, employment, and production. In

[72] Peter Hall, "Policy Paradigms, Learning, and the State: The Case of Economic Policymaking in Britain," *Comparative Politics* 25 (April 1993), 275–96.

contrast, the monetarist policy paradigm emphasizes the inherent stability and adaptability of the private sector and views traditional Keynesian efforts to manipulate the economy, particularly full employment strategies, as ineffective and possibly counterproductive.[73] Like the laissez-faire tradition, monetarism places faith in the long-run functioning of the market economy in lieu of government intervention.

More specifically, the monetarist paradigm posits that "the quantity of money has a major influence on economic activity and the price level and that the objectives of monetary policy are best achieved by targeting the rate of growth of the money supply."[74] This view has its roots in the classical monetary economics of the eighteenth century but rose to prominence in the 1970s, in part due to the work of Milton Friedman. The chief implication of the theoretical and empirical studies of this school of thought is that strict control of the money supply is the best way for governments to create the conditions for stable, low inflationary economic growth and employment. Inflation results from the overexpansion of the money supply and can thus be avoided if governments are willing to give up trying to manage aggregate demand with countercyclical fiscal and monetary manipulations.[75]

The key policy prescription of the monetarist camp centers on monetary targeting. Setting goals or targets for a stable, predictable annual increase in the aggregate money supply, monetarists argued, is the best way to avoid inflation and provide an environment conducive to economic growth.[76]

Monetarism was also thought to provide a solution to a key element of the macroeconomic policy dilemma that policymakers faced: the incompatibility of the Phillips Curve, which had guided government policymakers throughout the 1960s and early 1970s, with this changed

---

[73] This discussion draws on Peter Johnson, "Unpopular Measures: Translating Monetarism into Monetary Policy in the Federal Republic of Germany and the United States, 1970–1985" (Ph.D. diss., Cornell University, 1991), chap. 1; Peter Hall, ed., *The Political Power of Economic Ideas: Keynesianism across Nations* (Princeton: Princeton University Press, 1989); and Thomas Mayer, *The Structure of Monetarism* (New York: W. W. Norton, 1978).

[74] Phillip Cagan, "Monetarism," in John Eatwell, Murray Milgate, and Peter Newman, eds., *The New Palgrave: The World of Economics* (London: Macmillan, 1991), 449.

[75] In part, activist macroeconomic policy is viewed as ineffective because it is impossible for governments to time such policies correctly.

[76] The classic statement is Milton Friedman and Anna Schwartz, *A Monetary History of the United States, 1866–1945* (Princeton: Princeton University Press, 1963).

economic environment.[77] In 1958, A. W. Phillips had shown that there was a strong historical relationship between the unemployment rate and the inflation rate.[78] Over almost a century, as inflation rose, unemployment fell, and vice versa. Thus, postwar policymakers generally acted on the belief that expansionary monetary policies, while causing some inflation, would also decrease unemployment. This relationship held throughout the 1960s for most industrialized countries, but in the 1970s, governments for the first time confronted conditions that contradicted the Phillips Curve relationship. Inflation and unemployment seemed to move together: high rates of inflation were matched by high rates of unemployment and slow growth, producing the stagflation experience of the 1970s.

Monetarists offered an interpretation for the deteriorating relationship between unemployment and inflation: the Phillips Curve never existed in the first place. Friedman argued that each economy has a natural, "non-accelerating inflation rate of unemployment," independent of the rate of inflation and impossible to change through monetary policy.[79] Thus, there is no permanent trade-off between unemployment and inflation, but neither does price stability lead to higher unemployment.

This viewpoint was strengthened by rational expectations theorists, who argued that workers and employers, when faced with increasing levels of inflation in the late 1960s and early 1970s, began to expect inflation and calculate it into their decisions about wages and prices. The result was that people no longer viewed expansionary monetary policy as a boost to the economy but rather a harbinger of higher inflation. They began to focus on the real value of their wages and

---

[77] Jeffrey D. Sachs and Felipe Larrain B., *Macroeconomics in the Global Economy* (Englewood Cliffs, N.J.: Prentice Hall, 1993), 452–73, provide an excellent overview of the Phillips Curve and recent developments in theories about the relationship between unemployment and inflation.

[78] A. W. Phillips, "The Relationship between Unemployment and the Rate of Change of Money Wages in the United Kingdom, 1861–1957," *Economica* 25 (November 1958), 283–99.

[79] This proposition is rooted in the dynamic of the "acceleration principle," which focuses on the impossibility of holding unemployment below the natural rate without pushing inflation out of control. See Milton Friedman, "The Role of Monetary Policy," *American Economic Review* 58 (March 1968), 1–17, and Edmund Phelps, "Money Wage Dynamics and Labor Market Equilibrium," *Journal of Political Economy*, 76 pt. 2 (July–August 1968), 678–711.

demand increases in nominal wages to match the new level of antici-pated inflation.

These theorists concluded that if economic actors are rational in using information to guide their behavior, policymakers should adopt a credible anti-inflationary policy to restrain inflationary expectations. Moreover, unemployment can be attacked only with policies directed at the supply side of he economy, which seek to eliminate structural barriers to employment growth, such as heavy taxes and inflexible hiring, firing, and work rules.

A version of the monetarist approach that added fixed exchange rates to the monetarist agenda became part of the policy arsenal of many European governments in the late 1970s because it offered an alternative to and a justification for the ineffectiveness of traditional postwar government policy to achieve the goals of full employment and growth without unreasonable inflation. This pragmatic monetarism was promoted by experts in international organizations such as the OECD, in policy reports written for the European Community, and in eco-nomic policy circles inside the national governments. For example, a largely monetarist viewpoint was articulated in an important survey issued by the OECD, the McCraken Report. Noting the "severe deterio-ration" in the relationship between unemployment and inflation, the report called for governments to make clear to all that "they will not—and, in the end, cannot—pursue policies which will permit or accommodate high rates of inflation."[80]

The linkage between the advocacy of the monetarist viewpoint and the decision to pursue fixed exchange rates in the EMS was clear early on in the policy debate.[81] This linkage is most evident in reports prepared in the mid-1970s by the OPTICA group of economic experts,

---

[80] Paul McCracken, et al., *Towards Full Employment and Price Stability* (McCracken Report) (Paris: OECD, 1977), 13, 18. This document is couched in extremely diplomatic lan-guage, but one of its basic points is that inflation fighting should take precedence above all other goals. The report is evaluated in Robert Keohane, "Economics, Inflation, and the Role of the State: Political Implication of the McCracken Report," *World Politics* 31 (October 1978), 108–28.

[81] See, for example, the proceedings of a high-level roundtable discussion among European policymakers and economists in which the discussion focuses on the need to return to fixed exchange rates as a way to impose discipline on national authorities so that they will pursue price stability. Randell Hinshaw, ed., *Domestic Goals and Financial Interdependence: The Frankfurt Dialogue* (New York and Basle: Marcel Dekker, 1977), 104.

invited by the EC to prepare an analysis of national economic policies and the prospects for restarting the EMU project. The group took as their starting point the argument that "on the effectiveness of monetary policy economists are divided, although there is a growing consensus that, in long-run situations, monetary policy is unable to affect the level of real activity, but only affects the rate of price inflation."[82] Thus, fixing exchange rates and moving toward EMU should be considered an optimal strategy as "a member country, after a short period of time, *is able to forgo an independent monetary policy without any significant real costs.*"[83] The 1975 report also urged EC governments to reformulate their monetary policies by targeting the growth of the money supply, as in Germany, to lower the expectation of inflation and provide the necessary policy framework for a new fixed exchange rate regime.

Indeed, the pragmatic version of monetarism had its first real trial runs in West Germany. There, as Fritz Scharpf notes, in summer 1974 the Bundesbank turned to "an explicitly monetarist strategy—long before similar switches occurred in Britain and in the United States," with the addition of exchange rate management.[84] German officials were not hesitant about making their views known: at a conference of high-level economic policy experts in 1977, Helmut Schlesinger of the Bundesbank stated, "The German catalogue of goals rules out a trade-off between inflation and unemployment . . . the recognition is wide-spread—and not only in light of the experience of the last few years—that, except in the very short term, nothing can be gained from more inflation either for economic growth or for employment . . . [thus] government and public opinion reject" such a reflationary course.[85] Scharpf notes that this policy "had the full support of the dominant opinion among the professional economists in Germany," typified by "the standard textbook on economic policy by Herbert

---

[82] Directorate General for Economic and Financial Affairs, *OPTICA Report 1975*, II/909/75-E Final (Brussels: Commission of the European Communities, January 1976), 3–4.

[83] Ibid., 24. Italics added.

[84] Fritz Scharpf, "Economic and Institutional Constraints of Full-Employment Strategies: Sweden, Austria, and Western Germany, 1973–1982," in John Goldthorpe, ed., *Order and Conflict in Contemporary Capitalism* (New York: Oxford University Press, 1984), 284. Forms of monetarism had also been followed throughout the postwar years in the Netherlands and Belgium. See Kurzer, *Business and Banking*, 228.

[85] Quoted in proceedings of Hinshaw, ed., *The Frankfurt Dialogue*, 32.

Giersch, one of the most influential members of the German Council of Economic Advisors."[86]

In France, the monetarist assumptions of Prime Minister Barre, a former professor of economics, informed the French post-1976 orthodox economic orientation. The principles of controlled growth of the money supply and the primacy of inflation reduction quickly became the centerpiece of government policy after Barre became prime minister in 1976. By 1979, for example, an official French economic planning document, prepared in part by Barre, stated in blunt monetarist terms that France was "rejecting the mirages of a 'general expansion' that would certainly reduce unemployment temporarily but would make inflation and the balance of payments deficit and consequently, in the longer term, unemployment, worse."[87]

Monetarist orthodoxy also marked the Bank of Italy's stance during the second half of the 1970s. The fit between the experience of policy failure and the intellectual pull of monetarism was made closer by the fragmentation of Italian domestic institutions. Because the scope for controlling macroeconomic policymaking was politically limited, "The instruments available dictate[d] emphasis on monetarist policies, firstly because the Bank of Italy is a uniquely efficient (though autonomous) politic-economic institution and secondly because the alternatives are either subject to particularistic pressure from within the governing parties or largely escape coordinated governmental control."[88]

Monetary targets were used to buttress more restrictive policies across the majority of continental European governments by the mid-1970s—a further indication of monetarism's influence on policymaking.[89]

Although monetarism was important in aiding the creation of a policy consensus in Europe, the governments of Europe did not accept

[86] Scharpf, "Full-Employment Strategies," in Goldthorpe, ed., *Order and Conflict in Contemporary Capitalism*, 284.

[87] *Rapport sur les principales options du 8e plan* (Paris: La Documentation Française, April 1979), 33.

[88] Furlong, "Economic Recession in Italy," in Cox, ed., *European Recession*, 190.

[89] The European countries used different measures of monetary growth and the size of their targets varied. For details of the transition to targeting in Europe, see OECD, "Monetary Targets and Inflation Control," *Monetary Studies Series* (Paris: OECD, 1979),

its precepts wholesale. One monetarist theorist, Phillip Cagan, lamented that the policies followed by the OECD countries "are monetarist only in the sense that one or more monetary aggregates are an important indicator of policy objectives; they fall short of a firm commitment to a steady, let alone non-inflationary, monetary growth rate." Instead of the virtually automatic, slow, and steady year-to-year increase in the money supply advocated by Friedman and others, even the German Bundesbank has viewed the growth of the money supply as an "art" of adjusting to circumstances."[90] Moreover, monetary targeting was widely adopted after the first oil crisis as only one tool among several that governments used to restore price stability. Fixed exchange rates in the EMS were viewed as a means to reinforce monetary rigor, whereas monetarists would argue that exchange rates should be allowed to float, because the only appropriate target for monetary policy is the money supply, not the exchange rate.[91]

When considering the relative importance of monetarist ideas, it is crucial to remember that monetarism was not the only possible prescription for the economic crisis faced by the EC governments. Monetarism was not a purely functional response to the demands of the international economy. Indeed, many of its basic tenets, such as the notion of a NAIRU, were extremely difficult to verify empirically. As one observer has commented, although the crisis was confusing for policymakers "who had become used to seeing inflation and employment as rival evils," the economics profession was "in the midst of revising its long-held views on the proper role of fiscal and monetary policies ... The validity of traditional econometric models and their use in the preparation of economic policies were increasingly questioned, and new models were not accepted easily either." For example,

7. On target types, see F. Giavazzi, S. Micozzi, and M. Miller, eds., *The European Monetary System* (New York: Cambridge University Press, 1988), 269.

[90] Cagan, "Monetarism," in Eatwell et al., eds., *The New Palgrave,* 453; David Marsh, *The Bundesbank: The Bank That Rules Europe* (London: Heinemann, 1992), 24.

[91] Fixed exchange rates as a reinforcement to national price stability are advocated in *OPTICA Report 1976,* II/855/76-E Final (Brussels: Commission of the European Communities, February 1977). For a discussion of the difference in the European and American approaches, see Johnson, "Unpopular Measures," chap. 1. For an overview of the differences in monetary practices, see U.S. Congress, Joint Economic Committee, "Monetary Policy, Selective Credit Controls, and Industrial Policy in France, Britain, West Germany, and Sweden, *Staff Study, Joint Economic Committee* (U.S. Government Printing Office, June 26, 1981).

in 1977, the president of the American Economic Association (AEA), Franco Modigliani, made the defense of more traditional demand management policies the theme of his speech to the organization's annual meeting. His choice of topic was prompted by "the spread of monetarism . . . in the form of growing influence on the practical conduct of economic policy, which influence, I shall argue presently, has played at least some role in the economic upheavals of the last three years."[92]

In his speech, Modigliani argued that because the inflation following the oil crisis derived from a supply-side shock, governments and theorists were incorrect in rejecting Keynesian stabilization policies. In fact, sufficiently accommodating, that is, expansionary, monetary and fiscal policies could have offset the shocks and preserved full employment by shifting the nominal supply of money to meet the change in real demand that occurred after the oil shock.[93] Modigliani provides an extensive review of the historical evidence and asserted that the monetarist prescription of slow, steady growth in the money supply would leave the majority of economies *worse off* than if countercyclical demand stabilization were undertaken to deal with the normal run of exogenous shocks.

In this assessment Modigliani was joined by others, such as James Tobin, who lamented the "prevailing attitudes" of "fatalism and complacency; not much can be done, not much needs to be done about unemployment . . . The lesson learned by many policymakers, influential citizens and economists is that unemployment cannot be cured [by expansionary policies] without unacceptable risk of inflation. This view is more solidly entrenched in Europe than North America." Tobin argued that the "dismissal of expansionary macroeconomic policies is in my opinion a misreading of, at least an overreaction to, the events of the 1970s" and continued to marshal evidence to promote the idea of coordinated reflation in response to the two oil crises as "the key to progress against unemployment."[94] Despite these prominent dissenters, monetarist views dominated the EC policy agendas.

[92] Rijckeghem, "Benelux," in Boltho, ed., *The European Economy,* 602. Franco Modigliani, "The Monetarist Controversy or, Should We Forsake Stabilization Policies?" *American Economic Review* 67 (March 1977), 1–19.

[93] Modigliani, "Monetarist Controversy," 2.

[94] James Tobin, "Unemployment in the 1980s: Macroeconomic Diagnosis and Prescrip-

Policy Emulation and the Role of Germany

While most of Europe was struggling with stagflation after the first oil crisis, West Germany stood out as the one EC member state that was successful in managing its economy. Over the period from 1972 to 1980, German inflation averaged 5 percent, whereas it was roughly double that in the other EC states; furthermore, unemployment averaged only 2.5 percent in Germany but 5.3 percent in the rest of the EC.[95] Germany offered an example of monetarist-informed policy success at a time when national governments were searching for new approaches. Its success was a particularly strong influence on the Giscard government in France, which believed that keeping up with the German economy, so as to ensure a balance of power within the EC, could be best achieved by emulating Germany's "winning" ways. As I will explain further, this policy emulation was also spurred by the fervent proselytizing of German officials on the virtues of price stability and facilitated by the increasing importance of institutionalized interactions among national economic policymakers with the EC. These interactions aided the transnational learning process

Germany has historically followed more conservative monetary policies than the majority of the EC neighbors (see chapters 4 and 5). Throughout the Bretton Woods era, German policy had been marked by the pursuit of price stability, in conjunction with policies to promote industrial adjustment to international economic conditions. Despite a brief flirtation with demand management and expansionary policies that began in 1966 under Economic Minister Schiller, Keynesian policies were used only sparingly in the Bretton Woods years, because the emphasis on countercyclical demand policies was "effectively preempted by another set of policies, oriented toward the supply side and the social market economy" and was characterized by tight money policies.[96]

Not surprisingly, Germany's response to the first oil crisis was on the whole restrictive and emphasized price stability: "Most industrialized

---

tion," in Andrew J. Pierre, ed., *Unemployment and Growth in the Western Economies* (New York: Council on Foreign Relations, 1984), 79, 87, 109.

[95] These figures are calculated from European Commission data. See also Tables 9 and 10 in chap. 7 for more data on economic performance in the EC.

[96] Christopher Allen, "The Underdevelopment of Keynesianism in the Federal Republic of Germany," in Hall, ed., *The Political Power of Economic Ideas*, 263.

countries in 1974 registered double digit inflation, but the Bundesbank took on the role of the world's anti-inflation ice breaker." Interest rates were kept very high, and in 1974, the Bundesbank began publishing monetary aggregate targets, with Germany becoming the first major European country to use this monetarist policy instrument. The need for price stability was promoted constantly. At the ceremony inaugurating him as the new president of the Bundesbank in 1979, Karl Otto Pohl declared, "The world is being inundated by a new wave of inflation. . . . There can be only one answer to the evident signs of danger to stability—to keep money tight. . . . The experience of the last few years has shown quite clearly that stability policy is the best growth policy. . . . Stability is the basis of our economic position in the world, and of our country's prosperity."[97]

This policy stance of the Bundesbank permeated German politics. Legally autonomous and in practice highly independent, the Bundesbank "played the leading role in macroeconomic policy after 1974" within the German government," its tight money and strong currency policies were "basically accepted by the Social-Liberal government."[98] German unions went along with this orientation, subordinating their wage demands to the necessities of stabilization policies. As in the other major European states, the overall declining position of the unions in German economic policymaking would have made an alternative policy difficult to promote effectively, even if they had been able to formulate a coherent approach.[99]

The effects of these tight policies on inflation control were impressive; together with a long-standing societal commitment to economic stability and a high degree of social cohesion, the policies allowed

---

[97] Marsh, *The Bundesbank*, 192; Joint Economic Committee, "Monetary Policy, Selected Credit Controls," 109; Helmut Schlesinger, "Recent Developments in Western German Monetary Policy," in S. F. Frwoen, A. A. Courakis, and M. H. Miller, eds., *Monetary Policy and Economic Activity in West Germany* (London: Surrey University Press, 1977); quoted in Marsh, *The Bundesbank*, 47.

[98] Edgar Grande, "West Germany: From Reform Policy to Crisis Management," in Damgaard et al., eds., *The Politics of Economic Crisis*, 56.

[99] For example, the formal consultations between government, unions, and business organizations in the "Concerted Action" program begun in 1967 effectively ended with the adoption of the Bundesbank policies of restrictive targeting of the money supply. Ibid., 62–63. See also Kenneth Dyson, "Germany," in Cox, ed., *European Recession*, 32–64. Peter Gourevitch emphasizes the overall continuity of German macroeconomic policy and societal arrangements in his *Politics in Hard Times*, 204–8.

Germany to experience less political and economic disruption than the other European states in the wake of the first oil crisis.[100] This is not to say that West Germans were completely pleased with the country's economic performance. There was considerable angst and conflict over the expansion of the federal deficit to 5.8 percent of GDP in 1975, mostly because of an increase in employment and regional programs under the governance of the Social Democrats. Unemployment continued to rise into the 1980s as well, bringing much consternation to a society used to very low levels of joblessness. Yet inflation, at least, was kept low, and decreasing long-term interest rates indicated that the restrictive monetary policies were having the desired effect of dampening inflation expectations.[101] Thus, "in comparative terms, German policies and performance still remained an example for the rest of Europe."[102]

Germany was thus generally seen by European policymakers and economists as the nation that had adjusted most successfully after the demise of Bretton Woods and was thus a monetarist example worth following in the aftermath of the wrenching experience of policy failure. The long-held German view that stable prices are essential to investment in real growth and long-term employment began to be echoed in other national capitals by the late 1970s. This contagion effect was helped along by the Bundesbank's evangelical proselytizing. David Marsh describes the process in the following terms:

> The Bundesbank spreads its doctrine of monetary probity not only through its decision-making rigeur, but also through the compulsion of logic and argument. The past two decades have yielded remarkable success. Insistence on Bundesbank-style *Stabilitätspolitik* now forms the core of international economic policy. Since the late 1970s, the conviction has been enshrined in a thousand summit communiqués and ministerial declarations. Bundesbank officials are the evangelists of world finance. As they sometimes admit, arrogance is not far below the surface. One Bundesbank representative once put it, with commendable straightforwardness: 'We are arrogant because we are good'. . . . The Bundesbankers are secure in

---

[100] On this point, see Michael Emerson, ed., *Europe's Stagflation* (Oxford: Clarendon Press, 1984), chaps. 1 and 2; and Boltho, eds., *The European Economy*, chap. 16.

[101] OECD, *Country Surveys: West Germany* (1977), 35 and passim.

[102] Klaus Heinrich Hennins, "West Germany," in Boltho, ed., *The European Economy*, 499.

the knowledge that, by defying inflation, they are pursuing the brightest and most meaningful lodestar in the sky. Their devout wish is that others, too, will follow.[103]

Such statements as "The example of German policy is in my opinion a lesson for us all and perhaps a hope for the world" were not uncommon in economic policymaking circles by the second half of the 1970s.[104] An EC report on economic policy and monetary integration asserted in 1975 that "monetary rules, such as those introduced in Germany at the end of 1974 and renewed at the end of 1975, act to correct the formation of inflationary expectations, thereby helping gradually to dampen down inflation without generating substantial social costs . . . *it would be of the greatest interest for the Communities to develop methods for assessing in a rough way the likely consequences of . . . policy targets in Germany.*"[105]

The most striking example of overt policy emulation occurred in Giscard's France. Although French policy emulation was rooted in the objective view that Germany had done a better job of adjusting to the changes in the international economy, it was also driven by traditional realist objectives. The French leadership wished to restructure the French economy along German lines so that France could better compete with Germany, thus ensuring that the two countries carried equal weight in the EC.[106] The relative success of Germany was a recurrent theme in comments by the French president, Giscard d'Estaing.

For example, in the speeches and writings collected for Giscard's book *L'État de la France* (1981), which describe the economic challenges that France faced, Germany was often used as a point of reference and an example of success that France must emulate. France had to learn how to have strong but "sober" or noninflationary growth because the influence and independence of France in Europe and the world depended on a high level of economic development. In particular, Giscard argued that France's industrial production should be situated

---

[103] Marsh, *The Bundesbank*, 16.
[104] These are the words of Lord Robbins, a member of the Court of Governors of the London School of Economics, at the concluding session of a high-level policy discussion in 1977 transcribed in Hinshaw, ed., *The Frankfurt Dialogue*, 162.
[105] *OPTICA Report 1975*, 60; emphasis in the original.
[106] Giscard interview in *Le Monde*, October 18, 1978.

by mid-1980s at a level comparable to that of West Germany.[107] Giscard further cited Germany as a worthwhile example of a country with a low level of inflation, achieved not through price controls but because of its laudable social consensus on the need for price and wage restraint.[108]

The example of Germany was equally evident in the thinking of Prime Minister Barre as he prepared his economic austerity plan of 1976–77. His hope to push France "towards realism" in its economic affairs was based on an intellectual commitment to the precepts of monetarism but was also reinforced by the success of this policy for the Germans during the 1970s.[109] Emulating the German monetary example of targeting the money supply, keeping a tight reign on inflation, and maintaining a strong currency was central to this view; at the same time, Barre's perspective extended to other aspects of German political economy.[110] For example, Barre's attempt to dismantle price controls was accompanied by the claim that because Federal Germany had successfully curbed inflation without such controls, they could be abandoned with equanimity.[111]

The efforts of Giscard and Barre led critics on both the left and the right to deem "the obsession of the present rulers of France with Germany's economic success" and the desire to achieve equal economic status with Germany "absurd and dangerous." Opposition parties, notably the Communists and Jacques Chirac's Gaullists, accused the government of subordinating French interests to Germany in its pursuit of European integration and sound money.[112]

[107] Originally from a television interview, "Une heure avec le président," June 19, 1979, text excerpted in Giscard D'Estaing, *L'état de la France* (Paris: Fayard, 1981), 34.
[108] Reprinted from Giscard's earlier book, *La democratie française* (London: Methuen, 1983), 124.
[109] See Amouroux, *Monsieur Barre*, 280.
[110] The idea that France should follow the "Modell Deutschland" more generally was embodied in a bestselling 1978 book, *La grande menace industrielle,* by Christian Stoffaes. The argument was that France was in danger of losing its competitive position in West German markets unless it transformed the French economy into the more "sophisticated" German model of production and economic policy. See Story, "Convergence at the Core?" in Hodges and Wallaces, eds., *Economic Divergence in the European Community,* 173.
[111] Hayward, "France," in Cox, ed., *European Recession,* 125.
[112] Daniel Biron and Alexander Faire, "Le marc souverain," *Le Monde Diplomatique,* November 18, 1978, cited in Ludlow, *The Making of the European Monetary System,* 199; Story, "Convergence at the Core?" in Hodges and Wallace, eds., *Economic Divergence in the European Community,* 183–84.

Although Germany was an important example for France and Italy beginning in the mid-1970s, the smaller countries of Europe had long followed the German example. Those countries (the Netherlands, Belgium, and Denmark) had been long committed to a strong currency and close emulation of Germany's policies. Yet policy emulation may not be the best way to characterize their behavior. The success of German policies played some part, but more important may be the fact that the small states's room for maneuvering was much more circumscribed than that of their larger European neighbors. The higher level of openness to international trade and financial flows and the overwhelming importance of Germany as a key trading partner dictated a longstanding concern for price and exchange rate stability. In the small states, this concern has been matched by corporatist institutional configurations that provide strong support for stability. The mini-Snake countries, linked closely to the German mark, had a better price stability record in the turbulent 1970s than did countries outside the Snake that were not following German-style policies. This record may also have contributed to the larger countries' view that their own increasingly open economies had to adjust to the external constraints in the same way.

Finally, the process of policy emulation was encouraged by institutionalized interaction among national policymakers within European Community institutions. The existence of several forums for EC policy coordination and interaction facilitated policy emulation and gave a forum for those in the European Commission who viewed Germany as an example for the Community to follow. In particular, the Council of Economic and Finance Ministers (ECOFIN), established in the late 1950s, provided a significant ministerial-level platform for economic policy coordination. The Monetary Committee, established during the same period, has been a forum for the exchange of information and background preparation for the meetings of ECOFIN.[113] Finally, since the mid-1960s, interaction and policy emulation was facilitated by the creation of the Committee of Central Bank Governors (superseded by the European Monetary Institute in 1994), which met regularly to oversee the operation of the fixed exchange rate regime and coordinate

---

[113] The Monetary Committee was made up of representatives from the central bank and the finance ministry of each state, plus European Commission representatives.

policy. Gradually, these groups developed a rapport and an increasing influence on efforts at policy coordination and the choice of national strategies, concurrent with the convergence of the national policies around the German model in the 1980s.[114] As one central banker commented, "The atmosphere in the Committee of Central Bank Governors, and now in the European Monetary Institute, was very professional—people do not come to meetings with distinctive national positions, but instead we all share a very common agreement on the correctness of a monetary policy model very close to that of Germany."[115] Though not intensive or comprehensive enough to have produced policy consensus by themselves, the institutions of the EC did play a role in fostering the consensus that underpinned the EMS.

The dynamics of the EMS throughout the 1980s reflected the process of policy emulation. Since 1982, Germany has essentially set the monetary target for EMS participants, strengthening exchange rate stability in the EMS, as member states made a clear-eyed assessment of the costs of policy divergence and exit from the system. The German mark's privileged position within the exchange rate regime combined with the Germany's special role as the source for domestic macroeconomic policy emulation were vital to the success of the EMS in the 1980s.

[114] The development of routinized interaction among the European central bankers was singled out as a major factor in transnational learning by European Commission officials and members of the Committee of Central Bank Governors (interviews, Brussels, October 1991 and May 1994). See also Gros and Thygesen, *European Monetary Integration*, 22–23; and Niels Thygesen, "International Coordination of Monetary Policies—With Special Reference to the European Community," in John E. Wadsworth and François Leonard de Juvigny, eds., *New Approaches in Monetary Policy* (The Netherlands: Sijthoff and Noordhoff, 1979), 205–24.

[115] Interview, Brussels, May 1994.

CHAPTER SEVEN

The Drive toward
Economic and Monetary Union

By the mid-1980s, exchange rate stability in the European Monetary System led many to believe that the European Union had entered a new phase of cooperation and integration. This impression was furthered by the 1986 Single European Act (SEA), an ambitious EU program to remove barriers to trade in goods and services, to labor mobility, and to capital flows within the single European market. The 1989 Delors Committee's decisive relaunching of the EMU project sought to capitalize on this new "Europhoria." The EMU integration initiative came to fruition with the Treaty on European Union agreed to in Maastricht, the Netherlands, in December 1991. Despite a problematic national ratification process and currency crises in 1992 and 1993, European leaders seem poised to go forward with plans for EMU. What does the past EMS experience tell us about the probability that the European states will indeed take this momentous step? And what are the implications of the transition to EMU for politics among and within the EU states?

THE HARD EMS

The EMS displayed an unprecedented degree of stability in the second half of the 1980s. For example, whereas the early period of the EMS (1979–83) had been marked by multiple currency realignments, the frequency of realignments slowed over the next few years until there were none at all between January 1987 and September 1992.[1] The neoliberal policy consensus began to have effects on the real economy as EU member states' inflation rates gradually converged downward (see Table 9).

Table 9. Average yearly inflation rates in the European Union

	1971–1980	1981–1990	1991–1995
Belgium	7.1	4.6	2.5
Denmark	10.4	5.8	2.0
Germany	5.7	2.6	3.1
Spain	15.1	9.3	5.0
France	9.8	6.2	2.2
Ireland	13.9	6.9	2.5
Italy	14.6	9.9	4.9
Luxembourg	6.5	5.1	2.8
Netherlands	7.5	2.3	2.6
United Kingdom	13.3	6.0	4.2

SOURCE: *European Economy* 59 (1995), Table 27.

The institutional reforms of the Basle-Nyborg Agreement of 1987 also contributed to stability in the EMS by modifying the rules governing the operation of the exchange rate mechanism. The agreement, drafted by the Committee of Central Bank Governors in Basel and agreed to in Nyborg by the national economic and finance ministers, was prompted by particularly contentious discussions surrounding the January 1987 realignments. The most important operational change was to make financing more readily available for intramarginal interventions, that is, before a currency reached the limits of the fixed band, allowing for preemptive strikes against market pressure. The credit period for financing exchange rate interventions also was extended from forty-five to seventy-five days, and the debtor quotas were doubled. A general recommendation was issued stressing the need for balance among interventions, exchange rate flexibility within the margins, and

---

[1] A historical survey of the realignments can be found in Daniel Gros and Niels Thygesen, *European Monetary Integration* (London: Longman, 1992), chap. 3; and Dorothee Heisenberg, "The Mark of the Bundesbank," (Ph.D. diss., Yale University, 1996), chaps. 5 and 7.

the use of interest rate changes to support currency values. Although by themselves these agreements would not have produced a "hard EMS" without the underlying neoliberal consensus, they did ease the burden of adjustment somewhat for the weaker currency states.

Perhaps more significant for the exchange rate stability of the late 1980s was the increasing credibility of the EMS as an institution. A positive linkage seemed to have been forged among the initial domestic neoliberal policy changes undertaken by the member states, the development of the EMS into a credible cooperative institution, and an improvement in the level of policy convergence within the EU. The key to this dynamic is the increasing role that credibility has played in maintaining price and exchange rate stability as capital flows and market integration have increased. This phenomenon may be explained in analytical terms by invoking the rational expectations revolution and the "time-inconsistency problem" in macroeconomics.[2] Whereas stability in the EMS was built on a policy paradigm that rejected the argument that expansionary policies can produce any positive real effects in the medium and long run, a "surprise" expansion of the monetary supply can still have a one-time impact before inflationary expectations are revised. Thus, governments may be tempted to try such a one-time expansionary policy. The existence of this incentive—and therefore the *potential* for inflationary surprises—can itself create inflation. Thus, a government could increase the credibility of its domestic commitment to low inflation in the eyes of the financial markets by participating in an international institution such as the EMS. Both the practical constraints of keeping a fixed exchange rate in a system based on the strong, stable German mark and the political importance of the EMS to the EU's integration prospects can thereby contribute to sound money policies.

Policymakers have stated their belief that such a "virtuous circle" developed in the 1980s, in which the EMS served to reinforce the

[2] The classic theoretical statement on the credibility approach is Robert Barro and David Gordon, "A Positive Theory of Monetary Policy in a Natural Rate Model," *Journal of Political Economy* 91, no. 4 (1983), 589–610; on its application to the EMS, see Francesco Giavazzi and Marco Pagnano, "The Advantages of Tying One's Hands: EMS Discipline and Central Bank Credibility," *European Economic Review* 32 (June 1988), 1055–75. For an overview of these issues in the context of the EMU project, see John Woolley, "Policy Credibility and European Monetary Institutions," in Alberta Sbragia, ed., *Euro-Politics* (Washington, D.C.: Brookings Institution, 1991), 157–90.

initial neoliberal domestic policy changes of the late 1970s and early 1980s.[3] At the end of the 1980s, for example, Niels Thygesen, a member of the Delors Committee on monetary integration, commented on the benefits of the EMS:

> The benefits of continued EMS membership prompted the adoption of domestic policies of budgetary consolidation and deindexation [and other institutional reforms] which are anyway desirable, but would have been more controversial in the absence of the EMS. . . . Though these reforms were desirable in themselves, it was a perception of the longer-run incompatibility of previous arrangements with the rules of a system to which the country wanted to adhere that made their adoption possible. In this qualitative sense, the EMS has contributed to disinflation and convergence.[4]

Tommaso Padoa-Schioppa, a prominent EU and Italian economic official, shares this view: "Acceptance of the principles and objectives of the system has reinforced policy cooperation both *among* member countries and *within* member countries, between such policy-making bodies as central banks, fiscal authorities, trade unions and employers organizations." Yet, as Jean-Jacques Rey of the National Bank of Belgium has said, "From the point of view of a practitioner, relying on his own intuitive experience," the EMS did not by itself produce the set of policies and developments that led to greater price and thus exchange rate stability. "Rather, the reverse is true," he states. "Participation was seen to entail feedback effects in the form of incentives towards price stability, but the 1st round sequence goes from the policy reversal to ERM sustainability, not the other way round."[5]

---

[3] This interactive dynamic sheds some light on the reasons social scientists have not been able to demonstrate that the EMS has had an independent disciplining effect on national economies. For example, see Francesco Giavazzi and Alberto Giovannini, *Limiting Exchange Rate Flexibility: The European Monetary System* (Cambridge: MIT Press, 1989); Susan Collins, "Inflation and the European Monetary System," in Francisco Giavazzi, Stefano Micossi, and Marcus Miller, eds., *The European Monetary System* (New York: Cambridge University Press, 1988); and Paul De Grauwe, "The Costs of Disinflation in the European Monetary System," *Open Economics Review* 1 (March 1990) 147–73, among others.

[4] Niels Thygesen, "Introduction," in Giavazzi, Micossi and Miller, eds., *The European Monetary System*, 9–10.

[5] T. Padoa-Schioppa, "The EMS: A Long Term View," ibid., 372; Jean-Jacques Rey, "Discussion," ibid., 137.

By the end of the 1980s, it seemed that the EU, which in 1972 had failed miserably at creating a European-wide exchange rate regime to replace the U.S.-dominated Bretton Woods system, had triumphed against the odds. Small wonder that the success of the EMS soon brought back into the limelight the much more ambitious idea of creating a European economic and monetary union and a single European currency.

ECONOMIC AND MONETARY UNION

Monetary union has been on the agenda of the EU for a long time. In 1970, the Werner Plan proposed that the member states of the European Community move in three stages to an integrated monetary system by 1980. The short-lived currency "Snake" was the first and only stage of this plan to be implemented (see chapter 5). But by the second half of the 1980s, European leaders began to warm to the revival of the EMU project. At the June 1988 European Union summit in Hanover, the national leaders charged Commission president Jacques Delors with developing a plan for EMU. The committee formed to address this goal delivered the Delors Report to the European leaders at a summit in Madrid in 1989. The report's conclusions formed the basis for the subsequent Treaty on European Union, signed by the European heads of state and government in Maastricht in December 1991.

The treaty agreed to in Maastricht called for EMU to be achieved in three stages.[6] Stage I, which began immediately, had as its goals the removal of all capital controls, the reduction of inflation and interest rate differentials among the member states, the increasing stability of exchange rates in the EMS, and more extensive policy coordination. Stage II, begun in January 1994, is devoted to the transition to EMU. In this stage, a new body, the European Monetary Institute (EMI) was

[6] See Barry Eichengreen, "European Monetary Unification," *Journal of Economic Literature* 31 (September 1993), 1321–57; Michele Fratianni, Jürgen von Hagan, and Christopher Waller, "The Maastricht Way to EMU," *Essays in International Finance*, no. 187 (Princeton: Princeton University, June 1992); and Gros and Thygesen, *European Monetary Integration*. On the politics of the negotiations, see David Cameron, "Transnational Relations and the Development of European Economic and Monetary Union," in Thomas Risse-Kappen, ed., *Bringing Transnational Relations Back In* (New York: Cambridge University Press, 1995).

created to aid in the increasing coordination of national economic policies and the encouragement of convergence in economic fundamentals. The EMI is meant to lay the procedural groundwork for the European Central Bank (ECB), which comes into being in Stage III along with a single currency, subsequently named the Euro. The national central banks are to continue their existence as members of the European System of Central Banks (ESCB), carrying out the policies of the ECB, somewhat like the U.S. regional federal reserve banks.[7]

The starting date of the final stage of EMU was left indeterminate in the treaty. EU heads of state were required to meet by the end of 1996 to determine whether a majority of countries were ready for EMU and to set a date for the move to Stage III. As no date was set by December 31, 1996, Stage III is to begin on January 1, 1999, even if only a minority of countries are deemed ready to participate.[8] The Maastricht Treaty sets out conditions that must be taken into account when considering the move to Stage III. These "convergence criteria" were a necessary concession to those states, most importantly Germany, that feared EMU would be inflationary if the participating economies were not prepared adequately. The criteria are not set in stone, however, but allow heads of state to make their own judgments about which states should go ahead into Stage III and on what timetable.

The first criterion relates to inflation convergence: the average inflation rate of the applicant country should not exceed by more than one and a half percentage points the average of the three lowest-inflation EU members. The second criterion relates to nominal exchange rate stability: exchange rates must be maintained within the "normal" EMS bands for two years prior to EMU, although the numeri-

---

[7] The details of financial market integration and regulation and the exact procedures for the formulation and implementation of monetary policy are not in the treaty but are to be worked out by the EMI and adopted by the ECB. See the discussion of these issues in Jürgen von Hagen and Michele Fratianni, "The Transition to European Monetary Union and the European Monetary Institute," *Economics and Politics* (July 1993), 167–86, and Peter B. Kenen, *Economic and Monetary Union in Europe* (New York: Cambridge University Press, 1995).

[8] Those governments deemed not ready to join an EMU are termed "member states with a derogation." Their potential for membership must be reviewed at least once every two years. Also unstated in the treaty is the date at which a single currency comes into being for Europe, because Stage III and the ECB may initially come into being with the currencies fixed irrevocably against one another (the functional equivalent of a single currency) before a single currency is actually created.

cal meaning of "normal" is not specified and was made more ambiguous by the widening of the EMS bands in 1993. The third criterion is that a country's long-term interest rate should be no more than two percentage points above the rates of the three lowest-inflation member states.

The fourth and last criterion relates to fiscal convergence by establishing guidelines to ensure that EMU is not destabilized by member states with "excessive" budget deficits or public debts. The Maastricht Treaty establishes a numerical standard: budget deficits should not exceed 3 percent of GDP, and public debt should not exceed 60 percent of GDP. The treaty also includes an escape clause, however: states that are moving toward meeting these standards or that have "exceptional and temporary" deviations from these standards may still be considered to have met the rule. Although EMI officials argue that the criteria must be interpreted to the letter, EMU's political supporters urge that they be seen as guidelines, not binding preconditions.[9]

Clearer guidelines are laid out for the statute of the ECB regarding independence from political control and a price stability mandate. The treaty prohibits the ECB from seeking or taking any directions from "Community institutions or bodies, from any government of a Member State or from any other body."[10] The ECB is further directed to make price stability its primary objective, to reinforce this mission, the treaty bars the ECB from financing national budget deficits. Also, the ECB's personnel and oversight procedures are designed to keep external political pressures to a minimum to best ensure that price stability will be credibly maintained.[11] One member of the European

[9] Interview, EMI official, Florence, Italy, December 1996. Commissioner Henning Christopherson, at the time the EU official in charge of economic and monetary affairs, stated publicly that "it has always been understood that the judgement on whether a member state fulfills the conditions for participation in Stage 3 would be based on an assessment and not on a mechanical application of the convergence criteria. In other words, the treaty provides for a certain flexibility." Presentation at CEPS business policy seminar, "European Monetary Union: This Century or Next," Centre for European Policy Studies, Brussels, Belgium, February 22, 1994.

[10] Treaty on European Union, Title IX, Chapter 2, Article 107 (Luxembourg: Office for Official Publications of the European Communities, 1992).

[11] The Maastricht Treaty sets up relatively long terms for ECB officials. None of these individuals is allowed to hold any other position while on the Governing Council, and all are to be appointed "from among persons of recognized standing and professional experience in monetary or banking matters by common accord of the Member States." Treaty on European Union, Title IX, Chapter 3, Article 109a.

Commission and the president of the European Council can participate but not vote in the meetings of the Governing Council. Responsibility for exchange rate agreements and revaluations is kept under the purview of the Council of Ministers in Stage III. These two aspects could appear to dilute somewhat the independence of the ECB, although only to a very small degree.[12] Overall, the Maastricht Treaty reflects clearly the neoliberal "consensus of competitive liberalism" that developed in Europe after the first oil crisis.

CONSENSUS AND CONSTRAINT

Most fundamentally, European integration is the result of a conscious effort on the part of politicians to achieve peace after the ravages of two world wars. This security concern still holds true today: in the aftermath of the collapse of the Soviet Union, the Maastricht Treaty's deepening of integration has been viewed by many of its signatories as a way to safeguard the cohesion of Western Europe. Monetary integration fits neatly into this overall framework, for a single European currency has a unique potential to provide both a potent motor for and symbol of political integration. Relatedly, a single currency would allow Europe to have a greater weight in international economic negotiations. This rationale is one most often mentioned in private interviews with French government and European Commission officials, for whom the notion of Europe as an actor on the world stage is particularly important.[13]

But equally important for the EMU agreement are the two facts that shaped cooperation in the EMS: the increasing constraints of international capital mobility and the neoliberal consensus on monetary policy, "the consensus of competitive liberalism." In chapter 6, we saw that by the late 1970s, rising capital mobility had foreclosed states from simultaneously achieving exchange rate stability and independ-

---

[12] Alberto Alesina and Vittori Grilli argue that the degree of independence in the institutional structure of the ECB is equivalent to that of the Bundesbank. See "The European Central Bank: Reshaping Monetary Politics in Europe," in Matthew Canzoneri et al, *Establishing a Central Bank: Issues in Europe and Lessons from the U.S.* (New York: Cambridge University Press, 1992).

[13] Interviews, Brussels, 1994.

ent monetary policies. The success of the EMS was based on the willingness of governments to give up autonomous monetary policies for exchange rate stability. In the late 1980s, however, the quickening pace of financial flows both globally and within the EU increased dramatically, putting further pressure on states.

In Europe, the Single European Act of 1986 initiated reforms to create a single market within the EU by mandating the elimination of barriers to the free movement of goods, services, capital, and people by the end of 1992.[14] One of the follow-ons from the act, the 1987 banking directive, gave already high levels of capital mobility within the common market a boost by liberalizing the European banking sector, as did the commitment to eliminate all capital controls by 1991 even though it was not fully met.[15] Foreign exchange markets—an indicator of capital decontrol—have grown exponentially in Europe and elsewhere. The daily global foreign exchange turnover in 1995 had reached approximately $130 trillion, more than double the 1989 figure of $620 billion. The ratio of global official reserves to the daily foreign exchange turnover has dropped dramatically, from 14.5 to 1 in 1977 to 1 to 1 in 1995. The amount of reserves is expected to fall below the amount traded in one day.[16] Today, governments must maintain total commitment to the neoliberal policy consensus; at the slightest sign of diminished credibility, foreign exchange traders have challenged European governments' commitments to the EMS with massive speculation.

This capital constraint was evidenced in the foreign exchange crises of 1992–93. Over the course of the crises, the British pound and the Italian lira were driven out of the system; the Spanish peseta, the Portuguese escudo, and the Irish punt were involuntarily devalued,

---

[14] The politics of the SEA are recounted in Wayne Sandholtz and John Zysman, "Recasting the European Bargain," *World Politics* 42 (October 1989) 95–128, and Andrew Moravcsik, "Negotiating the Single European Act," *International Organization* 45 (Winter 1991), 19–56.

[15] Peter B. Kenen, "Capital Controls, the EMS, and EMU," *Economic Journal* 105 (January 1995), 181–92; and Geoffrey R. D. Underhill, "Market Beyond Politics? The State and the Internationalisation of Finance," *European Journal of Political Research* 19 (1991), 197–225.

[16] Data is from Mahbub ul Haq, Inge Kaul, and Isabelle Grunberg, *The Tobin Tax: Coping with Financial Volatility* (New York: Oxford University Press, 1996), tables A.1 and A.2, 291 and 292; see also Bank for International Settlements, *Central Bank Survey of Foreign Exchange and Derivatives* (Basle: BIS, 1996).

causing many to fear the demise of the European monetary integration project. Concrete economic and political problems contributed to the crises, but the root causes were exacerbated greatly by capital mobility, which has raised the stakes of cooperation in the EMS.[17]

A major cause of the crises was misalignments among the EU currencies that had built up over the years of the "hard EMS." Convergence in economic fundamentals was not complete, despite the commitment to monetary rigor, and fixed rates could not be sustained for such a long period without the markets applying pressure on traditionally weak currencies. In addition, German reunification had presented exactly the type of large asymmetrical and exogenous shock that economic theory has posited as the biggest threat to fixed exchange rates and monetary integration.[18] Economic fundamentals cannot explain all of the crises or their timing, however. Also critical was the political context. The EU states had agreed to the most extensive plan for monetary integration ever conceived in the modern era, yet the fate of Maastricht referenda in France and Denmark remained uncertain. The markets decided to test the EU's commitment to exchange rate stability and thus the EMU plan. The existence of the narrow 2.25 percent fluctuation band made things worse by giving currency traders a "one-way bet," since their gains could be huge if they sold a currency short and it broke out of the narrow band. If the currency managed to stay within the narrow band, traders' losses would not be large.

Despite an unprecedented volume of exchange rate speculation, the political commitment to the EMS held up in the majority of the countries. On August 2, 1993, the fluctuation bands were widened to 15 percent on either side of the central rate in an effort to remove

[17] This is explored in Barry Eichengreen and Charles Wyplosz, "The Unstable EMS," *Brookings Papers on Economic Activity* 1 (1993), 51–143; more generally, see also Christopher Johnson and Stefan Collingnon, eds., *The Monetary Economics of Europe: Causes of the EMS Crisis* (Rutherford, N.J.: Fairleigh-Dickinson University Press, 1994).

[18] The fiscal costs of folding the relatively undeveloped East German economy into that of West Germany prompted the Bundesbank to tighten monetary policy in an effort to control inflation. The resultant strengthening of the German mark put pressure on the rest of the European countries to raise their interest rates to fend off speculation against their currencies. On asymmetric shocks, see Barry Eichengreen, "A More Perfect Union? The Logic of Economic Integration," *Essays in International Finance,* no. 198 (Princeton: Princeton University, June 1996); and Erik Jones, "The European Monetary Trade-off: Economic Adjustment in Small Countries," paper presented at the 9th Annual Conference of Europeanists, March 31–April 2, 1994.

some of the incentive for speculation, and indeed the core EMS currencies soon returned to the previous, narrower margins and remained within them. The Italian lira remained outside the EMS, however, floating downward against the rest of the EU currencies over the next four years and spurring protests by import competing interests in the member states, which feared that Italian products were gaining an unfair price advantage. The Italian government continued to seek reinstatement in the EMS, seeing their inflation rate rise and their prospects of participating in EMU dim. In November 1996, the lira reentered, just in time to meet the Maastricht requirement that countries participate in the EMS for two years prior to EMU's start. The United Kingdom remains out of the exchange rate mechanism, however.

Although cooperation in the EMS has proved resilient, continuing pressure from financial markets makes it hard to believe that the EMS will not suffer another destabilizing crisis. One solution to this conundrum is to limit capital mobility. Yet this option has not received serious consideration by EU leaders, notwithstanding the use of temporary capital controls by some EMS states during the early 1990s. The technical difficulties are not insurmountable, but the political collective action problems inherent in sustaining a coordinated capital control program are quite high. In addition, it is difficult to see how erecting barriers to capital movements could co-exist with the political commitment made by the European leaders to the Single Act's emphasis on open markets, both ideologically and in terms of the domestic political interests in favor of capital mobility. A different solution would be to abandon the effort to fix exchange rates and to move instead to a floating rate regime. This is equally unlikely, however, as fixed rates continue to be a priority for political leaders.

Indeed, governments are instead seeking to move forward with monetary integration, not roll it back. With full monetary integration in an EMU, capital mobility would no longer have the potential to destabilize exchange rates across the European Union: there would be a single European currency, the Euro, and a common central bank setting monetary policy. Paradoxically, in an EMU, member states can partly regain their lost monetary policy autonomy without creating exchange rate instability within the single European market. In this

169

sense, EMU is a solution to the challenges of economic governance in a world of high capital mobility.

The logic of monetary union as a way to overcome the incompatibility of fixed exchange rates, independent monetary polices, and free capital flows had begun to be recognized by European leaders even before the Delors Report of 1989. Tommaso Padoa-Schioppa warned that the Single Act had created "an inconsistent quartet," adding the single market as the fourth element and arguing that national monetary policies should be merged into an EMU.[19] Both Padoa-Schioppa's "inconsistent quartet" and Mundell's Holy Trinity began to be picked up by others in Brussels policy circles as a justification for going to EMU, particularly after the crises of 1992–93. For example, this constraint was cited by Henning Christopherson, at the time the European Commission official responsible for EMU issues, as a key reason to move to a single currency.[20] In its official documents, the European Commission repeatedly has argued that the benefits of a single, integrated market for goods, labor, and services cannot be realized without a single currency.[21]

The Neoliberal Consensus Revisited

The neoliberal consensus that underpins the EMS will be crucial to the success of EMU, both to ensure political support during the transition and because the same level of tolerance (or intolerance) for inflation must be shared across the participants if the common monetary policy formulated by the European Central Bank is to be politically sustainable. Certainly, the EU governments had a strong enough policy consensus to reach agreement at Maastricht on a low-inflation,

---

[19] Tommaso Padoa-Schioppa, "The European Monetary System: A Long Term View," in Giavazzi, Micossi, and Miller, eds., *The European Monetary System*, 373–76.

[20] Christopherson is quoted in *CEPR Report* (London: Centre for Economic Policy Research, Spring 1994).

[21] Beyond EMU's potential to solve the Holy Trinity paradox, the economic costs and benefits of EMU are much less clear. Although there is agreement that transaction costs would be lowered with the use of a single currency in Europe, the savings are not that large. See Commission of the European Communities, "One Market, One Money," special edition of *European Economy* (March 1988), for the optimistic European Commission view of the benefits of a single currency. Barry Eichengreen offers a more negative assessment in "Should the Maastricht Treaty Be Saved?" *Princeton Studies in International Finance* 74 (December 1992).

German-model style EMU. But how strong is this policy consensus, and is it likely to continue? Since shared beliefs cannot be measured directly, it is difficult to answer this question definitively. Evaluating the three sources of the neoliberal consensus—policy failure, policy paradigm, and Germany as a policy example—suggests, however, that the consensus may still hold in the area of monetary policy. More problematic is what EMU signifies more broadly for the political economies of Europe, in particular its demands on the fiscal politics of the EU states and the impact of these demands on the monetary consensus.

First, European policymakers are still influenced by the experience with devastating inflation and Keynesian policy failure in the 1970s. If the EMS offered a way to reinforce their domestic fight against inflation, then EMU represents an even more ironclad way to lock in these disciplining monetary policies, while at the same time providing member states with a seat at the policymaking table in the ECB.[22] The rules and structure of the ECB embody the continuing belief that price stability is a crucial starting point for government policy, unlike the 1970 Werner Report on monetary union. By pooling authority for monetary policy, the ECB might provide more credibility for inflation-fighting than would be possible for the national central banks to achieve on their own (except, of course, in the case of the Bundesbank).

Even so, whereas the past ten years have been marked by historically low rates of inflation in Europe, unemployment has risen throughout the 1980s and, in the mid-1990s, averages about 12 percent in the EU (see Table 10). The unemployment situation, ever-present in political discourse, was in large part responsible for the spring 1997 Socialist victory in France. The focus on unemployment has drawn attention away from the strengths of the EMU project while raising questions about the effectiveness of the EU in the economic sphere. Although EU leaders have promised repeatedly to address the unemployment problem, for example, at the June 1997 Amsterdam summit, they have not taken any concrete policy steps in this direction. The European Commission's *White Paper on Growth, Competitiveness, and Employment* is

---

[22] This view strongly influenced both the French and Italian governments' attempts to move the EC toward a formal, symmetrical system of monetary coordination based on a European central bank. Gros and Thygesen, *European Monetary Integration*, 311–13; see also Sandholtz, "Choosing Union," 27–30.

an example of the difficulty the neoliberal consensus creates for the EU in dealing with unemployment. It warns against the "false prophets of inflation and of a return to exchange rate variability" and favors instead

Table 10. Unemployment rates in the European Union

	1971–1980	1981–1990	1991–1995
Belgium	4.6	10.7	9.0
Denmark	3.7	7.6	9.6
Germany	2.2	6.0	5.4
Spain	5.4	18.4	20.1
France	4.1	9.2	10.5
Ireland	7.7	15.7	17.4
Italy	6.1	9.7	10.9
Luxembourg	0.6	2.5	2.5
Netherlands	4.4	10.1	8.6
United Kingdom	3.8	9.7	9.5

SOURCE: *European Economy* 59 (1995), Table 3.

shrinking budgets deficits and monetary union.[23] Macroeconomic policy is thus ruled out as a policy instrument, yet the Commission does not offer a coherent alternative policy for combating unemployment. Instead, the White Paper relies on a mixture of tepid proposals, mostly national-level reforms. The centerpiece proposal is the establishment of trans-European infrastructure network that includes information-technology projects. Although few political leaders in the EU countries advocate a return to traditional Keynesian expansionary policies, the unemployment crisis has certainly made more appealing the calls for a loosening of monetary policy through the reduction of interest rates. In this environment, a strongly independent ECB that puts price stability first should be less attractive, but the neoliberal ideas of financial orthodoxy continue to hold sway, despite rumblings from the French about the need for more balance in EU economic policymaking. It seems most likely that labor market reforms and investments in job retraining programs, such as those advocated by the new British prime minister, Tony Blair, and his Labour Party, will be the policy areas undertaken by the EU states.

[23] European Commission, *White Paper on Growth, Competitiveness, and Employment* (Luxembourg: Office for Official Publications of the European Communities, 1993), 12.

Second, the neoliberal policy consensus has been based on a pragmatic version of monetarist theory, one that advocates a monetarist emphasis on price stability while departing from monetarism in advocating fixed exchange rates. The development of EMU itself has been shaped by advocates of this policy paradigm. The "All Saint's Day Manifesto" of 1975, a public call for the revival of monetary integration in Europe published in the *Economist,* was essentially the work of a group of economists sympathetic to monetarism, many of whom acted as advisers to the Commission during the 1970s.[24] Many of the academic economists working on the EMU issue a decade later, for example, preparing the Commission's *One Market, One Money* study and advising the Directorate General in charge of economic and financial affairs, also work within this modified version of monetarism. Wim Duisenberg, the new head of the European Monetary Institute, who will presumably be the president of the ECB should EMU occur, is also a monetarist noted for his emphasis on monetary rigor while the Dutch central bank governor.

As a guide for policy behavior, however, monetarist theory has come under attack. The difficulties of accurately measuring the stock of money makes monetarist targeting of the money supply problematic, and uncertainty about the stability of the links between the money supply and inflation has damaged the reputation monetarism enjoyed in the late 1970s and the first half of the 1980s.[25] But Europe's neoliberal consensus has never embodied a pure version of a monetarism, relying instead on monetarism's general principles and prescriptions while fashioning it to the European context. Equally important, the lack of any coherent alternative to monetarist principles has lessened the impact of these critiques.[26]

Finally, the third factor contributing to the convergence of policy preferences—emulation of the German model—is problematic but has not been supplanted. Europeans continue to see Germany as an

[24] "All Saint's Day Manifesto," *Economist,* November 1, 1975, 33.

[25] See, for example, "Auf Widersehen, M3," *Economist,* May 28, 1994, 84; and the analysis provided in "New Maps of Policy," *Economist,* September 19, 1992, 24–30, of the special survey "The World Economy."

[26] Benjamin M. Friedman, "The Role of Judgement and Discretion in the Conduct of Monetary Policy: Consequences of Changing Financial Markets," *NBER Working Paper,* no. 4599 (December 1993).

example for policy emulation, just as they did in the decade following the first oil crisis, in part because Germany's economy is still regarded as the most capable of achieving long-term low inflation and export-led growth, despite the shocks of reunification. Reflecting this view, the Maastricht Treaty's provisions for the ECB are very much modeled on the structure of the Bundesbank. Still, the high interest rate policies Germany continues to follow in the wake of reunification are not well suited to the needs of the other European governments, whose domestic institutional structures cannot as easily support monetary rigor. German policy has been acknowledged by Alexandre Lamfalussy, the former head of the European Monetary Institute, to no longer be foolproof. But Lamfalussy has said that following the German example of targeting the monetary supply remains a better policy than the alternative—which he characterizes as "flying blind."[27]

The neoliberal consensus on monetary policy necessary for EMU to be implemented and sustained thus seems to be intact but not immutable. Political leaders in Europe continue to pledge that EMU will happen by 1999, at least among a partial "core" group of member states. Italy's November 1996 rejoining of the EMS's exchange rate mechanism improved the chances of that founding EU state meeting the conditions for entry into EMU. Despite mixed signals on EMU from the new French prime minister, Lionel Jospin, long-term yields in the European bond markets and interest rate swap markets are converging, indicating that the markets believe that EMU will happen on schedule. European firms, particularly the banking sector, have been devoting substantial resources to prepare for the technical and logistical demands of the transition to a single currency.[28]

The Limits to Neoliberal Reform

Although many in Europe now assume that a group of EU states will go forward with monetary union in 1999, political tensions may

---

[27] Kathleen R. McNamara and Erik Jones, "The Clash of Institutions: Germany in European Monetary Affairs," *German Politics and Society* 14 (Fall 1996), 5–30; Lamfalussy quoted in Tom Buerkle, "In Search of an EC Money Policy," *International Herald Tribune,* October 25, 1993.

[28] On market beliefs, see "North Americans Begin to Believe Bird Will Fly," *Financial Times,* December 10, 1996, p. 2, and "How to Calculate the Odds in the Monetary Union

yet erupt and jeopardize EMU's future. This book has argued that the neoliberal policy consensus underpinning cooperation in the EMS is an elite-level phenomenon. It encompasses a series of shared beliefs about the goals and instruments of monetary policy—a new consensus of competitive liberalism—that has replaced the embedded liberalism of the early postwar period. Although the neoliberal policies of monetary rigor have had important effects on the macroeconomies of Europe, they have not been subject to intensive mass political debate or electoral contention, nor have they stimulated significant interest group politics.

All this could change, however, for EMU both exacerbates and makes visible what was previously obscured, that is, the social costs of neoliberal reforms and the democratic deficit inherent in European integration more generally.[29] The element of the EMU process that may prove the most problematic politically is the fiscal retrenchment demanded by the convergence criteria, as well as the "stability pact," which will go into effect once EMU begins. To enter EMU, states are supposed to have budget deficits of 3 percent or less of GDP and public debts not exceeding 60 percent of GDP, although some room is left for political maneuvers over the application of the criteria. In virtually all of the states save Luxembourg, meeting these targets is requiring stringent fiscal austerity. A variety of "one-off" budgetary measures are being taken in the national capitals to meet the convergence criteria, but it is unlikely that the criteria can be anywhere close to being met without deep cuts.[30]

Additionally, in an attempt to guarantee that fiscal discipline is maintained by the single currency states, German finance minister Theo Waigel proposed in December 1995 that a stability pact should be mandatory among EMU members to promote balanced budgets in an EMU. After much negotiation, the heads of state meeting in Dublin

---

Stakes," ibid., November 19, 1996, p. 2. On the banking preparations, see "Banks' Early Confidence on EMU Starts to Erode," *Financial Times,* December 3, 1996, p. 3.

[29] The broader history of European integration is marked by the principle of elite governance and technocratic policymaking rather than attention to democratic participation. Some of these issues are taken up in Robert Dahl, "A Democratic Dilemma: System Effectiveness versus Citizen Participation," *Political Science Quarterly* 109 (Spring 1994), 23–34.

[30] "Rush to Qualify for EMU Condemned," *Financial Times,* October 29, 1996; "EU Single Currency; Bankers Clash with Brussels," ibid., November 7, 1996.

in December 1996 came to a preliminary agreement on a system of penalties for states that run deficits of more than 3 percent of GDP after EMU begins. The agreement allows for exemption from sanctioning when a country is in a severe recession, defined as a drop in GDP of at least 2 percent over a year. When GDP has fallen between .75 percent and 2 percent, EU finance ministers will have some discretion in applying the fines, if a case could be made that circumstances warranted the deficits. At the insistence of the French, the agreement is being called the "Stability and Growth Pact," but it will most likely have deflationary effects on the EMU states. Although the fines themselves may not be unbearable, the loss of prestige implied in being sanctioned by the other EMU states will be a deterrent to deficit spending.

Economically, the importance of fiscal rectitude for the functioning of EMU is still much debated; instead, microeconomic reforms such as labor market flexibility and a monetary union-wide automatic fiscal stabilizing system are the focus of recommendations from the optimal currency area literature. It seems most likely that the stability pact may be necessary politically to calm both international capital markets and German fears, particularly in the Bundesbank, about possible inflationary consequences of an EMU that includes weaker currency states.[31]

Several factors make this fiscal retrenchment more socially costly and politically difficult than the monetary rigor demanded by membership in the EMS. First, the neoliberal monetary cooperation of the EMS was itself eased by the use of fiscal policy to cushion the effects of monetary rigor. When exchange rate stability increased in the 1980s, so did budget deficits throughout Europe, as unemployment benefits and public spending programs were used to promote political and broader economic stability.[32] Today, the fiscal option is receding at a

[31] Paul de Grauwe argues that the criteria "serve a political necessity" of allowing Germany "to restrict the number of countries that are going to participate in the union, so that it can keep a dominating position in the monetary policy making process." De Grauwe, "The Political Economy of Monetary Union in Europe," *The World Economy* 16 (November 1993), 660. On the optimal currency area literature, see Paul De Grauwe, "Reforming the Transition to EMU," in Peter B. Kenen, ed., "Making EMU Happen: Problems and Proposals," *Essays in International Finance*, no. 199 (Princeton: Princeton University, August 1996).

[32] For example, see the evidence on fiscal expansions in Geoff Garrett and Peter Lange, "Political Responses to Interdependence: "What's Left for the Left?" *International Organization* 45 (1991), 539–64.

time when it may be even more necessary, given the institutionalization of neoliberal monetary policies in EMU and continuing economic recession in Europe.

Second, the societal dynamics of fiscal retrenchment are fundamentally different from those of the monetary realm. The analytic uncertainty and collective action problems of monetary politics are not nearly as prevalent in budget cutting, where the effects of pruning particular programs are immediately obvious to their constituencies, be they public workers, pensioners, or businesses. The "embedded liberalism" of the welfare state is thus likely to be more resilient than any other policy area in the face of increased pressures for reform, and popular opposition to EMU could accelerate in the face of overburdened pension funds and declining social services.[33] The sanctioning of non-compliant states under a stability pact would heighten the visibility of the linkage between austerity and monetary integration, possibly fanning political dissatisfaction with European integration more generally. Already there is discontent in Europe, evidenced by the Socialist victory in the French parliamentary elections, but the connection has not yet been tightly drawn between the cutbacks and the EMU project. A nonelected governing body of central bankers in a European central bank may provide the perfect scapegoat and political cover for further reforms, or it may renew criticisms about the lack of accountability in EU institutions. Aware of these issues, French officials have suggested that the EU's Council of Economic and Finance Ministers should act as a counterweight to the political independence of the ECB, but this idea clashes with the German determination that monetary policy must be protected from politics and fiscal profligacy. The question is to what degree over the next few years EMU will force these issues out in the open and subject to overt political discourse within Europe.

A more politicized monetary integration process would be welcome, despite the complexities of this policy area, for EMU's outcome will greatly affect the daily lives of the citizens of Europe for decades to come. Some may strive to make the process of monetary integration one that is "disembedded," where economic motives and logic are

[33] Paul Pierson, "The New Politics of the Welfare State," *World Politics* 48 (January 1996), 143–79.

separated from the broader concerns of society, but the relationship between the international economy and domestic political authority cannot be so easily divorced. EU governments continue to have choices about the path of economic and monetary integration: although capital mobility and the neoliberal policy consensus appear to have painted these governments into a corner, it is important to remember that they have themselves wielded the brushes that put them there.

Index

Cornell Studies in Political Economy

A Series Edited by

PETER J. KATZENSTEIN

National Diversity and Global Capitalism edited by Suzanne Berger and Ronald Dore
Collapse of an Industry: Nuclear Power and the Contradictions of U.S. Policy
   by John L. Campbell
The Price of Wealth: Economics and Institutions in the Middle East
   by Kiren Aziz Chaudhry
Power, Purpose, and Collective Choice: Economic Strategy in Socialist States
   edited by Ellen Comisso and Laura Tyson
The Political Economy of the New Asian Industrialism
   edited by Frederic C. Deyo
Dislodging Multinationals: India's Strategy in Comparative Perspective
   by Dennis J. Encarnation
Rivals beyond Trade: America versus Japan in Global Competition
   by Dennis J. Encarnation
Enterprise and the State in Korea and Taiwan by Karl J. Fields
National Interests in International Society by Martha Finnemore
Democracy and Markets: The Politics of Mixed Economies by John R. Freeman
The Misunderstood Miracle: Industrial Development and Political Change in Japan
   by David Friedman
*Patchwork Protectionism: Textile Trade Policy in the United States, Japan, and West
   Germany* by H. Richard Friman
Ideas and Foreign Policy: Beliefs, Institutions, and Political Change
   edited by Judith Goldstein and Robert O. Keohane
Ideas, Interests, and American Trade Policy by Judith Goldstein
Monetary Sovereignty: The Politics of Central Banking in Western Europe
   by John B. Goodman
Politics in Hard Times: Comparative Responses to International Economic Crises
   by Peter Gourevitch
Cooperation among Nations: Europe, America, and Non-tariff Barriers to Trade
   by Joseph M. Grieco
Nationalism, Liberalism, and Progress, Volume 1: The Rise and Decline of Nationalism
   by Ernst B. Haas
Pathways from the Periphery: The Politics of Growth in the Newly Industrializing Countries
   by Stephan Haggard
The Politics of Finance in Developing Countries edited by Stephan Haggard,
   Chung H. Lee, and Sylvia Maxfield
*Rival Capitalists: International Competitiveness in the United States, Japan, and Western
   Europe* by Jeffrey A. Hart
The Philippine State and the Marcos Regime: The Politics of Export by Gary Hawes
Reasons of State: Oil Politics and the Capacities of American Government
   by G. John Ikenberry
The State and American Foreign Economic Policy edited by G. John Ikenberry,
   David A. Lake, and Michael Mastanduno
The Nordic States and European Unity by Christine Ingebritsen
The Paradox of Continental Production: National Investment Policies in North America
   by Barbara Jenkins

Kathleen R. McNamara is Assistant Professor of Politics and International Affairs at Princeton University.